STANDING UP TO HITLER

STANDING UP TO HITLER

RESISTANCE IN NAZI GERMANY

NORMAN RIDLEY

FRONTLINE BOOKS

STANDING UP TO HITLER
Resistance in Nazi Germany

First published in Great Britain in 2025 by
Frontline Books
An imprint of Pen & Sword Books Ltd
Yorkshire – Philadelphia

Copyright © Norman Ridley

ISBN 9781036136314

The right of Norman Ridley to be identified as Author of this work has been asserted by him in accordance with the Copyright, Designs and Patents Act 1988.

A CIP catalogue record for this book is available from the British Library.

All rights reserved. No part of this book may be reproduced, transmitted, downloaded, decompiled or reverse engineered in any form or by any means, electronic or mechanical including photocopying, recording or by any information storage and retrieval system, without permission from the Publisher in writing. NO AI TRAINING: Without in any way limiting the Author's and Publisher's exclusive rights under copyright, any use of this publication to "train" generative artificial intelligence (AI) technologies to generate text is expressly prohibited. The Author and Publisher reserve all rights to license uses of this work for generative AI training and development of machine learning language models.

Typeset by Lapiz Digital
Printed and bound in the UK by CPI Group (UK) Ltd, Croydon, CR0 4YY.

The Publisher's authorised representative in the EU for product safety is Authorised Rep Compliance Ltd., Ground Floor, 71 Lower Baggot Street, Dublin D02 P593, Ireland.
www.arccompliance.com

For a complete list of Pen & Sword titles please contact

PEN & SWORD BOOKS LIMITED
47 Church Street, Barnsley, South Yorkshire, S70 2AS, England
E-mail: enquiries@pen-and-sword.co.uk
Website: www.pen-and-sword.co.uk
or
PEN AND SWORD BOOKS
1950 Lawrence Road, Havertown, PA 19083, USA
E-mail: uspen-and-sword@casematepublishers.com
Website: www.penandswordbooks.com

CONTENTS

List of Plates vii
Prologue ix

Chapter 1   Internal Resistance Before 1938 1
Chapter 2   Defending Traditional Values 14
Chapter 3   Left-Wing Resistance.................................... 21
Chapter 4   Youth Resistance 32
Chapter 5   Intellectuals against the Nazis........................ 38
Chapter 6   The Churches 42
Chapter 7   The Oster Conspiracy 48
Chapter 8   The War in the West..................................... 65
Chapter 9   Harro and Libertas Schulze-Boysen 68
Chapter 10 Mildred Fish and Arvid Harnack 86
Chapter 11 Die Rote Kapelle 92
Chapter 12 The von Scheliha Group 104
Chapter 13 Herbert Baum and the Jewish Resistance 109
Chapter 14 The White Rose 113
Chapter 15 The Kreisau Circle 124
Chapter 16 Hitler and his Generals 133
Chapter 17 20 July 1944 157
Postscript.. 164

Appendix 1   Shulze-Boysen/Harnack Group Members 165
Appendix 2   Members of the Uhrig Group 170
Appendix 3   Members of the von Scheliha Group................... 171

Appendix 4 *Members of the Baum Group* 172
Appendix 5 *Members of the White Rose* 173
Appendix 6 *Members of the Kreisau Circle* 176
Appendix 7 *White Rose Court Proceedings of Hans and Sophia Scholl,*
              and Christoph Probst 178
Appendix 8 *Plötzensee Prison* 180
Appendix 9 *Draft of Governmental Declaration by Beck and Goerdeler,*
              summer 1944 (excerpts) 182
Notes 183
Sources 196
Index 201

LIST OF PLATES

1. Erika Gräfin von Brockdorff, executed by guillotine on 13 May 1943
2. Eva Maria Buch, executed by guillotine on 5 August 1943
3. Hans Coppi, executed by hanging on 22 December 1942
4. Hilda Coppi, executed by guillotine on 5 August 1943
5. Arvid Harnack, executed by hanging on 22 December 1942
6. Mildred Fish Harnack, executed by guillotine on 16 February 1943
7. Harro and Libertas Schulze-Boysen, Harro, executed by hanging on 22 December 1942, Libertas executed by guillotine on the same day.
8. Rudolf von Scheliha, executed by hanging on 22 December 1942
9. The lone bomber Johann Georg Elser
10. Erwin Gehrts, executed by guillotine on 10 February 1943
11. Adam Trott zu Solz, executed by hanging on 26 August 1944
12. Helmuth James Graf von Moltke, executed by hanging on 26 August 1944
13. Karl Behrens, executed by hanging on 13 May 1943
14. Liane Berkowitz, executed by guillotine on 5 August 1943
15. Friedrich Rehmer, executed by hanging on 13 May 1943
16. Sophie Scholl, executed by guillotine on 22 February 1943
17. Christof Probst, executed by guillotine on 22 February 1943
18. Poster for the 1943 'Soviet Paradise' exhibition
19. Swing Youth resistance group showing off their style
20. Claus von Stauffenberg (left) with Hitler at Wolf's Lair in July 1944 only days before he planted the bomb in an attempt to kill him. The look of Stauffenberg's face speaks volumes.

21 Wolfs Lair after the explosion of 20 July 1944
22 The execution building Plötzensee prison
23 The Guillotine at Plötzensee prison
24 Roland Freisler, head of the Volksgerichtshof (People's Court)

PROLOGUE

When you think about all that and the sun is shining like it is now, when you consider how young we are, you can't believe in death. Sometimes it all seems like a bad dream from which I must wake up at any moment.
Liane Berkowitz, 28 February 1943

Liane Berkowitz was two days short of her twentieth birthday when she wrote the following letter to her mother from her cell in in Berlin's Plötzensee prison,

Meine einzige teure Mamotschka
It's over. Today, when it will be dark, your Lanka will no longer be alive. My consolation and my hope is my little Irka (Irina), who, thank God, has no idea what is going on around her.

Raise Irka to be a smart, capable person, let her learn as much as possible. Teach her to have unshakable faith in God and in God's eternal love and justice.

I believe in God, in eternal life and that we will see each other again. I will pray for you and Inochka in the afterlife and protect you. I am calm and composed and am not afraid of death.

The last few months, especially the time since I separated from Ira, have been unbearably difficult for me and I am glad that this torment is now almost over. God has been very merciful to me. He has let me experience everything a woman can experience: He has given me a child. At least I have been a mother, even if only for a short time, and that is the most beautiful thing there is. . . . Now I turn my thoughts and mind to God and prepare myself to go to Christ in trust in His love and grace.

I embrace, greet, kiss you for the last time, kiss your hands and receive your blessing
Your quiet, unhappy Lanka

Having completed the letter, Liane was taken to a place of execution and beheaded by guillotine at 19.45 hrs on 5 August 1943. The 'crime' for which she had been convicted by the Second Senate of the Reich Military Court was 'aiding and abetting the preparation of high treason and aiding the enemy'.[1] The prosecution evidence against her was that on the evening of 17 May 1942 she, with others, had protested against a Nazi propaganda exhibition called *das Sokjet Paradies* (The Soviet Paradise) by posting stickers ridiculing it in the busy area between Kurfürstendamm and Uhlandstrasse. The stickers read;

Ständige Ausstellung
Das NAZI PARADIES
Krieg Hunger Lüge Gestapo
Wie lang noch?
Permanent Exhibition
The NAZI PARADISE
War, Hunger, Lies, Gestapo
How much longer?[2]

An appeal for clemency was rejected by Adolf Hitler and the death sentence was confirmed under the signature of Field Marshal William Keitel. The daughter, Irina, to whom she had given birth in another cell in the Barnimstrasse prison on 12 April of that year died a few weeks later on 16 October 1943 in Eberswald Hospital probably the victim of a Nazi euthanasia program, but she may also have died due to Liane's malnutrition during pregnancy.[3] The child's father, Friedrich 'Fritz' Rehmer had been conscripted and sent to the Eastern Front where he was wounded. While recuperating in Berlin's Britz military hospital, he had joined Liane's sticker campaign protesting against the Nazi anti-Soviet exhibition. He was arrested in November 1942 for undermining morale in the hospital by spreading stories about Nazi atrocities on the Eastern Front. He was sentenced to death on 18 January 1943 and executed on 13 May 1943 in Plötzensee prison.

Chapter 1

INTERNAL OPPOSITION BEFORE 1938

The road to resistance is in the last analysis a lonely one.[1]

The fundamental character of Nazi ideology meant that when it was imposed upon the German people after the Reichstag elections of January 1933 there would be significant repercussions detrimentally affecting large sections of the population. The new regime suppressed cultural pluralism and liberalism, all notions of individual rights or fundamental human equality and any expressions of nonconformity or independent thought. This radical reshaping of human nature, however, could only be enforced through a reign of intense propaganda and terror designed to crush the will of the German people to resist. When the Nazis took power they systematically set about eliminating all sources of opposition and resistance to their rule, by subverting social institutions and undermining the class structure. The ruthless and efficient way in which they achieved this meant much resistance could only manifest itself through the actions of individuals or small groupings acting out of personal convictions. These resisters came from all walks of life and were motivated by many different beliefs. Some saw their goal as the complete overthrow of the government while others found the courage to stand up, in the face of extreme danger, risking their lives to submit to the dictates of conscience and through their acts say that what was happening was simply wrong. Those voices came from a wide variety of political backgrounds from communists, from socialists, from conservatives, from the military and from the religiously motivated. Acts of disobedience and resistance took place very much in isolation under a regime that was enforcing total conformity through terror and punishing renegades with extreme violence.

Tracing the history of internal opposition to the Nazis relies on fragmentary evidence. By their very nature, dissident groups avoided leaving documentary traces and individual members were required to disguise their intentions by conformity. Not least of the difficulties is the shortage of personal testimony, given that so many resisters did not survive to tell their tales, and where it exists, allowance must be made for possible bias and ulterior motivation. Political agendas also skewed the narrative during the post-war years when the German internal opposition was variously seen as heroic or traitorous. General Hans Oster plotted to overthrow Hitler in 1938 and later betrayed secrets to Germany's enemies in 1940 was clearly a traitor to the Nazis but whether or not he was a traitor to Germany is another matter. Luftwaffe officer Harro Schulze-Boysen may well have been motivated by his opposition to everything the Nazis stood for, but by passing military secrets to the Soviet Union in 1941 in effect, became 'a cog in the machine of a foreign espionage organisation'.[2] The issue is neatly summed up in the title of Louis Eltscher's 2020 book, *Traitors or Patriots; A Story of the German anti-Nazi Resistance*.[3]

In the fetid political atmosphere of the Cold War, there was little enthusiasm for giving credit to those Germans who chose to act out of their communist beliefs in support of the Soviet Union's war efforts against their home country. Whereas in occupied territories, resistance was aligned with the national interest, no such argument can be employed in Germany where it was clearly out of step with the national effort and came close to being seen as treason which, for army officers at least, was an agonising dilemma. In such a situation, while many made what efforts they could to defend their personal class or status against intrusion, it was very much a matter of character and principle that motivated actual resistance to the Nazi regime.

Resistance, itself, is an extreme reaction. Taking responsibility for one's beliefs, whatever their political or religious foundations, involves a willingness to confront evil and take an unpaved and unmarked road in a landscape littered with menace and the real possibility of capture, torture and death. In Nazi Germany, where there was absolutely no room for dissent, opposition required that participants were willing to face the consequences of their actions. It also called for an understanding and acceptance that individual acts which carried such awful risk might, in the end, have no discernible influence on events. Men and women who took this path in the darkest of times 'reaffirmed the dignity of man' and there is every reason to acknowledge their deeds as 'a sacrificial act'.[4]

The German historian Martin Broszat separates German resistance into three stages. Only during the first and third stages was there any fundamental or significant opposition to Nazi rule. The first stage was during the early years of the Third Reich when the Nazis were struggling to impose their will on the German people by forming an alliance with traditional conservatives to suppress the labour movement and the left-wing political parties. During the next phase, most sections of German society and culture were penetrated and came under the control of special Nazi organisations and then in the third and final stage, the disenchanted conservative elites belatedly found it within themselves to act against the regime.

The basic precondition for the imposition of totalitarian rule was the violent and merciless suppression of communist and socialist underground opposition groups. Far from being a well-organised movement, however, this left-wing opposition was largely a spontaneous youth-led reaction to social degradation and Nazi violence which generated a cycle of punishment and radicalisation. Nazi power ensured that opposition was restricted to a few and the severe punishments for insurrection had the effect of supressing direct actions against the regime, leading to a period of increasing public support on the back of wildly successful diplomatic adventures and increased employment in the armament factories. During the second phase of 'passive resistance', when state power was becoming daily more oppressive, opposition was most likely expressed in private conversation or support for religious festivals and were more in the character of subversion rather than resistance. After the Anschluss and occupation of Czechoslovakia, those Germans who did not support the regime were generally sitting tight and waiting and hoping for the Nazi bubble to burst and then the spectacular successes over Poland, the Low Countries and France with the British humiliated at Dunkirk, left a lot of people quietly satisfied to see their country back in a dominant position in Europe.

In the third phase, however, when it was clear that Germany was losing the war and unlikely to reverse the momentum and news filtered in about the gruesome atrocities done in the name of the German people, more and more people cast off the mantle of passivity and conspired to rebel. In the diplomatic circle and the civil service and, most of all, in the military, the knowledge of what was really happening was in sharp contrast to the propaganda meted out daily to the rest of the population. Conspiratorial groups, such as the Kreisau Circle, emerged across the political spectrum with a wide range of ideologies but they remained essentially isolated from each other. Even within individual groupings of dissenters there were serious arguments over methods and objectives.

What Annedore Leber called the 'spectrum of resistance' included a wide variety of individual cases many of which are unrecorded. People from all corners of Germany and all walks of life, often acting alone, found themselves compelled to resist. Simply refusing to salute the flag or give the Nazi salute was the simplest act of defiance but helping the victims of persecution was something that individuals could do although this was of an altogether much more dangerous nature. For many it was a case of personal responsibility and a commitment to justice but to others it was the result of strong religious conviction.

Most of the 40 million Protestants were members of the German Evangelical Church comprising Lutheran Reformed and United traditions. This was one of the pillars of German culture and society, with a theologically grounded tradition of loyalty to the state. The Nazis had used the traditional ties between the Protestant church and the state to assimilate church dogma into their own ideology by putting their own people into positions of power in the church. Many Christians had been persuaded by the Nazi commitment, written into their 1920 platform to uphold 'the freedom of all religious confessions in the state, insofar as they do not jeopardise the state's existence or conflict with the manners and moral sentiments of the Germanic race'.

Historians now agree that the overall impact of resistance to the Nazis, whilst undoubtedly heroic in many respects, was limited even in the case of the French *Maquis* which puts German internal resistance into perspective. It cannot be said that there was a resistance movement in Germany in the same way that there were in Nazi-occupied territories during the war. While resistance in occupied countries had a modicum of support from the enslaved populations, in Germany, for the most part, the *Widerstand*, or resistance, was composed of individuals and small groups who operated independently of each other and without any 'social support'.[5] The resistance movement never had the public behind it in any organised manner. Consequently, it lacked the power to influence the course of events. Indeed, many of those who became active in the resistance had no love for either the masses or democratic government and did not seek to build that broad base of support. The Kreisau Circle was probably the only resistance movement that tried to bridge the gap between right-wing resistance and the working classes. Nevertheless, in the words of the post-war SPD leader, Willy Brandt, even though, 'there was very little resistance deserving of the name that was not soon discovered . . . the moral legacy of resistance retains its validity, irrespective of its limited effectiveness'.[6]

Most narratives about German opposition to the Nazis revolve around the failed attempt to assassinate Hitler on 20 July 1944 when Lieutenant Colonel Claus, Count Schenk von Stauffenberg planted a bomb at Hitler's *Wolfsschanze* (Wolf's Lair) headquarters. This moment had been long in the planning but was only one of several plots hatched over the war years by military and political leaders to bring an end to the war by eliminating the *Führer* and suing for peace. Stauffenberg's bomb exploded killing four and injuring most of the others in Albert Speer's annexe to Hitler's main bunker, but Hitler survived with barely a scratch. Stauffenberg, a 'tall, slim and agile [man] of decided personal charm' was arrested and executed along with some 200 others, many of them from the 'old elite' and most of whom had played no part in the actual conspiracy.[7] One who was on the periphery of the conspiracy, the writer and philosopher, Ernst Jünger, recorded in his diary his belief that it was 'the moral substance, not the political, which spurs [the plotters] to action' but it must be remembered that some of those involved who were subsequently lauded as martyrs or heroes, had they survived the war, might well have been in the dock at Nuremberg facing charges of war crimes.

Karl-Heinrich von Stülpnagel, the German military commander in France, had closely cooperated with the *Einsatzgruppen* in the mass murder of Jews when he commanded the 17th Army. The Quartermaster of the Army, Eduard Wagner, had coordinated *Einsatzgruppen* cooperation with the army and created the plans to starve Soviet prisoners of war, resulting in millions of deaths, and Arthur Nebe was leader of the Kripo (Criminal Police) and had commanded *Einsatzgruppe B* in the Soviet Union, responsible for the murder of over 45,000 Jews. Alexander von Falkenhausen as military governor of Belgium had assisted in the deportation of 28,000 Jews.[8]

The study of internal resistance to Nazism is unbalanced if the memory of the 20 July plotters is not offset against the tens of thousands of men and women who were imprisoned, tortured and executed, or died in concentration camps for their stand against the dictatorship. Most notable in this regard were the many communist groups, whose losses through arrests, imprisonment, and execution during the Third Reich were extraordinarily high. This book is concerned not only with revolt within the military but seeks to trace the evolution of other strands of internal opposition to Hitler some of which had their roots in a time well before the *Nationalsozialistische Deutsche Arbeiterpartei*

(National Socialist German Workers' Party, NSDAP) achieved its political ambition of controlling the Reichstag in January 1933.

Notions of resistance came up against a powerful propagandised version of reality which appealed to many Germans high and low, on both right and left of the political spectrum, with all its protestation of national pride and grandeur and of social conciliation in the near-religious appeal of a *Volksgemeinschaft* (national community).[9] The Weimar Republic had crumbled under the weight of revolution, rampant inflation, economic depression and political turmoil giving way to a new form of authoritarian government that came as relief to many who had seen their status, wealth and influence eroded. It was a regime they were more than willing to make compromises with. Indeed, German elites had been glad to see the back of democracy as manifest in the Weimar Republic and welcomed Nazism as 'the first ray of hope since 1918'.[10] Bourgeois institutions and political parties moved so far towards accommodating Hitler that within a year, even as they applauded his achievements, they barely registered the extent to which they were being further emasculated and soon would be barely able to find themselves amidst the throng of brown shirts, swastikas and torchlight extravaganzas.

The accelerating erosion of democracy and 'decay of power' in Germany occurred under conditions some of which were universal such as the world-wide depression and 'a decline in creative and religious forces and a cultural and moral crisis' and some of which were peculiar to Germany such as the war reparations and military restrictions imposed by the Treaty of Versailles. Any attempt to analyse the particular German reaction to the emergence of those 'dark forces forming the sediment of every modern society' must take into account the 'diabolical mixture of terror and propaganda which was characteristic of the National Socialist regime' and the economic necessities of everyday survival that made resistance such a precarious path. The German-Swiss philosopher Karl Jaspers recognised in Nazism a growth emanating from a 'seed of evil planted long ago'.[11]

For those who questioned the tightening grip of Nazism and looked outside the country for guidance, they found that even Winston Churchill was undecided when he wrote in 1935, 'We cannot tell whether Hitler will be the man who will once again let loose upon the world another war . . . or whether he will go down in history as the man who restored honour and peace of mind to the great Germanic nation'.[12] Even as late as 1938, the man who would later be the figurehead of implacable opposition to Hitler, wrote in *The Times* on 7

November that year, 'if Great Britain were defeated in war, I hope we should find a Hitler to lead us back to our rightful position among the nations'. Nevertheless, while many who found themselves defenceless and without legal remedy submitted to the powers of the fascist state, there were others who, to a greater or lesser extent, accepted the very real and terrible risks of taking the line of resistance.

The most active opponents of Nazism were the communists who had fought street battles with the ultra-right-wing *Freikorps* during the early Weimar years but failed to ignite a revolution powerful enough to oust the government. During the 1920s the *Kommunistische Partei Deutschlands* (KPD, Communist Party of Germany,), developed an impressive political-military apparatus for proletarian revolution under the leadership of the secret organisation *Militär-Apparat* that was in close contact with the state security services of the Soviet Union (the OGPU, then the NKVD). At its base was the *Roten Frontkämpferbund* (League of Red Front Fighters) which, together with the *Roter Jungsturm*, its youth organisation, trained militants to protect demonstrations and picket lines and fought battles for control of the streets with the *Sturmabteilung* (SA, paramilitary wing of the NSDAP). During 1931 alone there were 79 Nazi and 103 Communist deaths but then the KPD scaled down its activities after the *Rote Frontkämpferbund* had been banned and the *Sozialdemokratische Partei Deutschlands* (SPD, Social Democratic Party of Germany) showed its willingness to confront the communists, often alongside the Nazis. On 1 May 1929 it had been SPD leaders who had ordered the police to open fire on the communist procession in Berlin, killing thirty-three demonstrators. Then again on 17 July 1932, it was the police who had killed seventeen when they opened fire on KPD demonstrators protesting against a Nazi parade in Hamburg.

In January 1933, when the Nazis came to power: the communists reacted in several large cities with strikes and savagely repressed demonstrations. In February, the police invaded Karl-Liebknecht-Haus, the headquarters of the KPD, and outlawed the party but this ruthless suppression of democratic freedoms was done in such a way as to maintain a semblance of justice while using all manner of deception and falsehood. In these very early days of their reign, the Nazis understood quite clearly that they had to give the appearance of order, stability and rectitude to gain the trust and support of the people. The total abolition of democracy was the Nazis clear objective but it would be done not by violent insurrection and blatant law-breaking but by manipulation of induced crises backed up by oppressive authoritarianism. The banning of the SPD followed during the Summer which effectively neutralised it temporarily, as had been the case of the KPD, when many leaders went into exile.

When the Reichstag was gutted by fire on 27 February 1933 it was an excuse to blame the communists and 10,000 were arrested. A few weeks later, another 20,000 were swept up. Sixty camps, thirty special quarters in state prisons and sixty detention centres were specially opened to accommodate them. In every locality, private prisons and torture centres were established in cellars or empty factories. New concentration camps were built at Dachau and Oranienburg. When the Chief Superintendent of the Berlin Fire Brigade, Walter Gempp, questioned the official version of how the fire had started, he became a marked man. He would be arrested later for 'malfeasance in office' and was found strangled in his prison cell. The Nazis used the fire to justify the introduction of the Reichstag Fire Decree that abolished a whole swathe of civil liberties, including free speech and the right of assembly. A state of emergency was declared and a violent crackdown started against anyone who dared to challenge the authorities. In April, the SA were ordered to hand over their prisoners to the *Schutzstaffel* (SS), and terror was applied methodically and rationally. In June, they began the practice of hanging rebel prisoners held in concentration camps on the roll-call square in front of the camp population that was forced to stand to attention as it watched. The first to die in this way was the communist worker Emil Bargatzky.

When the communists won 81 seats in the 5 March elections, they were unable to take their seats in the Reichstag, an act which would have exposed them to immediate arrest. Then the Malicious Practices Act of 21 March made it a crime to criticise the new government. Anyone gossiping about or making fun of government officials could quickly end up in prison or in Oranienburg. In their drive to consolidate power the Nazis set about eradicating all vestiges of democracy which meant the removal of socialists and communists, Jews, artists and intellectuals who did not support Nazism. Where left-wing organisations existed, they were clearly identifiable and quickly closed down and had their assets confiscated. It was a catastrophic break in the political, cultural and intellectual traditions of the civilised world ensuring that Germany would become 'a state without justice' as the Nazi one-party state rigorously stripped the people of all freedoms.[13]

This was followed by the Enabling Act, formally called the 'Law to Remedy the Distress of the People and the Reich' brought before the floor of the parliament, surrounded by thousands of uniformed SA and

SS men, on 23 March 1933. Ninety-four very brave SPD members voted against it while twenty-six craven others abstained. The Act passed easily into law which gave the Reich government powers to issue laws without the consent of Germany's parliament giving Hitler practically unlimited powers only days after being sworn in as Chancellor.

By the end of March, the figure of political detainees had risen to 20,000 and by the end of that summer more than 100,000 communists, Social Democrats, union officials, and other 'radicals' were imprisoned. Over the course of the next few years, 150,000 communists would be incarcerated in concentration camps and some 30,000 others murdered. Whatever chances there had been of a left-wing coalition to oppose the Nazis quickly slipped away and disappeared almost completely when the SPD was banned, and its leaders were either imprisoned or fled the country.

About 15,000 opposition leaders fled into exile and those who remained fell into a number of categories. Those who were murdered, those who were thrown into concentration camps, those who continued in opposition by leafleting, selling papers, extending party organisations such as their union wing and even organising petitions and demonstrations, those who campaigned for better working conditions and those who remained passive. David Schoenbaum claims that the KPD itself, mistakenly centred its protests on economic rather than political issues and failed to provide an effective resistance.[14] A protest in 1934 called for non-payment of gas, rent, tax and electric bills but workers were reluctant to make overt statements of opposition to the government and risk falling foul of the Gestapo. The KPD also denounced the racist Nuremberg Laws and urged the membership to 'help our tormented Jewish fellow-citizens in whatever way possible'.[15] Despite the obvious risks involved, the party administration unwisely continued to maintain its old, centralised structure by keeping membership lists which ultimately proved to be a catastrophic mistake when these lists fell into the hands of the Gestapo.

Communist activities during the mid-1930 amounted to little more than distributing seditious pamphlets and illegal newspapers such as *Die Rote Fahne* (The Red Flag) whose last legal edition was printed on 27 February 1933 with the warning that 'the ruling class is dancing on a volcano'. There remained, however, an extensive underground movement financed by illegal subscriptions collected in factories and working-class areas. All sorts of information were assiduously collected and channelled out of the country to give a chilling view to 'an uncomprehending and deluded world' of what was happening in Germany but the world did not listen.[16]

Although seriously weakened by the arrests of so many of their cause, the communists had years of experience of revolutionary activity and opposition to government. For instance, for security reasons it was common practice for members of communist espionage rings to operate in ignorance of any cell but their own. They had weaknesses in their movement, however, probably the greatest of which, in the early years of the Nazi regime at least, was a belief that sooner or later the working class would rise up in a general strike and topple it as they had done in 1920 to see off the Kapp Putsch against the government but it was very much a case of relying on a historical precedent without understanding how much society and the methods of those in power had changed. Whilst essentially a revolutionary movement, the communists put their faith in the legalistic traditions of the trade union movement which, in fact, did not support the communist analysis. The Kapp Putsch had been an attempted coup d'état which had been opposed by the democratic forces but the Nazi government, had been put in power democratically, even though they had subsequently forced through anti-democratic legislation. They had, at least, some sort of legitimate authority and had built up their position step by step which gave the working class pause for thought and no single critical moment to ignite a country-wide revolt. Whereas wholehearted support for German communists against the Nazis might have been expected from Moscow, it was very much the case that Stalin held them back and even ordered some communists to cross over and join the Nazi Party in a united front against the Social Democrats.

There were many separate radical left-wing groupings often containing a high percentage of younger people who rejected social pressures to join official youth organisation. The *Jugenbund* had been formed in 1922 and a few months later was followed by the *Jungsturm Adolf Hitler* which was set up to train and recruit future members of the SA which itself was born out of the specialised German assault troops of the First World War. These Nazi youth movements were officially disbanded after the failed Beer Hall Putsch of November 1923 when Hitler was jailed but they continued to flourish underground. They reemerged in 1926 as the *Hitler Jugend Bund der deutschen Arbeiterjugend* (Hitler Youth League of German Worker Youth) which was later abbreviated to the *Hitlerjugend*. Many German youths did not identify with the movement and resisted calls to join, however. There were many separate radical left-wing groupings often containing a high percentage of younger people who rejected social pressures to join the official youth organisations but the hounding and persecution of their leaders did nothing to bring them together. Movements were infiltrated by Gestapo stooges and terror tactics against the most active members caused many to question whether the campaigns they were implementing, such as distributing underground newspapers and plastering city walls with anti-Nazi posters, were worth the risk. The growing power of the Gestapo, operating with impunity, meant that anyone apprehended faced brutal treatment and incarceration. Losses of activists mounted. Pragmatism demanded that active resistance cells protected themselves by careful selection of members and much greater secrecy in operation. but it is doubtful if the Gestapo interpreted a diminution of overt agitation and resistance as a falling off in support for the protestors. They remained alert to the threat but were distracted momentarily by an internal crisis within the Nazi hierarchy that might have offered scope for early action on the part of the resistance movement.

The Röhm Putsch of 30 June 1934 was a manifestation of the power struggle between the army and the SA. Ernst Röhm, the SA Chief of Staff was a longtime friend of Hitler, even though he was known to disparagingly refer to him as that 'ridiculous corporal'. The three million men under Röhm's command greatly outnumbered the *Reichswehr* (the official name of the German armed forces up until 1934) whose numbers had been restricted to 100,000 by Versailles. Röhm planned to use his forces to completely eliminate the German nationalist elites in a final consolidation of power for the Nazis but Hitler, still not securely in control of Germany, saw advantage in preserving these elites for his own purposes. He also feared Röhm's threat to his own position. The *Reichswehr* did not oppose Hitler's purging of the SA leadership. They, too, had grown fearful of what had essentially become Röhm's private army and were concerned that, in a battle for control of all the armed services, many of the army hierarchy would fall to Röhm's assassins.

The *Reichswehr* had already been seduced by Hitler's determination to reestablish Germany's military position in the world but mistakenly assumed that it would be able to withstand political pressures and eventually reassert its dominant role within the country. In general, while the army looked upon the Nazis as morally corrupt, they approved of Hitler's ruthless actions against the left-wing political parties and tacitly approved of his dictatorship with its repressive police and harsh judicial practices against political opponents. There is no doubt that the tradition of obedience to constituted authority in the German military played an important part in defining its response to Nazism, but neither can it be denied that the *Reichswehr* failed to take responsibility for establishing a viable power base to oppose the Nazi Party and allowed itself to be incrementally stripped of its ability to exert political influence.

They struck a deal with Hitler whereby they would accept the NSDAP as the legitimate political authority in Germany in return for Röhm's elimination. Hitler was more than happy to agree. Röhm was serious threat to his own position. Over the course of three days and nights, the SS murdered around 100 of the top SA leaders, including Röhm, and also took the opportunity to eliminate several other political opponents at the same time. The *Reichswehr* High Command was not sorry to see the back of Röhm and closed its eyes to the means of his removal. The regime had shown its true character by committing murder as an act of state but it was an act in which the army was complicit. The alliance between Hitler and the army was completed when military leaders supported Hitler on 19 August 1934 as he took the last key step toward full dictatorial control by assuming the title of *Führer* and Chancellor of the German Reich. The army was soon to find that Hitler's gratitude had its limits, however, and it was the SS that emerged from the crisis with enhanced power and influence.

Inevitably, the Night of the Long Knives, as the Röhm Putsch became known, stirred serious misgivings all through the German elites who were forced to acknowledge the reality of Nazi brutality and there were numerous circles forming in which 'the dignity of the human personality' became a rallying cry for opposition to the murderous regime.[17] There were various informal circles of friends or likeminded people such as groups instigated inside the armed forces by the Chief of the General Staff, Colonel General Ludwig Beck, and socially by Carl Friedrich Goerdeler, who famously called for 'the restoration of ordinary human dignity'.[18] The question was just how widespread had become the arousal of conscience in key positions within the state. Inside the *Abwehr* military intelligence, Admiral Wilhelm Canaris and his Chief of Staff, Colonel Hans Oster, were openly unenthusiastic about the regime but the most obvious opposition to Nazi ideology came from what Hitler called that 'witches kitchen', the *Auswärtiges Amt* (German Foreign Office). Again, it proved to be the pseudo legal nature of the Nazi regime that made it so difficult for any substantial resistance by high officialdom in the civil administration and the army despite the corruption and arbitrariness they were encountering on a daily basis but the contradiction between service to the state, with its warped *Weltanschauung,* and service to the country was lying heavily on the conscience of some.

When Joachim von Ribbentrop set up his own version of the Foreign Office in 1934 called *Dienststelle Ribbentrop* there emerged a concerted effort within the *Auswärtiges Amt* to keep the 'twitching wine waiter' out of matters that didn't concern him and that, in effect, catalysed within the *Auswärtiges Amt* the growth of opposition to the Nazis.[19] In the civil administration too there were the seeds of opposition. The Secretary of State in the Prussian Ministry of the Interior, Herbert von Bismarck was one who made protest at the illegal detentions and resigned. Goerdeler, the Burgomaster of Leipzig, was fundamentally opposed to all that the Nazis stood for and would go on to play a major role in the resistance to Hitler but, he remained in office and restricted himself to sharing his opinions with close friends with whom he worked for closer cooperation between opponents of Nazism inside and outside Germany. As late as 1935, he still believed that Hitler could be a force for good in Germany if he stopped listening to bad advice and his belief that sense and reason would prevail was unshakeable. He thought he could influence the *Führer* when he accepted the post of Reich Price Commissioner to tackle inflation in the economy but, in reality, his role gave him little power and his memos were ignored by Hitler and the President of the Reichsbank and Reich Economics Minister, Hjalmar Schacht.

What Goerdeler and those around him came to realise was that Germans were being 'led into the abyss by criminals and fools' and would be 'driven to death and mutilation'.[20] The Gestapo and the SS were establishing such a stranglehold on society that an unarmed civilian opposition had absolutely no chance of mounting a revolution against the regime. If this grip was to be broken it could only be by crushing the power of what amounted to the Nazi's private army. Only the regular army had the wherewithal to bring that about and if they acted it would mean civil war on a massive scale. The days when a general strike had been seen as the way to topple the Nazis were long gone. It was becoming clear that the new regime was competent and tough enough to retain and consolidate its power and the longer they held that power the harder it was becoming to challenge it. The consequences of active resistance to the Nazi regime were made crystal clear by Gestapo chief Heinrich Himmler when he said,

> We must have more concentration camps. The *Führer* has given me unrestricted powers to arrest anyone I consider suspect . . . We will have to deal not merely with the Army on land, the Navy at sea, and the Luftwaffe in the air; we shall have a fourth battlefield to look after: Inner Germany! Mass arrests on an unprecedented scale will be necessary . . . many political prisoners will have to be shot out of hand . . . the entire country must be occupied by a minimum of thirty Death's Head divisions . . . once the emergency arises, utter ruthlessness is essential . . . any war in which we neglected the internal battleground would lead to catastrophe.[21]

Chapter 2

DEFENDING TRADITIONAL VALUES

'Duty is my pleasure'. If you see duty in this way you will always derive the greatest of strength from it, in all situations in life.
Count Ulrich-Wilhelm von Schwerin von Schwanenfeld[1]

It was an opinion almost universally accepted immediately after the end of the Second World War that 'no [internal] opposition to Hitler worth speaking of ever existed'; that as a nation, the Germans had voluntarily associated themselves with a criminal regime either through blind obedience to the state or as followers of some baleful philosophy and who closed their eyes to the horrors of the Nazi regime.[2] It was only after the war started going very badly wrong for the Germans after Stalingrad, so this theory went, that members of the Wehrmacht General Staff really started to plot a coup against a leader who seemed hell-bent on taking them all down with him to an inglorious grave and leave a legacy that would scar the Junkers' reputation for all time. Even at this late date it might be possible to save themselves and salvage something from the wreckage. This was far from the truth. There were countless instances of personal heroism that testified to an underground of resistance, but it was a fragmented movement, if that word 'movement' could be applied at all.

Those in Germany who were among the first to recognise that the Nazis threatened their traditional values of law and honour were members of the old aristocracy, religious leaders, senior civil servants and monarchists who had never been comfortable with the democratic experiment embodied in the Weimar Republic and who advocated preservation of the old order, developed over many years and at the heart of which they stood. Compared to the rigorously authoritarian and dynamic organisation the Nazis were building, the traditional right, however, was fragmented and politically naïve with many members drifting towards acceptance of the Nazis as the least bad option to preserve some semblance of order. Rebellion for these groups was far from a natural reaction. Under normal circumstances they would have been the first to claim that active resistance to the government was akin to treason and so the question became one of the legitimacy of the regime. Many of them believed that their best interests were served by supporting Hitler and in so doing convinced themselves that they were serving Germany. The Nazi regime, despite being 'an upstart political movement whose leaders were corrupt, hypocritical, murderous, unpleasant and vulgar', seemed to them to be their best hope of restoring the monarchist society that war and revolution had swept away. It promised a way of making possible the political and military revival of their country, and for them that was enough.[3]

They had, for the most part, remained aloof and indifferent, occasionally hostile, to the Weimar government's attempts to introduce democratic politics into Germany and had been primarily concerned with preserving their own inherited status and privileges. It had been their first response to the rise of the NSDAP to try and find common ground on which to stand against the communists and radical leftists whom they saw as the real threat to Germany, but it soon became clear that the Nazis were interested only in reinvented the whole concept of tradition according to their own particular warped agenda. More progressive traditionalists were appalled by the destruction of local parliaments, by the erosion of Germany's image abroad and by the shredding of the social fabric at home but for a long time they had restricted their efforts to fending off intrusion into their respective realms and simply concentrated on defending what was left of them.

Each of these groups eventually had to acknowledge the reality of what was happening and individuals within the groups faced their own choices over how to respond. While most adopted a 'wait and see' approach and hoped to preserve their privileges through compromise, for men and women of courage, integrity and personal conviction, many of them in the highest offices of the land, there could be no giving ground to the Nazis. They recognised that there was no security in compromise under their regime and chose the path of resistance instead, but they could not do so openly and hope to avoid attracting attention. It was necessary for these individuals to stay in office and operate from within the established structure and appeal to conform and in so doing they were forced to adopt a dual existence. This set them on a journey of what Richard Cobb called 'self-discovery' and 'self-renewal'.[4] It became an increasingly hazardous way to live given the tightening grip of the Gestapo and the skills required to live such a life could only be acquire through experience and there was little comfort or support for dissidence to be found in a society that was becoming traumatised by fear. Helmuth von Moltke would later say that while even ordinary criminals in occupied countries could be lauded as martyrs, in Germany martyrs were often looked on as criminals.

When the coalition government led by Hermann Müller collapsed on 27 March 1930, the fate of the Weimar Republic was effectively sealed and the right-wing parties looked to Heinrich Brüning, Franz von Papen, and Kurt von Schleicher to put an end to the failed experiment in democracy by leading the country out of crisis and establishing an authoritarian government. On 11 October 1931 a number of the most important organisations on the German right came together to discuss ways of cooperating in the battle against the left and take control of the political agenda after Brüning had failed to deliver for them. The NSDAP, the *Deutschnationale Volkspartei* (DNVP, German National People's Party), the *Stahlhelm* First World War veteran's organisation, the *Reichs-Landbund* (RLB< National Rural League), the *Alldeutscher Verband* (ADV, Pan-German League), the *Vereinigte Vaterländische Verbände Deutschlands* (VWD, United Patriotic Associations of Germany) all descended on the small resort town of Bad Harzburg to issue a brutal condemnation of Brüning's government and to lay the foundation for the transfer of power to the radical right. The meeting turned out to be a talking shop with few practical consequences but it was a clear indication of the willingness of various right-wing organisations to come together in a 'national opposition' to the Weimar Republic.[5] It proved to be a short-lived opportunity to rein in the Nazis and bind them to a broader coalition, however. Hitler may have gone along with the meeting for the sake of convenience and a way of calming traditionalist concerns over Nazism, but such values of tradition and patriotism that the meeting was supposed to uphold had no part in his philosophy. The preservation of the traditional social structure based upon mutual respect and responsibility was not a solid foundation stone upon which the Nazi intended to build their state but a stumbling block to be smashed into pieces.

The rule of law was the first to go. Opposition within the German Ministry of Justice to Hitler's *Gesunde Volksempfinden* (healthy national community) meant that he had to set up an entirely new court system of *Volksgerichtshof* (People's Court) and *Sondergerichte* (special courts for political crimes) on 24 April 1934. From the very beginning, these were instruments of political control but initially restricted to trying civilians. After 1939, however, the power of the *Volksgerichtshof* was extended to try officers of the armed forces if they had been accused of crimes in which civilians were also implicated. When this threatened to take proceedings into complex and dubious legal territory service personnel accused of political crimes were simply dismissed from the armed services and tried as civilians. Later, in 1944, the court's power was extended to cover all military personnel regardless of civilian connections. The *Führer* was empowered to order a retrial if he was not satisfied with the verdict even if the trail had been legally competent and the final judgement handed down and, as a last resort, trials could be repeated until the desired verdict was returned.

The man Hitler appointed to head the *Volksgerichtshof* was the fanatical ex-communist Roland Freisler, someone who, up to that time, was completely unknown in the German legal system. As a young man, Freisler had been a prisoner in Russia during the First World War and whilst there had become fluent in Russian and apparently converted to Bolshevism. After returning to Germany, however, in 1925 he suddenly emerged as a dedicated, fanatical National Socialist but remained a great admirer of Stalinist strategic terror attack on his supposed enemies within the Soviet Union and made a great study of Andrei Vishinsky's tactics as prosecuting attorney at the Moscow political show trials. Hitler knew that he has found the right man for the job and even called Freisler Germany's Vishinsky.[6] In his capacity as prosecutor, judge and jury combined, Freisler went to great lengths to show his devotion to Hitler and faithfully followed his directive that 'the legal profession [must] understand that the nation is not here for them, but that they are here for the nation . . . all clamour about injustice is nothing but a lack of insight into the political situation'.[7] Fiesler had cameras in place that would start filming whenever he gave a signal. At that point, he would begin ranting at the accused, often using obscene language and frothing at the mouth, to paint them as worthless criminals. A certain natural justice would prevail when, on the morning of 3 February 1945, a raid by a US bomber force on Berlin resulted in the *Volksgerichtshof* building collapsing on Freisler seriously injuring him before he died on the way to hospital.

By January 1933, the bourgeois parties, including the church and the military, had moved so far toward accommodating Hitler that he was able to destroy them within his first year in power before they fully understood the danger they were in. The eminent businessman and politician, Alfred Hugenberg, who served in Hitler's first cabinet, who had tried to restrain Hitler within the Reichstag by creating a conservative coalition, was soon swept aside as the new Chancellor implemented his *Gleichschaltung* (synchronisation, i.e. Nazification) policy towards German institutions. With so many of Hitler's policies genuinely favoured by the right, such as the attack on the Versailles Treaty, it is no surprise that conservative opposition was swiftly muted. In fact, they applauded much of what the Nazis were doing and not until the war clouds started gathering after 1935 did they see him and his movement clearly for what they were. A movement that many admired at the outset they now began to despise when they witnessed the terrible consequences of their lassitude. Edgar Jung and Gero von Boese had belatedly tried to establish a conservative opposition within the NSDAP government in 1934 and had been mercilessly cut down along with many other opponents of the regime in the Röhm Putsch. Any talk of opposition now took place in private but it focussed on the growing risk of war. It was common knowledge that the German armed forces were many years away from completing their rearmament programme to the point where they could risk precipitating a war with Britain or France. Domestic issues such as the subjugation of the working classes and the persecution of the Jews barely registered.

The dangers inherent within any movement or circle that actively plotted insurrection were glaringly obvious and that necessarily meant that where such groupings existed they were secretive and disinclined to advertise themselves. This meant that each was generally unaware of others and any possibility of cooperation was severely limited not least by the ever-present danger of infiltration by informers and *agent provocateurs*.

For many who looked to defend what they saw as traditional values the rule of law was not always sacrosanct but there were some for whom that was the foundation of a stable society and the way that the Nazis dismantled the edifice of justice was all it took for them to reject National Socialism entirely. Amongst those who stood up for the basic principle of justice for all was Adolf von Harnier Freiherr von Regendorf, a lawyer whose religious and philosophical belief in an orderly state founded on the rule of law led him to reject any use of force in politics. He had roundly condemned Hitler as early as 1923 after his failed Beerhall putsch and was a vocal critic of Nazism all through the following years. In August 1939 he was at a meeting of like-minded opponents of the regime when it was raided by the Gestapo after an informer had betrayed them. The whole group was thrown into prison and held for five years before being brought to trial. In his defence he declared himself to be an 'ardent monarchist' believing the monarchist order to be 'the happiest of all state institutions known in the history of mankind.' On the strength of 'natural human rights' he felt morally obliged, regardless of the 'public condition' of the fatherland to play an active part in its concerns. Found guilty of high treason, Harnier was sentenced to ten years imprisonment. It was said of him that he 'gave many fellow prisoners moral support in those dark times'.[8] On 12 May 1945 he was due to be released from Straubing Prison by the Americans but on that very day he died of typhus and general physical exhaustion.

Born in Saltcoats, Scotland, the son of a diplomat, Otto Karl Kiep was another lawyer who had served in the German forces during the First World War and went on to be part of the German delegation to the Paris peace talks and later to Versailles. He later became the German Consul General in New York but retired from the diplomatic corps in 1933 having found that the political part he was being called upon to play was the complete opposite of what he stood for. He was in England at the outbreak of the war but returned to Germany to enlist in the Wehrmacht. As Chief of the Reich Press Office he established ties with resistance circles, such as the one run by Johanna Susanne Elisabeth Solf and later with the Kreisau Circle but careless talk brought him to the attention of the Gestapo and he was arrested on 16 January 1944. Brought to trial, Freisler sentenced him to death and he was duly hanged on 26 August 1944 in Plötzensee Prison.

It is no surprise that so many opponents of the Nazis were trained lawyers and Ewald von Kleist-Schmenzin was another but he was, at the same time, a wealthy landowner who had grown up on his parents' estate in Pomerania. Kleist was first and foremost a patriot, a strong supporter of the Stahlhelm and the DNVP, but he resolutely rejected the NSDAP. The dilemma he faced after the Nazis took power was a painful conflict between his love of country and abhorrence of its government. It was something that he, like others, had to resolve within his own conscience. He put forward his views in pamphlets he wrote when he said that hundreds of thousands of decent people had supported Hitler because of the political vacuum in the space abandoned by the conservative. 'I no longer consider it acceptable', he said, 'that we continue to tolerate the fiction that National Socialism is a national movement. This madness must be destroyed.'[9] Arrested twice and imprisoned for short periods in 1933 for his opposition, it was clear to him that he would have to look beyond Germany's borders for help but it was no easy decision for him in 1938 to play an important part in the unsuccessful move to persuade France and Britain to stand up to Hitler over his threat against Czechoslovakia and again, in the following year, in what he called his 'patriotic duty', he tried to engage Sweden into acting as a mediator to prevent the German attack in the West.[10] Kleist fully understood the enormity of his actions and furthermore realised the vanishingly small chance that he would be able to make much of a difference. Echoing the sentiments of Adam von Trott at a sense of isolation and futility, he expressed his despair to a Swedish friend at one time by saying, 'I am now all alone'.[11] He became closely involved in von Stauffenberg's 20 July plot and when that failed, he was arrested and put on trial at Freisler's *Volksgerichtshof* on 23 February 1945 where he was sentenced to death. He was executed by hanging on 9 April 1945 in Plötzensee.

Someone else who came from the landed gentry was Count Ulrich-Wilhelm Graf Schwerin von Schwanenfeld whose held large estates in Mecklenburg and West Prussia. As a young man, he studied agriculture and built up close ties with other students, such as fellow aristocrat Peter Graf Yorck von Wartenburg, who all advocated the political renewal of Germany based upon Christian social values. Already dismayed by Hindenburg's weak response to Hitler's rise he came to the opinion that 'Germany could only be freed from the [Nazis] by Hitler's violent death'.[12] He became involved with other opposition members such as Adam Trott zu Solz, Hans Oster and Hans von Dohnannyi establishing a particularly close relationship with Colonel General Erwin von Witzleben and it was in his house that Oster held some of his meetings to plan the 1938 coup d'état to topple Hitler. Heavily involved in the Stauffenberg plot, Schwerin was arrested on 21 July 1944 and tried in Freisler's court on 21 August. He was hanged at Plötzensee on 8 September 1944.

Chapter 3

LEFT-WING RESISTANCE

All resistance borders on treason.[1]

Many Germans who had suffered the trials and tribulations of the First World War trenches were bitterly disappointed at the failure of the Weimar governments to give meaning to their traumatic experiences by bringing about a renewal of German society through the abolition of class differences and by focusing on social welfare. The democratically-elected governments of the German republic faced two insoluble crises not of their own making. One they inherited and the other hit them like a battering ram. Both the legacy of the Treaty of Versailles and the world-wide economic meltdown might have been survivable in the long term but the country was not given the chance to find peaceful solutions. This was primarily because government was constantly being attacked from within by extreme and powerful forces neither of which had any desire to prolong democratic rule. The communists and the NSDAP battled the establishment and each other and foiled all attempts by the centre politicians to govern responsibly and efficiently. Effectively the direction of German politics after 1930 was determined outside the Reichstag. Parliamentary democracy went on but, without the moderate politicians realising it, had become irrelevant. Their *Rechtsstaat* (Rule of Law) banner was being ripped to shreds by the storms of extremism.

The crucial battles behind the scenes were won by the NSDAP when Hitler became Chancellor. He did much to demolish the old class structure which seemed to be a move in favour of democratic rights of workers but he had insidiously and almost without the workers realising it, replaced it with a new form of oppression based on coercion and false promises. While the economy grew and employment levels increased significantly it was all on the back of aggressive rearmament, a cure that threatened consequences much worse than the malady. Rather than the people coming together for mutual benefit, they saw society disintegrating under the jackboot.

Many influential writers have ignored or marginalised the importance of communist resistance in Nazi Germany.[2] Claude David and Alain Desroches claim that there was no organised resistance in Germany at all before 1938/39 after which the Kreisau Circle became the 'first nucleus of the opposition to Nazism [that included] liberals and conservatives, aristocrats and clergymen, landowners and industrialists, lawyers and professors'.[3] Resistance within the working class was seen by David Schoenbaum as virtually absent in terms of political dissent and focussed almost totally on economic issues of wages and working conditions. Probably the most famous contemporary writer of the Nazi period, William Shirer writes only of the 20 July plotters.[4]

Received wisdom has it that Nazi repression of socialist and communist opposition was swift and crushing with the main Communist Party leaders arrested or driven into exile. In truth, while Christian and socialist resistance was carried out by individuals or small networks, this was dwarfed by communist resistance that embraced a wide spectrum of actions including propaganda, sabotage, guerrilla warfare, espionage and industrial action that had huge detrimental impact on the production of munitions and aircraft. As an example, the communist cell at the Hasag-Werke factory replaced the explosive charge of the Panzerfaust anti-tank rocket launchers with sand.[5] In the first half of 1944 there were as many as 200,000 strikers (of all nationalities) in Germany all during a time when the Nazi police had arrested 177,000 men and women. The Gestapo was forced to devote more and more resources to its internal security, Thirty new SS police battalions were formed, as well as detachments of armed Nazi militants.

In the 1920s, the KPD had been in close contact with the state security services of the Soviet Union (the GPU, then the NKVD) and with the clandestine apparatus of the *Westeuropäisches Büro der Komintern* led by Georges Dimitrov. The basis of its organisation was the paramilitary *Roten Frontkämpferbund* with more than 100,000 members, providing military training for the protection of demonstrations and picket lines and confrontations in the streets with Nazis. Banned in 1929, this reformed as the *Kampfbund gegen den Fachismus* and came into direct confrontation with the Nazis and the Weimar government who supported the Nazis in the name of maintaining law and order.

Before 1933, the German labour movement was the largest in the world with many years of experience behind it, but it failed to offer a united opposition to the Nazis mostly as a result of the polarity between the SPD and the communists. Immediately after the Nazis came to power, the SA launched a terror campaign with systematic attacks on organised labour at the same time as the NSDAP political leadership was professing to represent the true interests of the workers. By April 1933 almost forty trade union offices had been raided and occupied by the SA and SS. Full-time trade union officials were arrested and beaten and those who hoped that they could work with the NSDAP were disabused in June when Dr. Robert Ley's German Labour Front was installed as the state's compulsory association of workers and employers. By the end of the year few left-wing activists remained at liberty and those that did had to seriously consider the consequences of resistance. In 1934 the Gestapo noted in its reports that despite the arrests and sentences imposed on the Communists 'the KPD has an enormous apparatus of remarkable permanent staff who succeed, in the provinces, in reconstituting the party apparatus'.[6] By October 1935, 219 of the 1933 communist leadership had been imprisoned, 24 were executed and 125 had emigrated.

There were two years of organised resistance where tens of thousands took part in illegal union organisations or activities such as the distribution of anti-Nazi literature but intense Gestapo terror tactics took their toll and a growing realisation that the Nazi regime was not going to weaken and fade away had the inevitable effect of discouraging the working-class opposition but it did not die altogether. The 1936 Olympics in Berlin was an opportunity for the KPD to show the world that the whole of Germany was not behind Hitler. They planned a campaign of unrest and strikes to coincide with the games but the Gestapo anticipated it and carried out roundups of militant workers. There were many incidents of torn or burned Nazi flags and anti-Nazi slogans chanted in the crowd or painted on the walls. The large motor car factory 'Auto-Union' in Berlin went on strike and the regime was forced to grant wage rises to quell the propaganda disaster but immediately after the games were over, retribution fell upon those who had participated in the strikes. KPD activity persisted but the Berlin section, was violently dismantled in January 1940 and its leader Willi Gall, executed. It reappeared under Rudolf Hallemeyer in 1941 when *Die Rote Fahne* was published once more within a short time, its leaders, too, were wiped out.

Communist opposition continued in the concentration and extermination camps where KPD militants increasingly took over the roles of auxiliaries: chamber chiefs, barrack chiefs, office workers, team leaders in the construction sites and workshops as well as maintenance. Occupying one of these positions significantly increased the chance of survival. Wherever this happened, the condition of the deportees improved. Himmler offered the German political prisoners freedom if they joined General Dirlewanger's SS Brigade. Some 800 agreed to join but over half deserted to the Red Army. In the Buchenwald camp, KPD members were able to set up a highly developed medical system fully equipped with equipment stolen from the SS. It ensured food supplies for the sick and the Soviet prisoners of war deprived of food. It set up an information service and achieved remarkable success in sabotaging the war production of factories employing camp labour. In Dora where the V2 rockets were produced, 80 per cent of all production was not fit for purpose and at the Gustloff factory, production fell from 55,000 rifles to a few thousand and three quarters of the production was sent back by the Wehrmacht as unusable when camp labour was brought in. KPD organisations in neighbouring towns sent political material, food and sometimes weapons into the camps. In both Dachau and Saschenhausen the escapes of leading KPD members such as Herbert Tschäpe, Rudi Wunderlich and Richard Schmeink, was organised.

The following few accounts of people who chose the path of opposition are presented here as a tribute to the many thousands of others who did the same. Friedrich Husemann was an early casualty of Nazi persecution of the working class. Working as a miner, he had educated himself through evening classes and became vice president of the International Miners' Association before being elected as an SPD member of the Reichstag in 1924. He was first arrested on 10 March 1933 along with other executives of the miners' union and several more times over the next two years before ending up in Papenburg-Esterwegen concentration camp on 13 April 1935. Two days later it was reported that he had been 'shot while trying to escape'. More than 1,000 mourners attended his burial, many of whom were arrested on the spot by the Gestapo.[7]

One of the underground working-class organisations that took up the role of opposition after 1933 was the *Internationaler Sozialistischer Kampfbund* (ISK, International Socialist Fighting League) that set up clandestine trade unions in the Hamburg area. Walter Brandt was a member of the group printing and distributing pamphlets urging passive resistance but by 1935, they had been infiltrated and Brandt's fiancée was arrested. She was released after a few weeks but in the meantime, Brandt had come to the attention of the Gestapo when he protested at her arrest. He fled to Switzerland and the France but decided to return to Germany in the guise of an English student. He was quickly denounced by an informer in Munich. Friends who had been arrested earlier had no idea that Brandt had returned to Germany and thought it safe to give up his name under interrogation since he was out of the country. Brandt, aged 25, hanged himself in his cell in October 1937.

Hans Funger, who worked on the railways, was described in court on 3 December 1937 as a 'long-standing trade union functionary' when he was charged with the re-establishment of the illegal United Association of the Railwaymen of Germany. He was sentenced to fifteen years hard labour in prison. Friends believe that he died in Bergen-Belsen concentration camp at some time during the war. Heinrich Körner was a member of the Christian Trade Unions of West Germany where he specialised in setting up educational facilities for its members. He later became a member of the state parliament. He was arrested on numerous occasions throughout the war and ended up in Plötzensee prison where he died on 25 April 1945. Franz Leuninger was a bricklayer, a city councillor for Breslau and a nominee for the Reichstag when the Nazis came to power. During the war years he worked in the resistance with Goerdeler and Beck but was arrested and brought before the courts on 26 September 1944. He was executed in Plötzensee prison on 1 March 1945. Oswald Wiersich had been a prominent trade unionist since the early 1900s. During the 1930s he was under constant Gestapo surveillance but maintained a clandestine friendship with Wilhelm Leuschner through whom he also met Beck. Arrested on 22 August 1944, at the age of 72, Wiersich was executed in Plötzensee prison on the same day as Leuninger.

The SPD was outlawed on 22 June 1933 and its leaders arrested where they could be found. Taken into 'protective custody', they faced torture and incarceration in concentration camps. Members who did not have the option of flight were left feeling hopeless and isolated. Young people, especially, set about creating a new socialist movement built on traditions of solidarity but inevitably the organisation was localised and disjointed. A group with around 3,000 members, mostly university students in the Berlin area on the socialist fringe of the SPD, was formed calling itself *Roter Soβtrupp* (The Red Shock Troop) but it was quickly stamped on by the Gestapo and its leaders thrown into concentration camps.

A splinter group from the SPD calling itself the *Sozialistische Arbeiterpartei Deutschlands* (SAPD, Socialist Workers Party of Germany,) had already been formed in 1931 and now tried to take up the fight but it too was quickly crushed by the Gestapo. The ISK had been in existence since 1926 and was able to operate undetected right up until 1938 helping political refugees leave the country, conducting sabotage and distributing leaflets. Its most memorable act of defiance was on 19 May 1935 when members painted anti-Nazi slogans across many of the bridges over a new autobahn between Frankfurt am Main and Darmstadt that Hitler was due to drive down in an inauguration ceremony. The Nazi propaganda film of the event required extensive editing.

While the conservative opposition within the military and the civil service had chosen to hide in broad daylight, as it were, by working within the old establishment, the socialists had no such option available to them. Not for them the freedom to move around both within and without the country but, at least, their rejection of compromise freed them from the burden of conscience. It did, however, make them easy targets for the Gestapo The bulk of the SPD leadership had fled in 1933 to Prague and later to Paris in 1938 then London in 1940. By 1938, SPD underground groups inside Germany were instructed by the exiled leadership to stop distributing seditious pamphlets. The risks had become much too high for too little reward.

The KPD had been a powerful political force in Germany all through the Weimar years and it was they who held the largest street demonstrations against the Nazis. It was no surprise, therefore when the KPD was the first political party to feel the full weight of Nazi retribution as they set out to annihilate it. The SS launched a series of brutal raids into working-class areas of many major German cities. The ferocity of the actions took the KPD by surprise and their underground organisation was badly mauled with premises smashed and a great number of activists ending up in concentration camps without the benefit of trial. Despite this devastation, the communists continued to print the *Rote Fahn* newssheet and distribute it in beerhalls and workplaces. Through this medium, the working class were kept very well informed about the terror methods being used by the security forces. During the two years 1934–5, the Gestapo estimated that some three million illegal pamphlets were circulated. Then just at the time that the exiled KPD leadership in Switzerland were calling for the coming together of all anti-fascist forces both inside and outside Germany, the Ribbentrop-Molotov non-aggression pact was signed between Germany and the Soviet Union on 23 August 1939 and communist resistance became virtually comatose until 22 June 1941 when Hitler ripped it up the treaty with the launch of the Barbarossa offensive.

After 1933 there was little contact between the exiles and internal left-wing opposition. Despite the growing threat of reprisals for opponents of the regime, however, personal integrity and confidence in the fundamental rightness of their cause, motivated some to rise to the challenge of resistance whatever the risks. While the left was indecisive before 1933, they had the courage of their convictions afterwards to take on the regime even though many of their actions appear pathetically ineffectual, but that must be seen against the crushing forces of oppression and terror that were ranged against them rather than the weakness of desire. In contrast to the actions of the political-military opponents of Hitler their efforts were surely worthy of respect.

Wilhelm Leuschner was Minister of the Interior of the Hesse provincial parliament between 1928 and 1933. This 'quiet and composed' man had worked his way up from working-class trade-union roots by virtue of a personality described as both 'scintillating [and] unfathomable'.[8] His ambition was nothing less than the full integration of the working class into the state with political, spiritual and cultural equality before the law. Already marked out by the Gestapo as a troublemaker in 1933, he made a public stance against the Nazi Labour Union and its leader Robert Ley by refusing to act as its representative at the International Labour Conference in Geneva. For his intransigence he got a two-year jail term. Upon his release he had a chance to emigrate but remained in Germany and started up a small manufacturing business which gave him an excuse to travel widely within the country. He revived contacts, and made new ones, with trade unionists and socialists building up a secret political network of like-minded opponents of the Nazis, one of whom was the 'red general' Kurt Freiherr von Hammerstein-Equord.[9] He was well aware of the dangers inherent in such a development and summed them up by calling rebellion 'suicidal as if prisoners were to rise up against their heavily armed guards' but that thought did not deter him.[10] He joined the opposition forming around Carl Goerdeler in 1939 and for a time was considered as a candidate to become Chancellor in a post-Hitler Germany. Hunted after the failed Stauffenberg plot, he wrote that his pursuers would 'not find [him] a fainthearted figure among the accused'.[11] Caught and imprisoned facing the inevitable he wrote again, 'and I still love this world in spite of everything' before facing execution in Plötzensee Prison on 29 September 1944. After the war, numerous German schools, streets and squares were named after Leuschner.

Someone who worked with Leuschner was Hermann Maas, secretary of the German Youth Association whose clear-eyed convictions and resolute character galvanised his friends to think clearly and justify their actions with 'spiritual incorruptibility'. It was Theodor Haubach and Carlo Mierendorff, however, who had the closer ties with Leuschner. Both were decorated veterans of the First World War. The four men met with others at the home of the placid Ludwig Schwamb whom they trusted as a rare friend through good and bad. Haubach spoke at many meetings of young Germans advocating a spiritual revival of socialism while serving as Head of the Press Department of the Berlin Police Headquarters. This came to an abrupt halt in 1934 when he was arrested without charge and condemned to two years' hard labour in Esterwegen concentration camp. After his release he had links with the Kreisau Circle and ended up being arrested in the purges following the Stauffenberg plot. More dead than alive through serious illness, he was hanged on 23 January 1945 in Plötzensee Prison.

It was said of Carlo Mierendorff that in his hands every idea was transformed into action. A 'restless genius of a man', he was Leuschner's press chief before 1933 but broke with the SPD over its muted response to the Nazis.[12] His 'Iron Front' anti-fascist paramilitary organisation had organised mass protests against the Nazi Party after Hitler's appointment as Chancellor and he was quickly targeted by the Gestapo. Branded as 'corrupt', he was forced to flee Zurich to avoid arrest, but a sense of duty and responsibility saw him return after a few weeks. 'What will our workers think if we leave them there alone' he said.[13] He secretly remained at liberty for three months before being arrested, marched through the streets of Darmstadt 'like a captured beast' and thrown into Osthofen concentration camp where he was so badly beaten that he had to spend many weeks in hospital there. After four years of brutal treatment, he was released in 1938, when he made contact with opposition groups and joined the Kreisau Circle determined to 'move forward, to victory or to the gallows'.[14] He saw neither. He was killed in an air raid on Leipzig on 4 December 1943.

Adolf Reichwein had received a serious bayonet wound in the First World War trenches but survived to become a student and teacher of history. Not really a socialist but more of a campaigner for social justice, he worked in youth camps across Germany trying to bring to his charges the sense of what Goethe called 'the great inborn capacity of man' and a sense that they were the carriers of 'the holy flame of real human freedom' which they must preserve for future generations.[15] When his marriage broke up after the tragic death of their son, Reichwein went to the US and planned to drive coast-to-coast in an old Ford car but had his journey truncated by an accident in the Rocky Mountains. From there he went to Alaska working for a time as a trapper and lumberjack. He worked his passage on a ship to Japan and China before returning to California and heading south where he crossed Mexico on horseback. Back in Germany after a year's absence he was appointed as personal assistant to the Prussian Minster of Culture. Of the several initiatives he proposed perhaps none was more revolutionary than suggesting that students should be schooled only in the winter months and should be left to roam free and follow whatever interest they chose all through the summer. Taking up a teaching post in Berlin he put many of his ideas about education into practice with an emphasis on showing consideration to others. By 1939, his concern for the way in which German society was being eroded drove him to join the Kreisau Circle where he met Haubach and Mierendorff. By 1944 he was actively seeking out underground communist resistance organisations but perhaps too eagerly. On 4 July he went to a meeting with Anton Saefkow and Franz Jakob but their group had been infiltrated by a Gestapo agent. All three were arrested. Reichwein was executed in Plötzensee prison on 20 October 1944.

As a young mechanic, Anton Emil Hermann Saefkow had joined the *Sozialistischen Arbeiterjugend* (Socialist Workers Youth Party) and after serving in the First World War returned to become a member of oner of the revolutionary council of workers and soldiers. He joined the KPD in 1921 and, together with his wife, Thea, was forced to flee to the Soviet Union to avoid arrest by the police when he engaged in street violence against the state. After an amnesty, he returned to Germany in 1923 and after ten years of political activity was elected to the Reichstag but was never able to take his seat. Instead, he was arrested on charges of 'conspiracy to commit high treason' and given a sentence of twenty months hard labour in Sieburg Prison. Further arrests saw him spend time in Dachau until his release in 1939 when he resumed the underground struggle operating clandestine cells in thirty companies, including the largest war factories: Osram, Telefunken, AEG, Hasse und Wrede, Argus-Motoren, Siemens. [16] After 1942, together with Franz Jacob he led the Saefkow-Jacob-Bästlein underground resistance and sabotage movement which aimed to bring together the remaining, disparate resistance groups under a single leadership within the communist movement. This organisation became one of the biggest resistance groups in Germany, including not just workers, but doctors, teachers, engineers and artists. About one-quarter of its 400 members were women. When the group was rolled up by the Gestapo, some 280 arrests were made with around 100 perishing in execution chambers or concentration camps.

The court judgement of Saefkow and Bernhard Bästlein described them as 'old permanent communist officials, deeply animated by an unbounded hatred against our *Führer* and our State . . . they are hardened and incorrigible. The punishments they have already endured made no more impression on them than their stay in the concentration camps. Especially in the fifth year of the war, they were so successful in reconstituting the German Communist Party and working for the disintegration of the Wehrmacht that it resulted in the most serious perils for the Reich.'[17] Saefkow was executed by guillotine, known in Germany as *Fallbeil* or *Köpfmaschine*, on 18 September 1944. To his second wife Änne, he wrote, 'I want to thank you, my comrade, for the greatness and beauty that you have given me in our life together . . . I am militant and shall die bravely. I only ever wanted to do good.' Haubach was condemned by Freisler's *Volksgerichtshof* on 20 October and hanged on the same day.

Ernst von Harnack, the cousin of Arvid Harnack, had studied law and served in a number of government positions prior to being dismissed on 20 June 1932 as part of the *Preußenschlag* (Prussian coup d'état) when the legal government of the Free State of Prussia was dissolved and executive powers transferred to the Reich Minister of the Armed Forces. He was arrested in 1933 as an agitator after he had called for an investigation into the murder of the SPD politician Johannes Stelling who has been a victim of the Night of the Long Knives massacre. Upon his release, von Harnack set up a cloth-trading business in the centre of Berlin which allowed for people to contact him without drawing attention to themselves. Although he said of himself that he was not, by nature, brave and had to steel himself to overcome fear, through his business he provided refuge for victims of state persecution and helped Jews to escape from the country. He came into close contact with Goerdeler, Beck and Julius Leber and was part of the group under Oster that planned a coup in 1938. When that came to nothing, he knew that only mass revolt could unseat Hitler and that would require an unlikely alliance between the old trade union leaders and the military. He offered himself as a bridge between the two eventually allying himself with the Stauffenberg plotters. He was arrested two months after the failed plot and was executed on 5 March 1945 after spending weeks chained to the walls of his cell.

The tough and uncompromising Julius Leber served in the Reichstag as the SPD spokesman on military affairs between 1924 and 1933. Goebbels never forgot the day in 1929 when Leber had called him 'the clown of the Reichstag'.[18] The day after Hitler was made Chancellor, Leber and some friends were attacked and arrested. Upon his release he tried to enter the Reichstag and was again arrested. This time he got a heavy prison sentence for being the 'spiritual leader' of insurrection and served his time in Sachsenhausen concentration camp. From prison he wrote that he had one great duty which was not to lose faith in himself. His existence was conditioned by 'profound passion and strength of feeling which lights up all the avenues and rooms of the inner being and thus becomes reality,' he wrote. His detention was particularly harsh. He spent a whole year in a dark cell with neither bed nor chair nor table. The winter nights saw him lying on stone floors without heat or blanket. When he was restored some measure of ease, he wrote to a friend saying that he was 'in good heart' with his sense of humour 'unimpaired'.[19] Released from Sachsenhausen in 1937 he started a business as a coal merchant in Berlin secretly meeting Leuschner and Mierendorff. He was arrested on 5 July 1944 after being exposed by an informer. After refusing to break under torture, he eventually made a statement admitting his own guilt after being faced with threats against his family. On 24 October, Freisler condemned him to death for 'high treason to the state' but he was not executed until 5 January 1945. His last message to his friends was 'For so good and just a cause the sacrifice of one's own life is an appropriate price . . . It is not our fault that all turned out like this.'[20]

Chapter 4

YOUTH RESISTANCE

> We will begin again! Truly we will. The soil will be ploughed one last time to be ready for a new, good seed. It will – Oh it will![1]

After the National Socialists took power on 30 January 1933, the *Hitlerjugend, Bund deutscher Arbeiterjugend* (Hitler Youth) was the only legally sanctioned youth organisation in Germany. All other youth associations were banned, forced to disband, or affiliated with the *Hitlerjugend*. The growth of National Socialism owed much of its success to the way it appealed to the generation growing up during the turbulent years of the Weimar Republic, but a great number of young people stood up courageously and selflessly for the preservation of civilised values. For some it was a religious duty, for others moral or philosophical issues gave them purpose and strength to resist. Weimar had tried but failed, in the face of immense internal and external pressures, to give young people a solid foundation on which to build their lives but so many families were driven to destitution and education of the young was a luxury few could afford.

Youthful vigour and enthusiasm could not be quashed, however, and while some marched under the flag of the 'corruptly distorted patriotism' of the *Hitlerjugend*, others remained attached to what, under Nazi rule, would become illegal political youth groups such as the *Kommunistischer Jugendverband Deutschlands* (KJVD, Communist Youth Federation of Germany) and the *Socialistche Arbeiter Jugend* (SAJ, Young Socialist Workers).[2] It was not easy for the young to see beyond the false values and standards that the National Socialist leadership laid before them with such elaborate care but a great many did just that even as late as 1933 after which state-sponsored terror made it clear that the new regime would not tolerate any sort of independent youth movement. Where there was youthful hunger to discover a place in society and a set of values to live by, the state provided nourishment in the form of myths of Aryan racial superiority, lectures about the evils of the class structure and physical activities such as camping, communal singing, hiking and sport. All intellectual pursuits and independence of thought were vigorously discouraged. Liberalism and individualism became concepts which no Hitler youth could openly espouse and hope to avoid humiliation and expulsion from their seat by the campfire into the dark night beyond its glow.

The *Gedenkstätte Deutscher Widerstand* (Memorial to the German Resistance) in Berlin included four sections on 'youth opposition'; working-class groups, young Christians, the circles headed by Hanno Günther and Helmuth Hübener and Bündisch Youth, and Oppositional youth such as the *Leipzig Meuten* and Swing Youth. The Memorial is a recognition of just how important juvenile opposition was, not necessarily because of its marginal effects on the Nazi regime but as a testament to the willingness of some courageous young people to stand against it often with catastrophic consequences. It is shameful that these heroic youths were given so little recognition during the post-war years when they were categorised as naïve, idealistic or even criminal. In the twelve years up to 1945, a total of sixty-nine juveniles were dragged before the *Volksgerichtshof* on charges of high treason. Twenty-one were executed and forty-three jailed.

The term 'juvenile' was defined at the time as a person under eighteen years of age at the time of arrest or at the time the alleged offences took place and the crime of high treason had been defined by the Weimar government as attacks that threaten the head of state, attempts to change or alter the territory of the federal state, and violations of its constitution. There still remained the idea that juveniles were not fully responsible for their actions and it was still the case that courts should balance concern for the offender's welfare against the need to punish them for their crime. On 28 February 1933, however, the Nazis introduced a Decree of the President against Treason and High Treasonous Activities which widened the definition of political crime and an increase in the range of punishments and began a process of stripping back the rights of the accused. This was aimed particularly at dealing with the threat from the communists. The *Volksgerichtshof*, itself was created by decree on 24 April 1934 to take over the handling of treason cases from the Supreme Court and quickly gained a reputation as a 'terror court, notorious for the severity of its punishments, secrecy of proceedings, and denial of the accused all semblance of judicial process'. It was clearly not a court in the judicial sense but an instrument of Nazi terror.[3] At the same time the Penal Code was amended in relation to high treason. The death penalty was now mandated for (a) the establishment or reestablishment of an organisation conspiring to commit high treason, (b) the subversion of police and defence forces, (c) attempts to influence the masses through writings, records, pictorial images and radio broadcasts and (d) the importation of treasonous material. Death was an available, but not mandatory, sentence for incitement to commit high treason.

Juveniles were not immune from the bitter knowledge of the sort of retribution resisters faced. This was especially true once war broke out when executions of 'traitors' were widely advertised through hoardings. Here again we are faced with the question of what motivated individuals to perform acts of resistance. A number of factors may be considered including a propensity for anti-authoritarian behaviour, religious belief, susceptibility to adult influences or loss of friend or family member through war or Gestapo persecution. Analysis of the backgrounds of the cases studied by Geerling, Magee and Brooks suggest that a 'typical' resister was male, came from a stable family, was employed as an apprentice of some trade, was not particularly well-educated and whilst never enthusiastic about the *Hitlerjugend*, had no previous criminal record.[4] Probably the most important characteristics common to many was either a strong religious belief or a connection to the communists. The study also suggest that juvenile resistance had its own distinct characteristics. It tended to be carried out by small independent groups with little adult direction, focused on small-scale disruption with little impact and no broader strategic ambition; none of which might be described as particularly unusual juvenile behaviour. A fairly typical example is that of Friedrich Lachnit, an apprentice boat builder from Vienna. He had been in youth organisations before briefly joining the *Hitlerjugend* and then, after the German invasion of the Soviet Union, sent anti-war newssheets to troops on the Eastern Front. Charged with subversion of the armed forces, he was tried and executed.

One of the larger youth groups, the *Roter Stoβruss* (Red Combat Patrol) was formed in Berlin as early as 1933. It published a weekly newspaper declaring its commitment to 'a movement without party book or club badge'.[5] At a time when most people were willing to toe the line and say nothing, the *Roter Stoβruss*, with great enthusiasm and drive, spread its influence throughout the country bringing together many strands of left-wing resistance. Money was collected to help the families of those arrested and escape routes were established for wanted persons fleeing the country. Pamphlets were distributed urging the people not to vote for the NSDAP in the November elections. When those elections saw the last vestiges of democracy done away with, the *Roter Stoßruss*, along with other resistance groups, was stamped on very hard by the Gestapo. A wave of arrests saw many activists given long years of imprisonment. Altogether, over the coming years, some thirty leading members were executed and hundreds more thrown into concentration camps.

Helmuth Hübener was seventeen years old when he was executed by guillotine on 27 October 1942 in Plötzensee Prison. Born into a family that were members of the Church of Jesus Christ of Latter-day Saints (Mormon Church), Hübener had joined the Boy Scouts and then, after they were banned by the Nazis in 1935, he joined the *Hitlerjugend*. After finishing school, he started an apprenticeship in administration and began listening to enemy radio broadcasts from the BBC. He used the information he heard to compose various anti-Nazi and anti-war leaflets which also included insulting remarks about Hitler. They were distributed throughout Hamburg, by surreptitiously pinning them on bulletin boards, inserting them into letterboxes, and stuffing them in coat pockets. One such pamphlet read,

> German boys! Do you know the country without freedom, the country of terror and tyranny? Yes, you know it well, but are afraid to talk about it. They have intimidated you to such an extent that you don't dare talk for fear of reprisals. Yes you are right; it is Germany – Hitler Germany! Through their unscrupulous terror tactics against young and old, men and women, they have succeeded in making you spineless puppets to do their bidding.[6]

Denounced by co-worker and Nazi Party member Heinrich Mohn, Hübener was arrested by the Gestapo at the Hamburg Social Authority on 5 February 1942. Assessed as having an intelligence 'far above the average for boys of his age' he was brought before the *Volksgerichtshof* on 11 August 1942 and tried as an adult. He was found guilty of conspiracy to commit high treason and treasonous furthering of the enemy's cause and sentenced not only to death, but also to permanent loss of his civil rights, which meant the prison guards were allowed to torture and abuse him, and he was not allowed bedding or blankets in his cold cell. After hearing the sentence, Hübener faced the presiding judge Engert and said: 'Now I must die, even though I have committed no crime. So now it's my turn, but your turn will come.'

One of more than 2,000 Jehovah's Witnesses murdered by the Nazis was the seventeen-year-old Jonathan Stark. Talented in music and drawing, he was called up to military service on 1 October 1943 but he refused to bear arms and would not swear the oath of allegiance to Hitler. He was taken into custody in December of that year and taken to Moringen concentration camp for underage 'enemies of the Reich' in February 1944. In October the same year, not long after his eighteenth birthday, he was transferred to the Sachsenhausen concentration camp, where he was hanged on 1 November without ever having been brought to trial.

The Edelweiss Pirates

There were youth groups throughout Germany who refused to accept the rigidity and overt political nature of the *Hitlerjugend*. In Cologne, they called themselves the Navajos, in Essen, the Roving Dudes, and in Düsseldorf and Oberhausen, the Kittelbach Pirates. Members were generally 14 to 18 years old, wore a badge depicting an *edelweiss* flower for which they earned the common name of 'Edelweiss Pirates'. This loose grouping of working-class teenagers didn't do anything especially violent at first, preferring to spend time on camping trips but they were not averse to squaring up to *Hitlerjugend* patrols. Once the war started these young people, who had hitherto been little more than a pest to the authorities, began taking part in organised resistance actions such as helping and hiding escapees from concentration camps and distributing Allied propaganda. As the Gestapo terror escalated, the groups fought openly with the secret police, on one occasion killing Cologne's Gestapo chief. Himmler was furious and demanded action against them. Many were imprisoned, others forced into Nazi labour camps or youth concentration camps, while some were killed. The leaders of the Navajos were publicly hanged in 1944.

The Swing Youth

Before the war, many upper-class teenagers rebelled against the Nazis, amongst them a group the Nazis called the *Swingjugend* (Swing Youth). They idolised Anglo-American culture, especially swing music and big bands which the Nazis despised, and mocked Nazi aesthetics with their style of dress. Girls curled their long hair, wore makeup, and painted their nails while boys also wore their hair long, donned British-style hats and, often, Union Jack lapel pins. These teenagers also started secret dance clubs, where they would gather and listen to illegally imported jazz records. Their propensity to speak English baffled and enraged the Nazi authorities who marked them down as subversive even though they showed no particular political affiliation. Their acceptance of Jewish members and half-Jewish members did little to help. Once the war broke out, Himmler was freer to act and he did just that after a jazz concert organised by Swing Youth in Hamburg attracted an audience of some 500. When he received a report of the concert he read,

> The dancers made an appalling sight. None of the couples danced normally; there was only swing of the worst sort. Sometimes two boys danced with one girl; sometimes several formed a circle, linking arms and jumping, slapping hands, even rubbing the backs of their heads together; and then, bent double, with the top half of the body hanging loosely down, long hair flopping into the face, they dragged themselves round practically to their knees. When the band played a rumba, the dancers went into wild ecstasy. They all leaped around and mumbled the chorus in English. The band played wilder and wilder numbers; none of the players was sitting any longer, they all jitterbugged on the stage like wild animals. Frequently boys could be observed dancing together, without exception with two cigarettes in the mouth, one in each corner.[7]

Naturally, he demanded the arrest of the group's leaders. These were thrown into concentration camps and up to 300 members had their heads shaved.

The *Leipzig Meuten*

The *Leipzig Meuten* (Packs of Leipzig) was a youth movement born in the industrial city made up of loosely organised groups mainly within the working class. The members were from social-democratic and communist children's groups. They had been given this name by the Gestapo but preferred to call themselves the *Bündische Jugend* (Union of Youth). The names of individual groups were the *Hundestart* and the *Lile*, after a cemetery and plaza in Leipzig each with around forty members while another larger group, the *Reeperbahn*, was organised in the district of Lindenau. It is estimated that there were up to 1,500 adolescent members with up to one-third of them being female.

The style of dress within the movement was based on that of traditional youth hiking groups, the boys wearing lederhosen, while the girls wore dark skirts with checkered shirts, knee-high socks, and hiking boots. All wore red neckerchiefs and skull and crossbones badges with the insignia 'BJ'. Peaceable at first, these groups increasingly came into violent contact with the regime as they distributed anti-Hitler leaflets in the city. They started to attack members of the *Hitlerjugend* and broke up their meetings. After a crackdown, several leaders were tried and imprisoned for 'preparing high treason'. A year later, in 1939, mass arrests and imprisonments for pack members followed. The movement never really recovered from this.

Chapter 5

INTELLECTUALS AGAINST THE NAZIS

I have no choice but to tremble at every rattling of the keys in front of the door
    Letter written by Fritz Solmitz and smuggled out of the Fuhlsbüttel concentration camp.[1]

The National Socialist regime depended for its control on the absolute subservience of German citizens but political domination was not enough for the imposition of totalitarian ideology, all intellectual resistance had to be broken also. This required rigid control of the education system, the elimination of press freedom, blanket censorship and stifling propaganda. The most blatant manifestation of the Nazi's desire to supress free thought was the series of book burnings which took place in May 1933. Afterwards, hundreds of authors and scientists were forced to flee for their lives and those who stayed did so on the understanding that any attempt to disseminate anti-Nazi philosophies or plead for intellectual liberty would be severely punished. At the centre of anti-intellectualism was anti-Semitism which was presented as a scientific crusade based on warped theories of race. Jews all across Germany were barred from schools, universities, libraries and public events and, stripped of all human rights, were vilified and demonised.

    Abuses of power were widespread but for those who were prepared to defend their intellectual freedoms against the machinery of the totalitarian state it was a daunting prospect. They may have been united in their struggle but the sheer variety of professions under threat made it difficult for those who chose to resist to come together. Journalists were prevented from telling the truth, scientists were obliged to pay lip service to pseudo-science, medical practitioners were faced with the abominations carried out in the name of medicine such as euthanasia, forced sterilisation and hideous experimentation. By standing against corruptibility of the mind these people fought their own battles for the preservation of decency and humanity.

Carl von Ossietzky was one of the first to be arrested on the morning after the Reichstag fire. He had started his career as a civil servant but turned to journalism with *Das Freie Volk* ('The Free People'), the weekly publication of the *Demokratische Vereinigung* (Democratic Union). Despite poor health he was called to service during the First World War which turned him into a devout pacifist. Afterwards he became secretary of the *Deutsche Friedensgesellsschaft* (German Peace Society) and began publishing its monthly *Mitteilungsblatt* ('Information Sheet'). It was not enough to satisfy his ambitions and soon he accepted the post of foreign editor on the staff of the nonpartisan, democratic, and anti-war *Berliner Volkszeitung* ('Berlin People's Paper'). He wrote in a 'sparkling, flowing, aggressive style' that was often embellished with his scathing wit and developed into a critical attack on National Socialism.[2] His intolerance of Moscow's interventions in Western communist parties saw him pilloried from the left as well as the right.

In the late 1920s, Ossietzky became involved in a campaign to expose collaboration with the Soviet Union in the secret rearmament of Germany in violation of the Treaty of Versailles. At a court hearing in August 1929, he was charged with 'treason and divulgence of military secrets and sentenced to eighteen months in Spandau Prison. In 1933 he was given the chance to leave Germany but he refused to leave the country, saying that a man speaks with a hollow voice from across the border.

On 28 February 1933, he was apprehended at home by the secret police, sent to a Berlin prison, then to concentration camps, first at Sonnenburg and later at Esterwegen-Papenburg where he was forced to perform heavy labour even though he had already sustained a heart attack. In the following year a campaign was launched by Berthold Jacob to nominate Ossietzky for the Nobel Peace Prize, a campaign that included famous people in many parts of the world. Dangerously ill with tuberculosis, he was given the award in 1936 but the Nazis refused to release him from the concentration camp and demanded that he decline the Prize. He refused to do so. Goebbels told the world that he was free to travel to Norway to accept the prize but, in reality, he was refused the necessary documents. The German press was forbidden to make any comment about the award. He died in a civilian hospital on 4 May 1938, broken physically but whole in spirit.

His experiences of the First World War had also turned Fritz Solmitz into a pacifist. After the war he entered the civil service but turned to political journalism, alongside the young Willy Brandt, in 1924 with the *Lübecker Volksbote*, whose editor-in-chief was Julius Leber. After the Reichstag fire, Solmitz was arrested and marched through Lübeck with a sign with the one word 'Jew' hung around his neck. He was thrown into Lübeck-Lauerhof prison before being transferred to Fuhlsbüttel concentration camp. On 19 September 1933, after months of torture, he was found hanged in his cell.

Elisabeth von Thadden's 'large, robust stately appearance and natural self-assurance of bearing suggested that she had 'something of the east German nobility about her'.[3] Although someone to whom 'faith came as naturally as love for one's country', this devoutly pious woman was not without wit, charm or gaiety. In 1927, she founded a Protestant boarding school at Schloss Wieblingen, near Heidelberg but refused to allow her girls to join the *Bund Deutscher Mädel* (League of German Girls). Her contempt for Hitler was no secret and that resulted in her boarding school being closed down in 1941, after which she moved to Berlin and went work in the field of social and child welfare. She came into contact with an opposition group centred around Hanna Solf and members of the Confessional Church. For a while she worked in France as an assistant in a military leave centre but on a visit home she hosted a meeting of the 'Solf Circle' which, by then, had been infiltrated by a Gestapo agent, Paul Reckzeh. Many members of the group were arrested on 13 January 1944 and brought to trial on 1 July 1944. Along with Otto Kiep, Hilger van Scherpenberg, Herbert Mumm von Schwarzenstein, Fanny von Kurowsky and Irmgard Zarden she was charged with 'high treason, sedition, defeatism and favouring the enemy'. Thadden was further charged that she had 'aided and abetted wartime enemies of the Greater German Reich by undermining the war effort and by conspiring to commit high treason'. Up until her death on 8 September 1944, she was held in metal shackles but when she walked to the execution room the chaplain reported that she had walked 'unfalteringly and without trembling'.[4] Her final words before the guillotine fell were 'Put an end Oh Lord, put an end to all our suffering'.

Nikolaus Gross was the son of a labourer and started out his life as a coal miner but worked his way up to become a union representative and editor of the workers' newspaper *Westdeutsche Arbeiterzeitung*. He was a blunt critic of National Socialism and advocated a moral code based on Christian values. Arrested on 12 August 1944 as part of the massive Gestapo roundup after the 20 July bomb plot, he was sentenced to death on 15 January 1945. In a final message to his wife and seven children, he wrote, 'I think of you with deep love and gratitude . . . thank you my loved ones for all you have given me. And forgive me if I have hurt you or failed in my duty and responsibility towards you.' He was hanged in Plötzensee prison on 23 January 1945.[5]

Chapter 6

THE CHURCHES

> The cost of obedience towards God, loyalty to one's conscience, may be my or your life. But it is better to die than to sin!
> Bishop Clemens August Graf von Galen

Most of the 40 million German Protestants were members of the German Evangelical Church, comprising Lutheran Reformed and United traditions. This was one of the pillars of German culture and society, with a theologically grounded tradition of loyalty to the state. The Nazis had used the traditional ties between the Protestant church and the state to assimilate church dogma into their own ideology by putting their own people into positions of power in the church. Many Christians had been persuaded by the Nazi commitment, written into their 1920 platform to uphold 'the freedom of all religious confessions in the state, insofar as they do not jeopardise the state's existence or conflict with the manners and moral sentiments of the Germanic race'. Later in Match 1933, this view seemed to be reaffirmed when Hitler said, "The rights of the churches will not be restricted, nor will their relationship to the state be changed' but in reality any power that opposed total Nazi domination of the minds and hearts of the German people was doomed.[1]

The Vatican and Catholic leaders inside Germany were initially less enthusiastic about National Socialism not least because of the rabid anti-Catholic stance of leading Nazi ideologues such as Alfred Rosenberg. In addition, the *Deutsche Zentrumspartei* (Catholic Centre Party) had been a key coalition governmental partner during in the Weimar Republic and had ties with both the SPD and leftist *Deutsche Demokratische Partei* (DDP, German Democratic Party), which put it at odds with right-wing parties like the NSDAP. Some bishops had prevented Catholics in their dioceses from joining the NSDAP but this ban was dropped after Hitler's Reichstag speech of 23 March 1933 when he described Christianity as the foundation for German values and later on 20 July 1933 when he signed a concordat promising that 'the property and activities of those Catholic organisations and the associations whose aims are purely religious, cultural, or charitable... will be protected'.[2] A very large number of Catholics were swept up by their enthusiasm for the Nazi's anti-Communist policy and by their hope for the national renewal and regeneration offered by the Nazi propagandists but, in reality, the terms of the concordat were ill-defined and left much to interpretation which meant that the document turned out to be no more than a device to be applied as required to curb Catholic power in Germany.

The Nazi government brought in important changes to the Protestant churches in Germany and gave its support to the German Christian Movement, a group of Protestants who wanted to combine Christianity and National Socialism to 'exclude all those deemed impure' and embrace all 'true Germans' in a 'spiritual homeland for the Third Reich' and continue to practice their faith and at the same time show support for Hitler. They also urged Protestants to unite all regional churches under the leadership of Ludwig Müller, a man who wore a 'cross on his breast and the swastika in his heart' and who urged all Protestants to rally to the Nazi cause.[3]

Further support for the Nazis came from Paula Müller-Otfried, director of the Protestant women's organisations, who 'prayed' in her 1932 New Year address for a 'steel hardened' man powerful enough to save Germany from atheistic communism. The movement adopted Nazi ideology by classifying people not according to faith but by racial heritage and expelled all members with Jewish ancestry. Non-Aryan clergy were forced out of office and there were even attempts to have the Old Testament scripture banned because it was based on Hebrew teaching. Church leaders told their followers that 'the eternal God created for our nation a law that is peculiar to its own kind. It took shape in the leader Adolf Hitler, and in the National Socialist state created by him. This law speaks to us from the history of our people... One Nation! One God! One Reich! One Church!'[4]

Around the middle of 1934, the NSDAP launched its power struggle with the Christian churches by adopting a strategy of undermining their integrity and sense of security. All church services were actively and conspicuously monitored by the Gestapo to inhibit the preaching of anything that resembled anti-Nazi sentiments and on 20 July 1934, the Ministry of the Interior banned all church newspapers from describing themselves as either Catholic press or an Evangelical press and had to use only the collective 'German press'. Then, after the Röhm Putsch saw the murder of a number of the Catholic Church's anti-Nazi leaders, a programme was launched to extend the battle for young minds by transforming denominational schools into secular institutions with all crosses and crucifixes removed from classrooms. Nazi party members were encouraged to leave church congregations.

Some German Protestants were not willing to go along with what they saw as warped religion, however, and created a faction called the Confessing Church which tried to protect their religion from Nazi influences. They accepted that anyone could be baptised into the Confessing Church regardless of his or her racial descent but in many other respects did not take issue with Nazi ideology. Church member Martin Niemöller met Hitler to affirm church support for his domestic and foreign policies asking only for the right to disagree on religious matters. Hitler bluntly refused and demanded that Niemöller sign a statement of unconditional loyalty to him personally. Niemöller was equally obdurate and would not sign which henceforth made him a target for Gestapo surveillance and eventual saw him imprisoned in a concentration camp.

While Protestant and Catholic clergy and leading theologians openly supported the Nazi regime initially, over time, there emerged strong anti-Nazi sentiments as church and state clashed over the way that the Nazis were exerting control over all aspects of society. Statements of protest from church pulpits in 1935 saw the state clamp down on dissent by briefly arresting over 700 pastors and depriving them of the right to apply to the law courts to defend their religious freedoms. Throughout this period, however, there was little public opposition to anti-Semitism and no attempt by most church leaders to publicly oppose the regime on the issue of state-sanctioned violence against the Jews. Caution and compromise were the orders of the day from both Protestant and Catholic churches. That is not to say that there was total compliance within church communities. There were individual Catholics and Protestants who spoke out on behalf of Jews, and small groups within both churches became involved in acts of resistance.

The churches were wary of giving any support to religious dissenters, fearing that they would become the rallying point for others who did not act out of a commitment to Christian doctrine and, in so doing, bring down the wrath of the state upon them. The monstrous nature of Nazi persecutions, however, forced the churches to condemn the violent suppression of dissent and when it became known that euthanasia and the murder of patients of psychiatric hospitals were widespread affirmative action was sanctioned to save those potential victims who might be helped.

Jehovah's Witnesses were a small religious group of some 20,000 members in Germany who found it impossible to make compromises with the Nazis. Their faith often prevented them from serving in the army or swearing allegiance to the state which made them prime targets for persecution. The Nazis destroyed their national headquarters, outlawed their church, and sent many thousands to concentration camps or prisons, where more than 1,000 were killed.

Like other Christian churches at the time, the Catholics were caught up in a series of major crises which profoundly affected the exercise of their authority and influence. All across the Western world, people were finding their own moral signposts and spiritual identities and were increasingly moving away from the teachings and instructions of ecclesiastical institutions and rejecting the authority of religious dogmas. At the same time, the modern state was beginning to assert its own claim for supremacy over religion. The Nazis, like the communists, expedited the collapse of religious or moral restraint on state power and set about the wholesale manipulation of their populations for political ends. Nazism itself had almost become a religion in its own right. It had its own sacramental rituals for baptism and confirmation, marriage and funerals. Ash Wednesday became Wotan's Day, Ascension Day became the Feast of Thor's Hammer and they crowned the Christmas tree not with a star, but with a swastika.[5] This inevitably led to a corrosive decline in moral conduct and humanitarian ideals. Prominent theologians such as Karl Adam, Joseph Lortz and Michael Schomaus published articles urging a positive relationship between Catholicism and National Socialism. Democracy was no part of the Catholic worldview and many theologians and ecclesial leaders felt more at home in Hitler's state than they had done in the Weimar Republic. Inevitably Hitler's patience with the Catholics ran out. The priests, he said, were political enemies and his street thugs had taken that as a green light to smash cathedral statues and use crucifixes for target practice. The Munich Cardinal, Michael von Faulhaber, even had his house set on fire.

Erich Klausener had made a career in the civil service becoming head of the police department in the Prussian Ministry of the Interior in 1926. He was also active in the Catholic church as a layman but had to divest himself of a number of church duties when he was appointed to the shipping department of the Reich Ministry of Transport on 2 February 1933. Two weeks later he spoke to a gathering of some 40,000 Catholics in Berlin and aroused the indignation of Alfred Rosenberg a Hitlerite sycophant who spent his whole adult life pandering to Hitler's basest instincts. Klausener, Rosenberg wrote in the *Völkischer Beobachter*, sees the NSDAP as a movement of 'insufficient spiritual values' and warns his followers not to 'unthinkingly fit' into a state-sponsored system.[6] There was no immediate reaction from the state to Klausener's speech but one year later he spoke again, this time to a crowd of 60,000 at Catholic rally in Hoppegarten. A week later on 30 June 1934, Hitler launched his purge of the SA by assassinating Röhm and his henchmen. On that day in the early afternoon, an SS gunman, Kurt Gildisch, on instructions from Reinhard Heydrich, entered Klausener's office and shot him dead.

While the Nazis chipped away at the edifice of religion, it was the fundamental ideals and concepts of faith that motivated some religious leaders to oppose them unreservedly. Karl Friedrich Stellbrink was a Lutheran pastor with a 'broad understanding of life', a man of 'great learning and culture [and] sparkling wit'.[7] Unwilling to compromise with his commitment to his convictions, Stellbrink delivered a sermon on 29 March 1942, Palm Sunday, calling on his congregation to 'hear the voice of God', suggesting that the recent RAF fire-bombing of Lübeck was divine punishment. He had already been questioned by the Gestapo for helping persecuted Jews and had been under surveillance for some years. This most recent indiscretion resulted in a close examination of his activities and it was discovered that he, along with others, had been copying and distributing the anti-Nazi sermons of the Catholic Bishop Clemens August von Galen of Münster. He was tried in the *Volksgerichtshof* along with Johannes Prassek, Hermann Lange and Eduard Mueller. All were found guilty and executed by guillotine on 10 November 1943. After his death, Stellbrink's widow was billed for his court costs, imprisonment, and execution.

The lawyer Friedrich Justus Perels was legal advisor to the Brethren Council of the Prussian Union of Churches and was under no illusions about the dangers of succeeding the regional court judge Friedrich Weissler, who had been imprisoned in Sachsenhausen in 1936 and murdered there in 1937 for his publication in the foreign press describing concentration camps, arbitrary rule, the distortion of justice, and the persecution of Jews and dissidents. Perels was close friends with both Martin Niemöller and Dietrich Bonhoeffer which brought him into close contact with various cells of the resistance. A man of deep and unwavering Christian faith and a critic of the Nazi regime, he was swept up by the Gestapo in the wake of the 20 July bomb plot and subjected to torture and threats against his family. Accused of withholding information about the resistance movements, he was sentenced to death on 2 February 1945 but no formal execution took place. Instead, as Soviet troops entered the suburbs of Berlin in April he was dragged from his cell, taken out into the street and shot in the neck by a special detachment of SS.

Dietrich Bonhoeffer was a gifted child concert pianist who had not been particularly religious but the death of his brother, Walter, in the First World War caused him to turn to religion and became the associate pastor of a German congregation in Barcelona. declaring that 'the concepts of person, community, and God are inseparably interrelated'. [8] He went on to study for a year in 1930–1 in New York at Union Theological Seminary. It was at this time that he began to see the events of the world from the perspective of the marginalized and disenfranchised. Preaching to a congregation in Yonkers, he said, 'I stand before you, not only as a Christian but also a German, who loves his home the best of all, who rejoices with his people and who suffers, when he sees his people suffering'. Returning to Germany, he warned in a radio address that the German people must reject the temptation to make Hitler into an idol. He became particularly concerned with the persecution of the Jews and joined Martin Niemöller and others to form the Pastors' Emergency League with a doctrine of non-violent resistance.

His brother-in-law, Hans von Dohnanyi, introduced Bonhoeffer to *Abwehr* chief Canaris and Oster and he was given a role of a double agent, ostensibly using his ecumenical contacts throughout Europe to gather information for the Nazis but actually passing information about the resistance in the other direction. On 5 April 1943, Dietrich Bonhoeffer was arrested on tenuous charges related to his role in the *Abwehr*. He was sent to Tegel prison in Berlin but released after no incriminating evidence was found. He was arrested again in September 1944 when his name was discovered on documents relating to the 20 July bomb plot. He was executed by hanging at Flössenburg on 9 April 1945 along with his brother Klaus, von Dohnanyi and Rudiger Schleicher.

Chapter 7

THE OSTER CONSPIRACY

> If [the brake] lever is not applied here soon, with the object of arriving at a change of conditions which have become intolerable, and if the present anarchy remains permanent, then the future fate of the Wehrmacht in peace war and with it the fate of Germany in a future war can only in the blackest colours.
> Chief of the German General Staff, Colonel General Ludwig Beck[1]

Mistrust was one of Hitler's outstanding characteristics. His aide, Colonel Friedrich Hossbach, who was with him practically every day during the years 1934 to 1938, said of him: 'He was faithful to only a few, in the long run only to those who recognized his infallibility, praised him and devoted themselves to him unconditionally.' Shortly before the Fritsch crisis, Hossbach observed on Hitler's part a marked sharpening of mistrust toward the army. This was principally because realisation of his ambitions was coming more and more to rely on the full support of the armed services whose unswerving cooperation he knew he could not take for granted. He had often met resistance from the generals to his foreign political ventures, rearmament, and the reoccupation of the Rhineland after which he said, 'If I had listened to my generals, I would not be where I am today!' Later when he recognised the strength of army opposition to his war plans, Hitler fulminated, 'What kind of generals are they anyway, that the Chief of State may perhaps have to drive them to war! If things were as they should be, I should be hard-pressed to prevail against the urging of the generals *for* war!'[2] The General Staff's methodical mode of working was anathema to Hitler, the master of intuition. It's worth asking the question, what might have come of a combination of Hitler's often brilliantly perceptive political instincts and the orthodox planning of the General Staff if Hitler had allowed it, but he resisted the authority of the *Oberkommando der Wehrmacht* (OKW, Armed Forces High Command,) right to the very end sometimes by the hypnotic effect of his rhetoric and at other times by the brutal treatment he handed out to those whose objections went beyond the limits of his tolerance.[3]

Western countries thought they recognised a natural symbiosis between Prussian militarism and Nazism but, inside Germany, Goebbels saw no such bonding. For him there was an almost unbridgeable gap between the old, outdated aristocratic Junker mentality of the army and a new dynamic élite Nazi philosophy. This did not apply to the German navy, which was dominated by middle-class elements and, by its nature, more outward-looking and played only a minor part in German domestic politics. Neither did the Luftwaffe harbour dissidents to any great extent and, in fact, forged its military doctrine from scratch on the basis of youthful vigour and technical innovation very much in the Nazi tradition. Only in the army was there a significant reaction to the Nazi's unspoken but unmistakable ambition to launch another war but that was tempered by the undoubted benefits it accrued from that the vast amounts of money Hitler was pouring into his remilitarisation programme.

National defence was the *Reichswehr*'s overriding priority with threats to the nation's integrity evident in the east where the Bolsheviks and Poles were constantly manoeuvring for advantageous alliances and France in the Western Powers eager to keep a foot on Germany's chest now that the country was on the floor. National ambitions could only be realised on the back of a rejuvenated and powerful army and the High Command was happy to play its part in creating that force but, catastrophically as it turned out, did so on the mistaken assumption that once the 'Bohemian corporal' had laid the foundation for the army's return to Europe's top table he could be got rid of and the military would once again take hold of the levers of power in Germany. The generals took the pragmatic view that Hitler was simply a tool to be exploited for the purposes of strengthening national defence and the revival of military morale. In the meantime, to follow Prussian military tradition and remain aloof from politics was seen as the most convenient way. While it suited Hitler's purpose to keep the army out of politics, he was constantly infuriated by the sneering Junker attitude of aristocratic disdain and superiority towards him. The generals were disappointed to find that after enduring the turmoil of the Weimar years they could not recreate the bond between army and state that had existed under the Kaiser. Neither were they willing to allow the Nazis to gain much influence over the *Reichswehr*.

The *Reichswehr* was seemingly unconcerned, however, by Hitler's ruthless actions against political parties and made no protest over his repressive police and harsh judicial practices. They made no official comment about the building of concentration camps for political opponents and remained silent over the draconian measures being taken against Jews, Roma and the communists, amongst others. While the Nazi's commitment to creating a strong Wehrmacht to protect Germany's borders found favour with the generals, the insidious bleed of National Socialist elements into the armed services was very much not to the army's liking, however. There were those in the army who were never willing to tolerate the Nazis at any price and they began to distance themselves from the regime. Hammerstein-Equord was one who opposed the Nazis from the start. Appointed Commander-in Chief of the Truppenamt and General of the Infantry in 1930, he advocated a firm commitment to the Weimar constitution. In 1933, on behalf of the army, he approached Reich President Hindenburg, the great military leader who was looked up to with deep faith and veneration particularly by all soldiers young and old, about his concerns over allowing the National Socialists into government but by then Hindenburg was very much a spent force and he failed to act. Crucially for law-abiding Germans, the road to dictatorship had opened up without violating the constitution. There was no revolution, no bloodbath, no coup d'état. The reins of government were handed to Hitler in accordance with democratic principles. There was no reason for the Officer Corps of the Wehrmacht to view the new state leadership with antipathy or even with mistrust. Hammerstein-Equord saw no alternative but to resign early in 1934 to be replaced by Werner Freiherr von Fritsch, but he retained close links to civilian resistance groups and for a while was seen by them as the man who would personally make the arrest when the time was ripe to take action against Hitler.

During the Weimar years, the army under Hans von Seeckt had worked in the shadows to find ways of circumventing the terms of Versailles and this had caused it to take on a 'don't ask questions and you'll hear no lies' attitude to the government. It was able to retain its elitist Junkers philosophy and while this had within it the unspoken understanding that 'the army is the state', it avoided getting involved in the complex, fraught politics of the time. For the *Reichswehr*, it was a time of restraint. The unloved Weimar government was tolerated as a transient phase on the way to a reinvigorated sovereign state based on what the army saw as traditional values but what forbearance that had existed was eroded during the crisis of 1929–30 which hit Germany particularly hard as its massive US loans were undermined by bank failures on Wall Street. When, by 1932, a third of the German population was reduced to poverty, and the state was threatened with anarchy, the Reichstag was paralysed. Seven million unemployed and communists in control of the streets left the country with a simple choice between military dictatorship or the acceptance of Hitler's NSDAP as the ruling party. Nazism had been decidedly unwelcome in the *Reichswehr* and many recruits from the *Hitlerjugend* had to be re-educated to keep politics out of the army, but it was time for the army to look at the benefits of working with the NSDAP who certainly shared the *Reichswehr*'s aim of casting off the shackles of Versailles and allowing Germany to become, once again, a strong independent and united country with powerful armed forces but this rapprochement was fragile and was lacking in trust on both sides.

After Hitler had taken control of the Reichstag, the army once again drifted into the political background but it was not long before its military 'honour' was challenged by a recognition that by remaining aloof, it was effectively condoning a criminal administration. The murder of generals Kurt von Schleicher and Ferdinand von Bredow during the Night of the Long Knives caused indignation for some while the introduction of racial laws disgusted others. The developing relationship between Hitler and the Army was not altogether confrontational, however. The Nazi Party saw obvious advantage in remaining on good terms with the strongest of the three armed services and during the early years, Hitler often protected the army from the machinations of the Himmler who was constantly trying to undermine it and bring it under SS control. When it seemed as if the SS, now numbering some 400,000 men, was poised to launch a bitter attack on the *Reichswehr* in late 1934 Hitler feared that Himmler was preparing a putsch against himself and he made a speech to the leaders of the Party and many of the higher officers in the Berlin Opera House making clear his total faith in the *Reichswehr* and its High Command. Himmler was forced to back down. The cosy relationship could not continue, however, as the army found itself constantly having to defend itself against SS interference which Hitler, for the sake of keeping his subordinates at each other's throats, tacitly encouraged as long as it didn't go too far.

In February 1934, the Defence Minister Werner von Blomberg took steps to protect the army from interference by moving towards Nazification of the army in a process of *Gleichschaltung* (synchronisation). He had all the Jews serving in the *Reichswehr* given an automatic and immediate dishonourable discharge and a month later had the *Reichswehr* adopt Nazi symbols into their uniforms. Then the biggest blow to army independence came in August 1934 when all military personnel were obliged to take a personal oath of obedience to Hitler. Since 1919, the oath had been,

> I swear loyalty to the Reich's constitution and pledge, that I as a courageous soldier always want to protect the German Reich and its legal institutions, (and) be obedient to the Reich President and to my superiors.

Then in January 1933 it was changed to,

> I swear by God this holy oath, that I want to ever loyally and sincerely serve my people and fatherland and be prepared as a brave and obedient soldier to risk my life for this oath at any time.

After the death of von Hindenburg on 2 August 1934, another crucial change was made and now the oath became known as the *Führereid* (Hitler oath).

> I swear by God this holy oath that I shall render unconditional obedience to the Leader of the German Reich and people, Adolf Hitler, supreme commander of the armed forces, and that as a brave soldier I shall at all times be prepared to give my life for this oath

When compulsory military service was reintroduced in March 1935, the huge influx of recruits had a number of detrimental consequences. First of all, the speed and scope of its introduction saw a rapid dilution of the quality of the army and secondly it dramatically increased the possibility of the government launching unwise military adventures. There was a sense of apprehension that the government was not spending the nation's wealth on building a huge army if it did not plan to use it and the Nazis had their own very particular idea of how the new expanded army would operate. There began a process of transforming the 'hallowed' officer corps into a functioning National Socialist élite. Most of them viewed with genuine satisfaction a new program of making Germany into a great power once again opening up the possibility of a glittering career for them. These were days of rapid promotion for those who made the correct choices. Men who were particularly favoured by the Nazis found themselves on accelerated promotion programmes thanks to illicit bribes from the Party to those who controlled the process.

In March 1935, the Officer Corps welcomed Hitler's trashing of Versailles by announcement of the sovereign right to arm and a year later by the reoccupation of the Rhineland. In between there had been the conclusion of the Anglo-German Naval Treaty. What resistance there remained within the army was being undermined by the prestige he was bringing back to the country with this series of successful initiatives. Those generals who had made strong objections to what they had seen as reckless diplomacy lost ground when their fears proved to be unfounded.

The army was happy to enjoy the benefits of this burgeoning prestige and massive injection of capital into its rearmament but did not share Hitler's ambition for war and it was the prospect of war with Czechoslovakia that concentrated the minds of those like Beck. At the Hossbach Conference on 5 November 1937, the *Führer* revealed for the first time his foreign political objectives which could not be attained by peaceable means. A heated discussion followed in which Fritsch, Blomberg and the Foreign Minister, Konstantin von Neurath all strongly opposed his plans. It was not so much that they opposed war plans from a moral perspective, after all they were career military men who spent their days discussing and planning warfare. What alarmed them was the prospect of a localised war exploding into a wider conflagration for which they knew their forces were not yet ready. Of course, Hitler did not want to hear that sort of thing. What the army lacked in the way of resources would be made up for by his dynamic leadership. He scanned the room to identify the dissenting voices and made his plans to silence them.

The anti-Semitic Fritsch had been heavily involved with the illegal rearmament of the *Reichswehr* in cooperation with the Soviets during the late 1920s and early 1930s. He had long been in favour of rapport with the Bolsheviks against the common foe, Poland and was one of the Nazi Party's more vocal supporters in 1933. Hitler held in high regard this highly competent general, one of the creators of the new army, but was increasingly irked by his aristocratic manners and forthright opinions delivered emphatically and with unerring objectiveness. Blomberg had been the first Commander-in-Chief of the newly created Wehrmacht on 21 May 1935 which had made him a target for Göring and Himmler both of whom wanted to take control of the army. Both Fritsch and Blomberg posed a threat to Hitler by virtue of their very rational argument which, he feared, reflected the general mood of the more sober-minded members of the Officer Corps. The two men were becoming more than irritants. Hitler chose to utilise his growing political power which was giving him the confidence to reach out and realise his ultimate ambitions of creating a Greater Germany through war if necessary. He did not want to listen to reasons why he could not do it. His Nietzschean 'will to power' would be enough to overcome all obstacles but it would require the unquestioning loyalty of his armed forces. It was time to stamp his authority on the army once and for all.

Blomberg had married Erna Gruhn on 12 January 1938 but a police investigation found that she had previously worked as a prostitute and had posed for pornographic photographs. Marriage to such a person was far from the sort of behaviour expected of any serving officer, let alone a member of the OKW. Threatened with the exposure of his wife's criminal record, Blomberg resigned. One down, one to go. Fritsch's devotion to the army had left him no time for a private life and he had never married. Heydrich already had a file on him falsely accusing him of homosexual activity and Heydrich's boss, Himmler saw this as the perfect time to dust it off. To avoid a scandal, Fritsch too resigned. On 4 February 1938, Neurath was sacked as Foreign Minister to be replaced by Joachim von Ribbentrop, a sycophant much ridiculed among his contemporaries as a 'twitching wine waiter' but more to Hitler's liking.[4] The shameful treatment of the popular Fritsch offended the sense of honour of some of the Officer Corps and there were the first inklings of rebellion, but Fritsch would not involve himself in any conspiracy even from outside the *Oberkommando des Heeres* (OKH, Army High Command).

Hitler used the situation to weaken the traditional OKH by subordinating it to the OKW with the malleable Wilhelm Keitel as head of the OKW. Keitel was Hitler's ideal candidate because he lacked the strength of character to stand up to the *Führer* when he was in full flow. itler HitlerAt the same time Hitler fired a dozen corps and divisional commanders whose Junkers background was anathema to his idea of what a modern army should be. The role of Reich War Minister was abolished and any responsibilities that office used to hold would now come under his own direct control. This effectively gave Hitler a combined position of Supreme Commander and Commander in Chief of the Wehrmacht, an outcome to which the Commanders in Chief of the three services did not object believing that it would strengthen their own position viz-a-viz Himmler's SS.

At the Hossbach Conference, held in Berlin on 5 November 1937, Hitler had outlined to his generals a plan for incremental aggrandisement of the German Reich to ward off economic decline and build up strength to oppose 'its two hateful enemies, England and France', who were poised to oppose Germany at every turn. Sometime in the next five years, he speculated, Germany would have to achieve autarky (complete economic independence) by seizing areas of eastern Europe to prepare for a possible war with the British and the French.[5] Beck saw this a catastrophic miscalculation on Hitler's part and made his opposition clear with weighty memos to the Commander-in-Chief of OKH, Walter von Brauchitsch. Brauchitsch had succeeded Fritsch and immediately below Brauchitsch was Beck. Neither had been disturbed by the Anschluss but when the Sudeten crisis threatened to lead to war in July 1938, Beck called on the senior generals to resign simultaneously and urged Brauchitsch to save Germany by arresting Hitler. 'It is now a question of final decisions affecting the fate of the nation,' he told Brauchitsch. 'History will hold these leaders guilty if they do not act in accordance with their professional and political conscience. Their military obedience ends where their knowledge, their conscience and their sense of responsibility forbids the carrying out of an order.'[6] Although steeped in the Prussian tradition of service, Beck was more of a philosopher than a militarist and was far from being a typical German officer. He studied the deep correlation between warfare and politics and, like most of his fellow officers, had initially welcomed the rise of the Nazis with the assertion of discipline, the reestablishment of military primacy, and the revision of the Versailles Treaty.

Highly respected by his peers, Beck was described as 'refined and gracious in disposition, modest in outward appearance and behaviour'.[7] In all respects the perfect gentleman in his dealings with everyone, Beck's views were valued because of his self-control and self-discipline, lack of prejudice and willingness to listen to the views of others. While Brauchitsch did not disagree with Beck's views, he shied away from the terrible step of insurrection believing that he could prevent disaster through his personal influence on Hitler. Beck saw that his honour would not allow him to take responsibility for what was happening to Germany. His high position where conduct of war and policy merged and extended beyond his own service into all phases of the political affairs of state obliged him to act accordingly. He also resigned in the late summer of 1938 to be replaced by General Franz Halder.

By the end of August 1938, the mood within the OKH was sombre. They waited with great misgivings for the orders to invade Czechoslovakia which in their view would invite military intervention from France and Britain. Both Halder and Beck talked of 'practical opposition' and contemplated a coup if Hitler actually issued the order. The level of disquiet was measured now by the number of people who expressed support for the idea. Schacht and Goerdeler were the two most prominent but others included Hans-Bernd Gisevius whose position inside the Reich Ministry of the Interior gave him access to important information about the SS.

Hjalmar Schacht had been an ardent admirer of Hitler and would find himself in the dock at Nuremberg charged with having committed 'crimes against peace'; a charge of which he was acquitted but he was sentenced by a West German De-Nazification court in 1946 to eight years' imprisonment. He had praised the Nazi movement in 1932 as 'intrinsically so right and necessary'.[8] As General Plenipotentiary for the War Economy, Schacht had found extraordinary and creative financial solutions to facilitate the Nazi's rearmament programme but by 1938, he had been forced to resign as Reich Economic Minister for his opposition to excessive military spending and he moved closer to opponents of the regime such Gisevius and Goerdeler with whom he had worked in government. He became an enthusiastic supporter of the conspiracy, meeting many of the top generals and put himself at their disposal in any future post-Hitler government.

A plan of sorts was worked out by Colonel General Erwin von Witzleben which envisaged the occupation of Berlin after which Hitler would be forced to dismiss Himmler and Heydrich. It was the view of many that it was the malign influence of these two men that was diverting Hitler from a more rational strategy for Germany. The attack against Czechoslovakia was anticipated to start between 14–16 September but crucially there would be a 48-hour period between the order and the actual attack. It was then that the plotters would strike. They would require substantial support from army units in and around Berlin but one of their problems was that relentless German propaganda about helpless Sudeten Germans under daily and bloody assault from Czech police had a powerful hold on German public opinion and many servicemen were very much in favour of marching into Prague. Vital to the success of a coup would be the threat of a wider war involving Britain and France if the attack went in. If these two countries, that had certain military obligations to the Czechs, were seen to mobilise and threaten to bring to bear the full weight of their considerable forces against Germany's weak western defences then Hitler might have second thoughts about invading Czechoslovakia altogether which would seriously weaken his personal position. Many of his erstwhile supporters who had eagerly encouraged the invasion would be given pause for thought and the removal of Hitler and his cohorts would be much easier. Already a parade of a new panzer division through the streets of Berlin had been met with a distinct lack of enthusiasm. This show of force at a time of international crisis was ignored or watched in silence as the German people reacted with hostility towards the prospect of war. When Hitler tried to recover some prestige by appearing to a crowd on the balcony of the Reich Chancellery, the response was muted. It was clearly a time when Hitler self-confidence was wavering and was a perfect moment for the plotters to strike.

Central to the conspiracy against Hitler was the *Abwehr* Chief of Staff and second in command under Canaris, Hans Paul Oster. His early military career had been exemplary. Serving on the Western Front in 1916 he won the Iron Cross First and Second Class and the Knight's Cross with Swords. Promoted to the German General Staff, he was sufficiently highly thought of to be retained, in 1919, as one of the 4,000 *Reichswehr* officers permitted by Versailles. Oster's personal life was somewhat unbefitting an officer, however. In his book *Plotting Hitler's Death*, Joachim Fest called Oster, 'decisive, quick-witted, and diplomatically imaginative . . . an unusual blend of moral rectitude, cunning, and recklessness', but according to his biographer, Mark M. Boatner III, he was a 'brash, cynical, volatile, womaniser whom many peers and superiors regarded as unfit for general staff duties'. It was his irresponsible carelessness that led to an adulterous affair with a fellow officer's wife in 1932 for which he was brought before a court of honour and compelled to resign. It was apparently little more than a rap across the knuckles because his undoubted intelligence and overall popularity saw him recalled to active duty in the following year to serve in Göring's *Forschungsamt* a private intelligence organisation set up to spy on foreign diplomats and other leading Nazis on whom Göring wanted to create personal dossiers. He soon moved on from there and joined the *Abwehr* in counterintelligence work securing promotion to lieutenant colonel in 1935. He had been an enthusiastic supporter of the Nazis up until the Night of the Long Knives in which his good friend and former *Abwehr* chief Major General Bredow was murdered. This slaughter brought home to him the true nature of Nazism and his erstwhile acceptance of their regime turned towards a fundamental hostility towards them.

Over the next few years, Oster moved freely and made contact with others, both military and civilian, who shared his misgivings about the regime. In 1938 he was made head of the *Abwehr* central division turning it into a focal point for opponents of the regime. The following year he became Chief of Staff to Wilhelm Canaris under whose leadership the *Abwehr* provided cover for a conspiracy against Hitler, but Nazi Germany was an armed camp controlled by secret police in which active insurrection was immensely dangerous and difficult. The anti-Nazi Canaris was possessed of a nature that 'enjoyed intrigue for its own sake . . . but had a deep distaste for violence'.[9] After the Anschluss, when ordered to integrate Austrians into the *Abwehr*, Canaris had done so on the understanding that there were no 'damned Austrian Nazis' among them; he did not want 'any of those swine'.[10] He was sympathetic to Oster's position but made sure that he spent much of his time outside the country to avoid being implicated in any plots. This effectively left Oster in charge at *Abwehr* HQ and given free rein to guide the inner enclave of that organisation in the direction of active resistance to Hitler. After Beck's resignation, it was Oster and Goerdeler around whom the movement coalesced.

Carl Friedrich Goerdeler was born into a conservative Prussian family and after following family tradition with a successful career in the civil service, was appointed Burgomaster of Leipzig in 1930 turning it into one of the best administered cities in all Germany. His particular talents for administration and finance brought him to national attention in 1931 when he was appointed National Inspector of Price Control, a position he continued to hold under the new Nazi regime in 1933. He had, at one point, been put forward as a successor to Brüning as Chancellor but President Hindenburg would have none of it and went for Franz von Papen instead.

To everything he did, Goerdeler brought unlimited energies as well as an undaunted faith in the rationality and goodwill of mankind but it left him unguarded against the realities of Nazism which he only belatedly came to see as a calamity for his country and the whole world.[11] The rapid erosion of justice and good government was a bitter blow to his own administration but a man of 'iron nerve and his indomitable will', he trusted his own powers of reasoning and persuasion to influence government policy which made him stand out as somewhat optimistic and naïve.[12]

He was re-elected as Burgomaster for a twelve-year term in 1936 but his anger and frustration eventually brought him to a crisis when, during an absence from the city in November 1936, the NSDAP representatives in the City Administration forced through a decision to remove a monument to the Jewish composer Felix Mendelssohn, a decision which they knew Goerdeler had opposed. When his demands to have the monument be restored were ignored, Goerdeler then handed in his resignation and left office on 1 April 1937. At the time, he had been in Stockholm carrying a letter of introduction written by Schacht, to Marcus Wallenberg of the Enskilda Bank. The business relationship between Goerdeler and Wallenberg would develop onto a close personal contact that created a line of communication between the German resistance movement and the British Government.

By this time, he was well-known and admired throughout the business community in Germany and took up a post as adviser to the electronic company Robert Bosch GmbH in Stuttgart. The owner of the company, Robert Bosch, was a long-time opponent of Hitler and had gathered around him a circle of like-minded people within which Goerdeler felt at home. This rather loose contractual arrangement enabled Goerdeler to enter actively into opposition activities and gave him cover for an elaborate schedule of foreign journeys that took him to Belgium, Holland, England, France, Switzerland, Canada, the USA, the Balkan countries, Africa and the Middle East establishing connections with politicians, business leaders and economists wherever he went spreading knowledge about the existence of a Germany that was different from the one presented by the Nazis. In 1937, Goerdeler had also met Beck and the two men forged a strong relationship built on opposition to the Nazi regime and would go on to form one of only two groups, the other being the Kreisau Circle, that was able to develop a strategy that posed a genuine threat to the Nazis.

The British, especially, did not know what to make of Goerdeler. They thought him 'an honest fellow' but 'could not make out in whose interests he was travelling or with what precise purpose'.[13] Nevertheless, they accorded him every courtesy and treated him as a person of consequence. His first meeting with Under-Secretary at the British Foreign Office Sir Robert Vansittart in 1937 went very well, the two men taking to each other immediately. Vansittart understood what risks Goerdeler was taking said of him that he was 'an impressive person, wise and weighty, a man of great intelligence and courage, and a sincere patriot'.[14] Goerdeler, however, could never get the British to overcome their suspicions that the group within Germany whom he represented was little different to the Nazis in its hegemonial ideas and therefore did not constitute a creditable alternative to Hitler's expansionism. The clear impression the British got was that Goerdeler and Beck objected more to Hitler's methods than his objectives.[15] The Americans were worried that Goerdeler might, in fact, be an instrument of Nazi misinformation and could bring embarrassment to any who took him too seriously. While he roundly condemned the 'condition of lawlessness, of moral disintegration, of economic unreality and financial irresponsibility' inside Germany, his vision of a pacified Europe did not preclude a revision of Germany's borders to their pre-1914 limits and was vague over whether that meant a

Germany with a 'tamed' Hitler or one without him. Neither was there much criticism of Hitler's claims to the Sudetenland.

The British attitude to Goerdeler when he made his next visit in March 1938 was against the background of Fritsch's dismissal and his talk of resistance and a potential military coup seemed to be little more than a vague aspiration in the face of a brutal reality that had seen the dissenters inside the OKW given a severe rap on the knuckles. The resistance that Goerdeler represented, however, seemed to be supporting the same ideas of territorial expansionism that filled Hitler's speeches just in a rather less belligerent way. Vansittart began to question Goerdeler's status as a moderate. If the British allowed themselves to be inveigled into a plot to remove Hitler, there was no clear expectation that it would resolve many of the dark clouds currently hanging over European political landscape. There was also the risk that a coup might result in civil war and the only real beneficiaries of that would be Poland and the Soviet Union neither of whom would be slow to move in and scavenge on what was left of Germany after that.

Up until this point, Goerdeler had been very much a reformist in as much as he had what the British industrialist A.P. Young called an 'optimistic attitude' and did not seem to display fundamental opposition to the Nazis.[16] What he seemed to fear most was a power shift in favour of Himmler, Goebbels and Heydrich but after the pogrom of the *Reichskristallnacht* (Night of the Broken Glass) it was clear that even without such a change of leadership Germany was now set on a path to war and even greater authoritarianism. Goerdeler's attitude underwent a fundamental shift towards resistance and to signify this change he wrote a 320-page memorandum setting out his views on new economic, social, legal, constitutional and foreign policies urgently needed to save the German state. He had maintained close contacts with Beck, the German diplomat Ulrich von Hassell and the Prussian finance minister Johannes Popitz but there were virtually no formal discussions among the individuals who stood in contact with Goerdeler. The decisive political plans, which found expression in numerous memoranda by Goerdeler, were as a rule fashioned by him alone.[17]

Military preparations for a coup were by no means perfunctory. Witzleben and the Berlin Police president Graf wolf Heinrich von Helldorf were both very much on board and the Potsdam area commander Graf Walter Brockdorff-Ahlefeldt stood ready to act. The most serious threat to the success of the coup was the Munich SS Lifeguards who would race to Berlin at the first sign of trouble to suppress any rebellion and it would be the role of General Erich Hoepner's 1st Light Division in Thuringia to prevent that happening. Internally, the plan probably had sufficient resources to succeed as long as instability was created within the regime and that would only happen if Britain and France gave a clear ultimatum that they would intervene if German forces crossed the Czech border. Whether the conspirators ultimately had the will is another matter altogether.

Contacts between German opposition members and the British intensified. On 18 August it was Ewald von Kleist Schmenzin who, with the blessing of both Canaris and Beck, went to London and met both Winston Churchill and Vansittart to outline the German opposition plans. Kleist, a Pomeranian Junker, deeply religious and conservative to the bone was a fierce opponent of Hitler and had already made contact with the British Foreign Office through the News Chronicle journalist, Ian Colvin earlier in the year. Only the British government's credible determination to back Czechoslovakia with military force, Kleist maintained, would ensure that the German anti-war faction had the support it needed among the generals to move against Hitler. Churchill foresaw civil war in Germany if the plotters went ahead. When Prime Minister Neville Chamberlain heard about the meetings, he baulked at the thought of Britain being complicit in any sort of civil disobedience in Germany and was personally affronted by Goerdeler and Kleist whom he thought close to being traitors to their country; something that was entirely alien to his own philosophy. Overall, the British could see no reason to suppose that the opposition they represented would be able or willing to take the sort of action that might lead to the overthrow of the Nazi regime.

A few weeks later on 7 September, Theo Kordt, the German chargé d'affaires in London arranged through Chamberlain's adviser, Horace Wilson to meet the Foreign Secretary Lord Halifax in 10 Downing Street where, on behalf of 'political and military circles in Berlin', he outlined the movement's aims to explore ways of returning to 'conceptions of decency and honour among European nations'. 'If the desired statement [of intent] is made' then the leaders of the army were ready to 'proceed against Hitler by force of arms'.[18] One of the difficulties for Kordt was that the British, although unwilling to give the slightest hint at the time, were already planning their own solution. Apart from anything else, the other big problem for the British was that they really had no way of knowing exactly how much credibility these emissaries had or how much support they had within the Wehrmacht and the civilian administration of Germany. They were reluctant in the extreme to start beating war drums on the strength of what they had been told. It was far from clear that the plotters agreed on the basic issue of what to do with Hitler himself. One faction seemed to be advocating the complete overthrow of the regime accepting as a possible consequence of that the assassination of the *Führer* but the British government was unlikely to want to be seen to be complicit in the murder of a foreign head of state. For others, all that was needed was the removal of Himmler's malign influence and the disarming of the SS leaving Hitler in charge but, crucially, tamed. It was not an attractive proposition either, to facilitate a coup that would leave Hitler in place.

Meanwhile all was not well on the home front. Oster went to Hannover to meet General of Infantry Alexander Ulex, commander of XI *Armeekorps* and his intelligence chief Major Alexander von Pfuhlstein, while Gisevius went to Münster to meet General of Artillery Günther von Kluge and Goerdeler went to Leipzig to see General of Infantry Wilhelm List. The delegates outlined their plans and suggested that, as part of the coup, the army should march on Berlin and confront the Gestapo, which was an exceedingly dramatic request of generals who had sworn a personal oath of allegiance to Hitler and it was no surprise that none of the meetings went well. Excuses for inaction abounded. List said that a coup could not hope to succeed without the Luftwaffe, who would never support it. Leadership of a coup would have to come from the very highest level of the army command and although it was well known that Beck was not supportive of Hitler's plans, he was still a long way from launching civil war and few expected him to come out publicly and challenge Hitler. This lack of support from mainstream army commanders caused Beck to get cold feet and when Halder called on him to be ready to lead the revolt, he lost confidence and called it 'mutiny . . . a word that does not exist in the vocabulary of a German officer'.[19]

At a meeting with Chamberlain on 22 September Hitler acquainted him with new demands of allowing the Sudetenland to be occupied by the German army and having all other Czechs evacuated from the area within the week. The idea was rejected by the Czechs, the British cabinet and the French. The Czechs were ready to fight but needed Western support. The plotters chose 29 September as the day to act. Even Brauchitsch seemed willing to come into the plotter's fold but the whole plan was thrown into disarray when on 28 September, Chamberlain, the French Premier Édouard Daladier and the Italian leader Benito Mussolini announced that they were flying to Munich for further talks with Hitler. With its hint of the possibility of a peaceful diplomatic resolution to the crisis, this announcement completely derailed the planned coup. The Munich agreement the four leaders arrived at, without the participation of Czechoslovakia, on 30 September gave Hitler almost everything that he had been demanding. He had read the situation perfectly and manipulated the Western Powers to achieve his greatest foreign political success with peaceable and legal means and had strengthened his position tremendously, even within the Wehrmacht. Even the occupation of the rest of Czechoslovakia in March 1939, had been meekly accepted by the world without involvement in war.

It must be said that the conspiracy against Hitler of September 1938 was poorly planned and stood little chance of success. The British, while never actually saying as much to the plotters, suspected that Hitler was far too strong and well-protected by the SA and SS to be toppled by any half-baked scheme and nothing they were hearing showed the conspiracy in any other light than that. The vital element was to get access to Hitler and either kill him or kidnap him. Killing him, at that time, would not have been all that difficult but effecting a complete seizure of power afterwards without a bloodbath seems not to have been considered. Georg Elser, acting alone would later acquire explosives and make a time-bomb which he planted in a supporting pillar of the Bürgerbräukeller in Munich on 8 November 1939. It detonated killing eight people only minutes after Hitler had left the podium. With the resources available to Oster's conspirators, they could surely have done better if they had the will. To kidnap him would have been much more difficult. To get access to Hitler was difficult enough but to extract him was a different matter altogether and there is no evidence that plans to do that were ever discussed in any meaningful way either. There were serious differences within the conspiracy about what its objective was. Goerdeler, for instance was quite opposed to assassinating Hitler not only from a religious or moral perspective but because of his doubts about whether the plotters would be able to count on the immediate support of the majority of the German people after cutting down their leader in cold blood.

After the collapse of the Oster conspiracy of 1938, the window of opportunity for Hitler's removal was rapidly closing. It was one thing to justify a coup d'état as a means of preserving peace but quite another to expect support if war broke out and the whole German nation was engaged in another struggle for survival. In war the armed forces of a state have only one duty, to gain victory and everything that detracts from that goal is, in a military sense, immoral and reprehensible. Mutiny and sabotage are contrary to the military code of all nations while obedience is the foundation for the wartime effectiveness of any armed forces. Despite the fact that Hitler himself had written in Mein

Kampf, 'If a nation is being led to its downfall through the devices of the government in power, then rebellion is not only the right but also the duty of every citizen of such a country', it was extremely difficult for a military man to contemplate revolt primarily because of his personal oath to the *Führer* and secondly because high treason, whether or not it is morally justified, is a betrayal of country. Brigadier General von Tresckow said that it was impossible to move a victorious German Army to take action against Hitler.

Even in the late summer of 1939 there was still a strong desire to avoid war within the leading circles of the Wehrmacht but there was a distinct lack of personalities with the necessary will to act and break the spiritual bond of their calling. After the invasion of Poland, however, the Wehrmacht had enough on its mind without concerning itself with than the overthrow of the Head of State especially as everything appeared to be going very well indeed. Only a few in Beck's inner circle were not affected by the euphoria and, rather than believing in final victory for Germany, more than ever saw the danger of a Wehrmacht becoming the unwitting tool of a criminal leadership and these men continued to work unceasingly for the overthrow of the dictatorship.

Chapter 8

THE WAR IN THE WEST

Nothing is more successful than success.[1]

Immediately after the defeat of Poland, Hitler informed the generals of his intention to attack the Western Allies. Brauchitsch and Halder, already shaken by evidence of the vicious excesses of the SS in Poland feared that not only was it suicidal for Germany to attack west but that it would also widen the powers of Himmler's private army. It reinvigorated their old coup d'état spirit but, in the meantime, Brauchitsch thought he could to talk Hitler out of the venture. The two generals made their presentation to Hitler on 7 November warning the *Führer* that the army did not have enough supplies for such an invasion and that the weather at that time of year was against it. Possibly referring to the shock that many front-line soldiers had felt at what they had witnessed the SS doing in Poland, Brauchitsch nervously, because it was unwise, brought up the question of army discipline and morale which, he said, were not what they should be. This infuriated Hitler and he responded with a diatribe against the spirit within the General Staff itself which was where he said the whole problem of poor morale stemmed from. It would be stamped out, he roared, and the army would be ready for an invasion of Belgium, Holland, and France which would start on 12 November. Fearing a witch hunt, Brauchitsch and Halder hurried back to their headquarters and ordered that all documents hinting at a coup be burned and they went very cool on any idea of entertaining any mention of the issue for a long time.

In his position as head of the administrative office of the *Abwehr*, Oster did not have direct access to Hitler's invasion plans, but he was able to piece together information he gathered from briefings, and he had a good idea both of the direction and timing of the attack. He now believed that it was crucial to make Hitler's plans known to the Western Powers. He told them to the former head of the Operations Section of the Dutch General Staff and current Dutch military attaché in Berlin, Major Gijsbertus Jacobus Sas, whom he had known since 1932. Sas did not doubt that Oster's information was good and agreed to Oster's suggestion that he pass it along to the Belgians, French, and British. Brauchitsch and Halder, were now slavishly following Hitler's orders and made all necessary arrangements to prepare their men for battle on the agreed date but weather reports were distinctly unfavourable, and Hitler took this as an excuse to postpone the attack until 19 November. When it was postponed again and again well into December Sas was informed each time and each time he passed the intelligence along the line until it all started to sound like a case of crying wolf.

Oster did not rely on Sas alone, however. He also gave the same information to a 41-year-old lawyer named Josef Müller who had contacts with the Vatican in Rome. Müller was instructed to persuade the Pope that a credible resistance group existed in Germany with the intention of overthrowing the Nazi regime. The role of then Vatican would be to act as a communication channel between the conspirators and Germany's enemies once the Nazis were swept from power. In January 1940, the Pope called in the British ambassador to the Vatican, Sir Francis d'Arcy Osborne to inform him of Müller's message and find out what Britain's response might to an anti-Nazi German government but, crucially, one that likely would attempt to retain all the German territorial gains made up to that point. Britain doubted the reliability of Müller's intelligence and hedged by asking for time to consult with the French but Müller returned with an encouraging report suggesting that he had been well received in the Vatican. This gave the conspirators hope, especially Halder, but Brauchitsch was distinctly cool and eventually said he would not support any further moves in that direction calling it treason.

Then on 3 April, Oster told Müller and Sas about Hitler's plans to invade Denmark and Norway within the week. Clearly Oster's action was treasonable and might have resulted in the deaths of many young German servicemen, but he believed that it was his duty to rid Germany and the world of what he called 'this plague' of Nazism. The invasions, Oster hoped and believed, would turn out to be a catastrophic military blunder again putting the *Führer* in a weak position. The problem was that neither the Danes nor the Norwegians gave Sas's warnings any credence and the British somehow failed to get the intelligence about the date at all. When Denmark and Norway were quickly occupied, two more spectacular conquests were added to the German list and the Western Powers were humiliated by what appeared to the world as another example of the unstoppable German armed forces.

German generals now gave little thought to a coup and looked forward to an offensive in the West that would cement Germany's status as the preeminent power in mainland Europe. There were few who shared Oster's belief that it was still not too late to topple the Nazis from within. The invasions, however, had raised Sas's credibility in Brussels and The Hague which made them sit up and take notice when, on 3 May, Oster told Sas that the Germans were poised to invade France via Belgium and Holland and that the date of the attack was set for early May but the neutral countries, Belgium and Holland, were reluctant to mobilise against a possible German attack for fear of being accused of belligerence and provocation. On 10 May, the German launched *Fall Gelb* with attacks on France and the Low Countries successfully trapping half a million French and British soldiers at Dunkirk. France surrendered six weeks later and the military triumph made the grip of the Nazi regime on the German people more powerful than ever.

Hitler's victory fundamentally changed the relationship between Britain and the German politico-military opposition. For Britain under Churchill's leadership, the idea of a negotiated peace was fading quickly. At a stroke, this removed one of the main planks of the opposition argument calling for Allied support. The other important factor had been the apparent willingness of leading German generals to take part in a coup to remove Hitler and the SS. This particular strategy virtually fell apart on the day that France signed the Armistice document at Compiègne on 22 June 1940. Talk of Hitler's 'madness' became muted and those generals who had foretold disaster had been resolutely proved wrong and did not like to be reminded of the fact. Even if Hitler could be assassinated now, the rank and file of the German forces and the bulk of the German people would react with horror and surely would not support those who had delivered the blow. Many, like Moltke, who had played important parts in the failed diplomacy of 1938 and 1939 fell silent.

Chapter 9

HARRO AND LIBERTAS SCHULZE-BOYSEN

> I am characterised by a certain fanaticism in the construction of things that concern me.[1]

Heinz Harro Max Wilhelm Georg Schulze was born in the Baltic port of Kiel on 2 September 1909, the anniversary of the German victory over the French at Sedan in 1871. His father, Lieutenant Captain Erich Edgar Schulze served as Chief of Staff to the German naval commander in Belgium. He came from a traditional Prussian family that boasted judges, professors, high officials and military leaders in its background. Patriotism and loyalty to the Kaiser were the keystones of family values where servitude to the state, allied with modesty, were of paramount importance. Schulze's great-uncle on his father's side had been Grand Admiral Alfred von Tirpitz, a favourite of Kaiser Wilhelm II, but his was also a family that embraced a somewhat liberal ethos for the times both educationally and politically. His mother, Marie Luise (née Boysen), tended to place greater value on social status and was rather more of a snob than her husband. With her 'temperamental, restless almost passionate' nature she introduced a certain tension into the family especially as they struggled with the deprivations brought on by the First World War.[2]

When the guns finally fell silent in 1918 and the war-weary, embittered soldiers came home from the trenches they found Germany on the verge of a revolution which saw the end of the Wilhelmine authoritarian state and a new bloody power struggle being played out on the streets as forces battled to fill the ensuing power vacuum. In the Wilmersdorf suburbs of Berlin, the Schulze family experienced little of the day-to-day violence, but they felt the political ground moving beneath their feet. Harro's sister, Helga Mulachiè, said of Harro that, in his youth, he always showed 'great love of his country' which made him very conscious of the fact that many of the traditional values he had grown up with were being undermined as state power seemed to dwindle away.[3] His faith in stability and authority, epitomised by conservative role models such as his great-uncle, was severely shaken but by no means destroyed, however. Under the circumstances it is no surprise that, in such a volatile environment, even at such an early age, he began to take a keen interest in politics. The national humiliation that Germany had suffered at Versailles was something that he, along with many others, felt strongly about and was something that he would be motivated to address in later years.

The war years had taken their toll on the Schulze household. Along with others they suffered shortages and economic hardship, but Marie Luise was resolute in the protection of family values. The young Harro had health issues, however, and his mother used family connections to have him enrolled on a Red Cross scheme that temporarily saw him evacuated to Sweden. The Swedish Minister of Justice Berndt Hasselrot in Gripsnäs was one of those who had volunteered to take in vulnerable children from Germany and it was there that Harro went. The Hasselrot house was set in beautiful countryside on the shores of Lake Mäler facing Gripsholm Castle. After a few weeks there with clean air and good food, the boy's health improved significantly, and he returned home reinvigorated. The Hasselrots had found Harro to be polite, respectful and good company, all the things that his family would be proud of and the boy would be invited to return for holidays in the summer months during the following years while he continued his formal education in Germany.

It was not to Berlin that the thirteen-year-old returned, however. The father's naval career had come to an abrupt end after the Treaty of Versailles restricted the German navy to a maximum of 15,000 men and he had been forced to find civilian employment with a mechanical engineering company in Duisburg. It was a humiliating comedown for Erich Schulze further compounded by the new environment in which his family lived. Compared to Wilmersdorf, their new home was wreathed in industrial pollution from the grey, smoky, evil smelling industrial estates close to where they lived. Harro had come face-to-face with a manifestation of what he and many other Germans saw as the injustices of Versailles. It could not fail to heighten his political instincts but worse was to follow. In January 1923, French and Belgian tanks rumbled into the streets of Duisburg and other industrial centres of the Ruhr. Infantry and cavalry followed as German cities in the region were locked down under occupation. Germany had defaulted on its war reparations which had given the French an excuse to accomplish an objective, denied them at Versailles, of establishing a 'cordon sanitaire' against future German aggression, partitioning the Rhineland from the rest of Germany.

The occupation destabilised the government and economy of the entire Ruhr valley which, especially given the arrogant and overbearing attitude of the occupying forces, nurtured radical nationalist movements. Curfews were imposed. Business owners and workers alike protested. Passive, and in some cases violent resistance was stirred up among the local populations. Some activists were shot dead, others given hefty prison sentences and some, like Leo Schlageter sentenced and executed by a French military court. Like many other German youths, Harro was inspired to take part in demonstrations and was briefly imprisoned as a result. While he was careful to avoid giving the occupying forces any excuse to pick him up again, the bitterness and shame of his experiences stayed with him.

Despite the suppression of nationalist sentiments by occupying forces, his education at the Steunbart-Gymnasium remained very much in the German nationalist and militaristic tradition and nurtured his essentially conservative character. The bourgeoise nature of the school gave anti-Semitism free rein, despite the high number of Jewish students. It was an attitude that was not at all unfamiliar to Harro, but after at first flirting with prejudice in his new school, he was able to resist peer pressure and turn away from it thanks mainly to a home environment devoid of racist attitudes.[4]

The occupation ended in 1925 and, a year later, encourage by his father to do so, Harro joined the *Ordensjugd des Jungdeutschen Ordens*, the Young German Order's youth group. This was a kind of Boy Scout movement that involved communal outdoor activities such as hiking and camping which engendered a sense of camaraderie and belonging. At that time, there was little of the militaristic nature that would later pervade the organisation when the Nazis took it over and transformed it into the *Hitlerjugend*. It did, however, have a political agenda in as much as it called for a commitment to Prussian values and traditions where romantic images of the past became battle cries for a glorified renewal of German society. There was no question of submission or blind obedience to ideals but instead, what Harro later called, a voluntary, joyful submission to a communal movement. The young man bought into these ideas wholeheartedly with his love of nature and the outdoor life and proved to be one of the most zealous recruits, speaking out at meetings and rallies against partisanship and factionalism that had plunged the country into chaos. For him, it was a way of paying homage to the past before, what he called, 'a time of deepest disgrace' where the humiliation of Versailles and political strife of the early Weimar years had threatened to tear his country apart.[5] Newspaper reports of the time refer to Harro for the first time as Schulze-Boysen.

The time spent in Sweden and trips to England with the *Ordensjugd des Jungdeutschen Ordens* had broadened the young man's mind and allowed him to see Germany from the outside. This reinforced the ideals instilled into him by the movement which promoted an idealised, forward-looking state devoid of class structures but there were many other political movements competing for influence over the minds of young Germans and politics, as a whole, was beginning to dominate Schulze-Boysen's thoughts. He was not afraid to express his views and, when he did, it was with clarity and erudition. He graduated from his school with distinction in modern literature and a reputation as a clear-headed, persuasive and tenacious debater.

He remained close to his family and adhered very much to the values with which he had grown up. Circumstances in the home had become straitened through the Weimar years but the family had retained its pride and respectability. While they had maintained friendships with their middle-class friends, they had slipped behind many of them in their ability to maintain a bourgeoise lifestyle but they had held firm to their progressive philosophies and were willing to tolerate, even encourage, independence of mind in their children.

After leaving school, Schulze-Boysen enrolled in the Albert Ludwig University of Freiburg to study law and political science. It was a joy for him to escape from the dreariness of Duisburg and find himself in the clear, bright surroundings close to the Black Forest but he was appalled by the narrow-mindedness and arrogance of many students he encountered within the fraternities. For the purposes of assimilation, however, he had little choice but to join one of them but looked in vain for like-minded people who opposed the ruling system. In the end he applied to join a duelling fraternity, the Albingia, and was pleasantly surprised to meet what he called in his letters home, 'very nice people'.[6] He learned to ski and even learned to fence, coming to revel in the duels in which he acquitted himself well although it was not without mishap. Despite getting advice from Great-uncle Tirpitz to avoid getting into politics too early in life, the twenty-year-old Schulze-Boysen spoke to a meeting of workers during a visit back to Duisburg about the goals of young Germans to create an egalitarian society. For the first time, Schulze-Boysen began to find himself questioning the political views of his family role models but there was, as yet, no signs of a rift. Indeed, thanks to Schulze-Boysen's influence, his father had softened his own views to bring them more in line with those of the *Jungdeutschen Ordens*. Schulze-Boysen, himself, was aware of tensions that were growing between his natural desire for continuity of family values and what he saw as a need for decisive changes in German society.

Having only part completed his course at Freiburg, Schulze-Boysen signed up to study law at the Friedrich Wilhelm University in Berlin, taking up lodgings in the working-class Wedding district of the city close to relatives. In both city and university, he found a completely different political climate to that in Bavaria especially after the New York Stock Market crash of 29 October 1929 but at this point there is no evidence to suggest that he had moved appreciably to the left. What he did find in Berlin, however, was rampant anti-Semitism and a growing body of National Socialists in the student bodies. He reacted by arguing against 'blind hatred' and urged 'strong love for our German compatriots' but he struggled to make his voice heard amongst the chaos that was spreading on the streets of the city.[7] The methods of political discourse that were becoming ever more violent caused him much distress but he was compelled to do whatever he could to bring together what he called 'honest people' willing to 'join hands across party lines to rebuild Germany'.[8] He utterly rejected 'holy programs' and believed that only through independent leadership rooted in the people and responsible to the people could the country find stability. The best way forward seemed to be through the intellectual-nationalist group called the *Volksnationale Reichsvereinigung*, the People's National Reich Association.

At the same time, he was motivated to temporarily abandon his opposition to political parties and support the *Deutschen Stattspartei*, the German State Party, formed by the merger of the *Jungdeutschen Ordens* and the *Deutschen Demokratischen Partei*, the German Democratic Party. It was a vain attempt to create a collective movement to bring together the disintegrating middle-class in opposition to the NSDAP. Schulze-Boysen's father, however, had no confidence that a centrist party could bring salvation to Germany and favoured more right-wing groups. Schulze-Boysen accused him of abstaining in a debate of crucial importance and asked who or what did he believe in. Inevitably, the tensions that had started to appear in the between father and son grew but not beyond a point where they threatened the fundamental family relationships. It was clear, however, that reconciliation was out of the question when great uncle Tirpitz died on 6 March 1930 and Schulze-Boysen did not attend his memorial service.

Despite surviving on a tight budget with limited but regular funding from his parents, Schulze-Boysen moved out of Wedding into the more salubrious district of Halensee where he lodged with Emil Unger-Winkelreid, the publisher of the weekly newspaper *Deutsche Vervörts*. Schulze-Boysen was a great admirer of his landlord, who shared his views that the working class could only fight for its rights under bourgeoise leadership, and who epitomised for him of the sort of man who could provide it. There was no enthusiasm from either man for Marxism, however. Bands of entertainers from the Soviet Union who toured Germany at the time inspired Schulze-Boysen with their artistic excellence and, while he rejected their revolutionary message, he developed a powerful sense of the immense power of that country.

There was little time to delve too deeply into Soviet politics, however. The Brüning government had failed to get parliamentary approval for certain emergency measures which it considered necessary to alleviate the existing economic situation and called for a general election on 14 September 1930. It would prove to be an election of critical importance in the evolution of German political parties and democratic institutions.

A seismic political event shook Germany when the NSDAP got more than six million votes in the Reichstag elections. The *Deutschen Stattspartei* failed to make an impact with only a fifth as many votes as the Nazis. Schulze-Boysen reacted by arguing for the party to become more proactive and to radicalise the working class but the leadership urged caution. Support slipped away especially among the young leaving Schulze-Boysen bitterly disappointed. The Nazis puzzled him. Still blinkered by his upbringing, he could not see how a party, made up of 'rabble' and one so devoid of intelligence could succeed in a democracy, but he decided to try and see what its electoral appeal was.[9] He read Hitler's *Mein Kampf* and found it to be a '*Sammelsurium von Plattheiten*' (a hodgepodge of platitudes) containing 'nothing but nonsense'.[10]

It was clear that the appeal of the Nazis to their supporters was based not on logic or argument but what he saw as blind faith with an almost religious fervour. His greatest fear now was that any further increase in support for the Nazis would lead to civil war in which the communists would prevail. A central path which he believed to be the only way to avoid catastrophe was disappearing fast. He campaigned for moderation and met many Nazi supporters whom he found to be in broad agreement with him but who were not willing to stand up and be counted. Nevertheless, it was his firmly held view that the intellectual vacuum at the heart of Nazi ideology would condemn it to early failure. He wrote to his friend Rudolf Heberie on 17 January 1931 saying that, because of infighting, he believed that the Nazis had 'passed their peak' and that the 'NSDAP threat' was receding but he still had no clear idea of how to advance his own version of national socialism. The Nazis remained an enigma for him. He was ready to acknowledge that the movement was a, possibly necessary, transitional stage involving a dismantling of the bureaucratic, feudal structures of the bourgeoisie leading to the creation of a transformed society but try as he might he could not understand its appeal to the masses and the social dynamic, resulting from fear, that was propelling it to power.

Street violence, always part of the Nazi agenda, was never far away and on one occasion Shulze-Boysen feared for his safety when he was accosted by a group of Nazis. If the encounter was meant to intimidate him, it failed. He retained his faith in rational argument and denounced fascism in all its guises at a packed meeting at the university but, at the same time, did all he could to resolve differences of opinion and bring rival students together to talk rather than fight. It was not only movements such as the International Student Association, where he was a member of the action board, that he turned to, but he was ever willing to meet and debate with anarchist groups. Working on a project alongside the unemployed to build accommodation for them, for the first time he began to contemplate a career in politics but it was strictly non-partisan. His vision, as always, was for a 'people's community' where social background counted for nothing and where people were able to 'live sensibly again'.[11]

With the political and social environment deteriorating and affecting more and more people, the young, in particular, struggled to find purpose in their lives. There was absolutely no enthusiasm within the middle class, that had suffered most from the catastrophe, for the continuation of a capitalist economic model which had led to nearly five million unemployed. The danger was that the country was ripe for ideologues to channel the revolutionary fervour along nationalist lines. Schulze-Boysen took a keen interest in the economic theories expounded by the magazine *Tat*, edited at that time by Adam Kuckhoff. These included ideas on a planned economy under an authoritarian state where nationalists and socialists could come together in common cause against Bolshevism. It was not enough for Schulze-Boysen, however. He began his own campaign to raise funds for a new forum, *Politische Arbeitsgruppe zu Berlin* (Berlin Political Working Group). While he cast his net widely for support, there was no place for Nazis. This tended to lean the movement more towards the left than Schulze-Boysen might have wanted at first but more and more he found that, for him, socialism became inextricably linked with a struggle for national freedom. It was the struggle between capital and labour, central to his agenda, that inevitably drew him to radical Marxist economic theories and brought him into conflict with the leadership of the *Jungdeutschen Ordens* to which he had hitherto given his allegiance but which he now found inflexible and increasingly irrelevant. He believed that bourgeoise society had no answers to society's problems but, nevertheless, he was not willing to discard the traditional family values he had grown up with. It was simply a matter of saving what was good and genuine from his old life and integrating it with the new but, as yet, he had no real idea what the new would look like. He made contacts and developed relationships with activists from diverse backgrounds, including the Marxist playwright Bertolt Brecht, and explored different political philosophies to try and resolve contradictions, all the time playing a leading role by initiating discussions and speaking frankly about his ambitions.

He spent the summer of 1931 in France as a guest of André Germain. It caused Schulze-Boysen's mother some concern since she suspected Germain of homosexual tendencies and feared that his interest in Schulze-Boysen was not altogether political but her son was quick to reassure her that Germain was simply a man 'with an awful lot of feeling and soul'.[12] Schulze-Boysen had many issues to resolve in his attitude to France. First of all he blamed that country for being the chief sponsor of the Treaty of Versailles and that would not be easily laid aside. Secondly, he criticised the 'bourgeoise and cowardly' country for 'reclining on the laurels of many centuries' and refusing to make compromises with Germany to allow it to reclaim its place at the top table of European nations.[13]

Moving even further to the left politically, Schulze-Boysen could not avoid the inevitable showdown with his family. For him, a well-ordered bourgeoise existence had lost all meaning. The global economic crisis was hastening the abandonment of his social ties but politically, his firm commitment to avoiding ideologies and bureaucracy meant that he continued to abjure political parties. More than ever, he laboured to refine his own philosophy and create a new movement based on it. The parents, Erich and Marie Luise were not happy when Schulze-Boysen abandoned his legal studies in November 1931 to concentrate on politics but, by this time, they knew better than to try and dissuade him and concentrated instead on maintaining a sound relationship with him.

Franz Jung, who had been active within the *Kommunistischen Arbeitspartei Deutschlands* (KAPD, Communist Workers' Party of Germany) had started publication of a bi-monthly magazine in June 1931 called *Der Gegner* ('The Opposition'). It had close links with the French magazine *Plans*, both opposing liberal individualism and championing a collective left-wing solution to the economic woes of both countries. It was hardly a secondary matter that both periodicals saw the youth of both countries coming together to act in unison to create a new world order that would reject militarism and avoid the continent sliding blindfold into another European war. *Plans* arranged a meeting of what it called the *Treffen der revolutionären Jugend Europas* (Meeting of Europe's Revolutionary Youth) in Frankfurt am Main in February 1932 which it hoped would form the basis of permanent cooperation between European youth for the creation of a new post-capitalist political order. Schulze-Boysen took a lead in discussions with students from France, Germany, Switzerland, Italy and Belgium. The meeting recognised the leadership qualities of this charismatic young man who argued passionately on three main points. Abolition of the capitalist system was at the top of his agenda followed by revision of the terms of Versailles and the urgent need to allow Germany to determine its own future free of foreign control. Narrow ethnic nationalism, however, was not part of his philosophy for a community of peoples working for the common good.

Schulze-Boysen was invited to join the editorial team at *Der Gegner* and submitted his first article in January 1932 outlining his socialist ideals, but he was by no means overtly partisan. He claimed to have no 'stone truths' and he was still open to considering the merits of argument from all sides. His emphasis was on challenging the status quo but, crucially, without resorting to doctrinaire alternatives promulgated by either right or left. Two months later, on 5 March, Schulze-Boysen was appointed editor and pledged to build 'a magazine for a new unity' crossing all political landscapes in the cause of toning down hostility and polarisation. 'Todays' opponents', he wrote, 'will be tomorrow's comrades-in-arms for a new unity.'[14] The general tone of the magazine, however, was beginning to show a more socialist edge. Schulze-Boysen himself, who had always been beguiled by Russian culture now wanted to learn more about the politics of the Soviet Union, the only great power, in his opinion, that could help Germany cast off the burden of Versailles. He also began socialising more with members of the KPD and attended their raucous meetings that were often interrupted by Nazi thugs. Nothing convinced him of the validity of Marxist solutions, however, which he found simplistic.

He was still unable to break entirely from his bourgeoise roots and held firm to and idealised theory of society He believed that it would be from that strata of society that leaders would come to liberate the proletariat but quite how that would happen was not clear given Schulze-Boysen's rejection of parliamentary government which, in his eyes, had repeatedly shown itself to be incapable of overcoming domestic crises.

The Weimar democracy was in its death throes having exhausted every means of survival. At the state elections on 24 April 1932, the Nazis scored another major success, winning 162 of 428 seats and becoming the largest party in the Prussian *Landtag*. On 31 July, elections to the Reichstag resulted in a triumph for the Nazis who won 230 seats. When the Reichstag met two months later, the Nazis amassed an overwhelming vote against the new Chancellor Franz von Papen who promptly dissolved the chamber and fixed new elections for 6 November. In the elections, the Nazis lost nearly two million votes forcing Papen's resignation. After a chaotic two months, on 30 January 1933 a Papen-Nationalist-Hitler coalition was formed with the Nazis holding only three of eleven Cabinet seats: Hitler as Chancellor, Wilhelm Frick as Minister of the Interior and Hermann Göring as Minister Without Portfolio.

Strict press censorship was introduced after Göring's *Polizeierlaß* (police decree) of 2 February banned all demonstrations and meetings of the KPD. Staff at *Der Gegner* faced arrest if they transgressed. Shulze-Boysen advocated 'a certain degree of restraint' to avoid 'a heroic defeat'.[15] Passive resistance seemed to be the order of the day in the hope that political opposition was still possible but his optimism faltered when it became clear that leading representatives of industry and finance were giving tacit support to the Nazis whom, they believed, would safeguard their interests. He tried to reassure his mother, however, that his faith in the power of the people was not diminished. It would take the burning of the Reichstag on 27 February and immediate imposition of the Ordinance for the Protection of People and State to introduce him to the stark reality of the dangers he faced. On 3 March, in a clear warning, he was arrested and held in prison overnight without charge and released the next day. Clearly *Der Gegner* was not to the Nazi's taste. Although, the editorial team argued that the magazine avoided political statements and had no political tendency, an investigation by the Berlin State Criminal Police into the structure and activities of the Gegner association '[confirmed] the assumption that this association is radically communist'.[16] Schulze-Boysen was now clearly in the Nazi's sights. His father saw the danger and tried to persuade Harro to turn away from politics and study for a pilot's licence away from Berlin but all to no avail. He was clear in his mind that there could be no return to Weimar politics and he was not yet convinced that the Nazis could cling to power without suffering a backlash from the working classes who would rise up and impose a dictatorship of the left. The mood of the times allowed for not the slightest possibility of a democratic resolution.

When a meeting was held at the offices of *Der Gegner* on 26 April 1933 to discuss the position of the churches in relation to the political situation, men of the *Hilfskonnado Henze Sturmabteilung* burst in and began beating up all those present. They were flung down the stairs, hauled into waiting police vans and taken to the SS interrogation centre at Potsdamer Straβe. All but four were released twenty-four hours later. Two more were given their freedom a day later but Henry Erlanger and Schulze-Boysen were taken to a detention centre in Charlottenburg. Schulze-Boysen's parents frantically used all their contacts to locate the two men but by the time they arrived at Fürstenbrunner Weg, Erlanger, a Jew, was already dead, beaten to death in front of Shulze-Boysen who was now the subject of a debate among his captors as to whether he, as a witness to the murder, should be eliminated also. Shulze-Boysen's parents were able to negotiate his release but found him 'deathly pale with deep shadows under his eyes [and] his hair chopped off'. His back was covered in welts and a swastika had been carved on his thigh with a knife.[17] When Erlanger's murder was reported to the police, Schulze-Boysen was arrested again and suffered further beatings. After coming out of his ordeal with a mutilated ear and damaged kidneys, he took his father's advice and, in his own words, put his revenge 'on ice' then reported to the commercial pilot training school in Warnemünde, a covert military training base for what would later become the Luftwaffe, which was now under the control of the *Reichluftfahrtministerium* (RLM, Reich Aviation Ministry).

In many ways it was a welcome relief to someone who had come so close to a violent death but, despite having to study hard, Shulze-Boysen missed the challenge of intellectual debate. Politics was definitely not one of the subjects discussed either formally or informally in the Ministry. Theory and physical exercise dominated the curriculum since there was a serious lack of military aircraft, still banned by the terms of Versailles. Friends who visited him found a dispirited, almost despairing man far away from the mainstream of the politics and unable to engage with the issues that concerned him so much. His mood, like the political landscape, was darkening as the fascist counterrevolution was gaining momentum. The restrictive pseudo-military environment in which he now lived deprived him of the freedoms he had worked so hard to win for others. The frustrations that built up inside him could find no outlet. 'To hold on in spite of all forces', he wrote to his father, 'is also what makes you strong'. Despite the loneliness and 'inner emptiness' he was feeling, he was able to assure his father that he was building his strength and not giving in to depression.[18] While he conceded that his views and those of his parents would 'never coincide', he assured them that 'the bond that binds me to you more than ever shall not be broken again'. Locked away in his intellectual isolation, Schulze-Boysen immersed himself in the writings of Nietzsche and Goethe and even the Bible. He also continued his studies of Russian language and culture.

In the spring of 1934, the flying school converted from a commercial venture into a military one, albeit still technically illegal, and his time there came to an end. He returned to Berlin to find so many of his friends there now enrolled in the *Hitlerjugend* but he was not minded to join them. He applied to the RLM for a post in the newly created *Fremde Luftmächte* (Foreign Air Powers department) where he would be responsible for evaluating news from abroad about foreign air forces. Specifically, he would collect information about tactics, organisation, training and technology. His former superior, Hermann Becker was called upon for a reference and had no hesitation in saying that the candidate was 'a multi-talented and gifted young man with a genuine National Socialist outlook'.[19] In a society that was increasingly being closed off from the outside world, this access to foreign news placed him among a narrow elite.

Slowly, Shulze-Boysen was coming to terms with National Socialism but it was at a distance. His position in the RLM was poorly paid but that was the price he paid to stay under the Gestapo radar and he found the work interesting enough. At least, it gave him an opportunity to expand his foreign language skills, especially Russian to the point where he was able to read Dostoyevsky in the original and offered a way to fit into the system without making too many compromises with his convictions. It was the involvement of what he called big capitalists in the party that he could not accept. What he admired, however, was the way the NSDAP was led. Schulze-Boysen was an elitist at heart. He believed that only a very few had the ability to understand the issues and find solutions to the country's problems and what he saw in the NSDAP was a determination to revolutionise society. What he did not agree with, however, was the way that the Nazis prized militarism over 'political education'. Nevertheless, he was prepared to adjust to a regime that he still did not expect to last for long. He knew, however, that in the meantime he would have to learn to keep his opinions to himself.

Such softening of his radicalism, however, seemed to have taken a toll on his self-esteem. An old friend, Elsa Nuss, who met him having not seen him for a couple of years found a restless and nervous man struggling with 'deep disappointment'.[20] His slovenly appearance and downcast manner were quite out of character as the tedious and unrewarding work in the Ministry continues to take its toll. Although his immediate superiors were far from ardent Nazis, the party itself was well represented in the RLM and many seemed to be benefitting financially from the surge of investment the air force was seeing. The fact that Shulze-Boysen saw little of this munificence in his pay packet did little to assuage his sense of frustration. His only respite from the drudgery was occasional the weekend sailing trip on the Wannsee with his friend Richard von Raffray.

He worked hard, however, and built a reputation for himself within the Ministry and went, as its representative, on a number of foreign trips most notably to Switzerland. These visits outside the country expanded his vision and understanding of how the rest of the world viewed what was happening in Germany and he began to feel constrained by his inability to act and speak freely while employed at the Ministry. The lack of promotion opportunities seemed to stem from his lack of enthusiasm and history of left-wing activism so he started to look around for alternative employment but, despite the question marks over his commitment, he was so well thought of and made such a good impression with those he met that he continued to be chosen to represent German youth abroad. He went again to Switzerland to attend a series of lectures on League of Nations issues in August 1935 but this time he was accompanied by a friend, Libertas Haas-Heye. Jewish friends they met there tried to persuade the couple to stay in Switzerland, but both insisted that they would return to Germany and try to influence events there.

Libertas Viktoria 'Libs' Haas-Heye was the youngest of three children born in Paris on 20 November 1913 to Otto Ludwig Haas-Heye, a couturier to the aristocracy, and the noted pianist, Countess Viktoria Ada Astrid Agnes zu Eulenburg. Living at various times in London and Paris, the young Libertas also spent time on the Schloss Liebenberg estate, the ancestral home of her maternal grandfather Prince Philipp zu Eulenburg-Hertefeld in northern Brandenburg. Wilhelm Göring was an occasional guest at hunting weekends and would become an important contact for Libertas in later years. She had a Protestant upbringing and, at first had strong religious leanings, but they did not survive her childhood and had little significant residual influence on her world view. Her parents divorced when she was only eight years old, which was unusual for the times. Libertas and her sister stayed with their mother while the brother went to live with the father. She learned to act and take decisions independently at an early age. After two years schooling in Berlin, Libertas spent six years at the Zurich Municipal Girls' High School where she thrived and became hugely popular. She learned to play the accordion and wrote poems and articles for the school magazine. Her teachers considered her to be an 'enthusiastic and increasingly independent girl'.

After spending six months in London and Ireland, by the end of 1932 she was back in Germany and coming under the spell of Nazi spectacle. She had watched the SA columns march past the Reich Chancellery on 30 January 1933 and was moved by the drama of torchlight parades all of which motivated her to join the NSDAP and the *Bund Deutscher Mädel* in March 1933. Moving to live in Berlin a month later, she was hired by the motion picture company Metro-Goldwyn-Mayer (MGM) as a press officer. In this role she was required to write reviews about new films coming out. She and Harro had met while sailing on the 'paradise for yachting enthusiasts', the Wannsee, in April 1934 while both were guests of Richard von Raffey.[21] Libertas fell head over heels in love with the gallant young man. She later recalled those first weeks of romance with a poem describing 'the flickering of candles, the fragrant shimmer of red roses. 'I laid my heart in your hands,' she wrote.[22] For Schulze-Boysen, Libertas brought about what he called 'an intensification of his being'.[23] Many photographs of the couple bear witness to the intense feelings they had for each other. They soon began living together in an apartment in Hohenzollerndamm, in the Wilmersdorf district. This common law marriage did not find favour with Schulze-Boysen's parents but Libertas went to great lengths to assure them that their son received 'thousands of strengthening thoughts' and 'many lines full of love' every day.[24]

Early in 1935, Libertas spent six months doing voluntary work for the *Freiwilligen Arbeitsdienst für die weibliche Jugend* (Reich Labour Service) before returning to MGM. This experience had left her exasperated by the lowly status of women and the lack of opportunities in her role at the film studios further disheartened her. The restless energy that had characterised her early life now drove her to question the male domination of society and encouraged her to look to radical alternative ideas. She left the studios and took up freelance journalism, working first for the *National-Zeitung* of Essen and later taking employment with a cultural film organisation closely associated with Joseph Goebbels'

Ministry of Popular Enlightenment and Propaganda. At the same time, she started working for Schulze-Boysen's magazine *Wille zum Reich* ('Will to Empire') as a translator. The couple planned to marry despite it being clear that Libertas lived up to her name by being something of a libertine by eschewing conventional sexual morals.[25] The lawyer Rudolf Behse described her as 'a beautiful woman, with such sex appeal', a 'decided flirt' whose musical and athletic talents made her the centre of attention.[26] A friend Margrit Weisenborn said of her that 'she wanted to be desired by everyone'.[27]

At the start of 1936, Schulze-Boysen started a three-month training course at the *Luftnachrichtenschule* (Air Intelligence School) which required him to take the personal oath of allegiance to Adolf Hitler. At the end of his course, which was temporarily interrupted by a kidney problem that required hospitalisation, he was promoted to private in the reserves and moved to a new building in what was a rapidly-expanding RLM with new responsibilities and more interesting work. At the same time, he submitted a formal request to resign from the Nazi Party.

The wedding took place in the chapel of Liebenberg Castle on 26 July 1936. Many post-war accounts cite Hermann Göring as giving away the bride but, in fact he was not present at the ceremony.[28] Libertas, whose morals and general attitude to life were far removed from traditional values, had not made a good impression on her mother-in-law who tried, unsuccessfully, to encourage her to adopt the more domesticated role of *Hausfrau*. Her frivolous attitude to life was exactly the opposite of the steadying influence she thought her son needed. He, however, was happy to see Libertas out in the world living a semi-independent life and moving closer to him politically with every passing day. She, too, applied to leave the Party, somewhat disingenuously citing family commitments that left her no time to devote to the movement.

The lack of promotion despite the overwhelming approval of his work by his superiors, was a serious disappointment for Schulze-Boysen. So much so that Libertas took the opportunity to speak to Göring during one of his hunting weekends at Liebenberg and put in a word on behalf of her new husband. The chief of the newly formed Luftwaffe High Command had always been charmed by Libertas and promised to see what he could do to improve Schulze-Boysen's circumstances. As a result Schulze-Boysen was fast-tracked for promotion but only on the condition that he underwent further military training. This paid off with promotion to sergeant in August 1937.

Meanwhile the couple's house in Charlottenburg had become a popular meeting place for Bohemians and opponents of the Nazi regime from a variety of social circles. There were academics, workers, artists, doctors and military personnel. Guests included the sculptor Kurt Schumacher, his wife Elisabeth, the doctor Elfriede Paul, her friend Walter Küchenmeister, the writer Günther Weisenborn, the dancer and sculptor Oda Schottmüller, Marta Wolter and Walter Husemann. Schulze-Boysen brought along foreign newspapers he has acquired through his work to inform and stimulate discussions. After 1936, the main focus of conversation was the civil war in Spain where General Franco's fascists, with help from Italy and Germany, had launched a coup against the elected Republican government who, in turn, had looked to the Soviet Union for support. Whenever the friends met in Charlottenburg, the radio would be tuned in to a German-speaking station broadcasting on 29.8 metres short wave from Barcelona. This German Freedom Station was being operated by the KPD under orders from Moscow. It gave news of events in Spain and called for resistance to Hitler's regime.

The general character of the meetings, however, was not so much conspiratorial as a means of establishing and maintaining solidarity within the group. That is not to say that anti-Nazi sentiments were not openly expressed. Some actually found the tone of some discussions so disturbing and dangerous that they stopped coming. Ernst von Salomon and a friend, Ille, were guests at the Schulze-Boysen house on one occasion when they were taken along by Ardvid Harnack. While Salomon had not been unduly concerned, Ille left the meeting in some distress. 'Promise me will never go there again' she said as they left, 'I don't want to have my head cut off'. These 'well-dressed, decent-looking people', including at least one whom Ille recognised as a member of the SS spent the evening 'acting like socialising lunatics . . . all hammering away like villains in an old-fashioned melodrama', calling the Nazi leadership 'utter fools' and passing secret messages from one to the other.[29]

In the face of evidence to the contrary Schulze-Boysen, however, believed that the authorities could not object to what he saw as 'normal social interaction'. There was clearly a blinkered attitude where these people, many from privileged backgrounds, who met and behaved this way believed themselves to be somehow immune to persecution. Schulze-Boysen's own experiences should have shown him that this was far from the case. The Gestapo was well aware of what was going on but chose to just keep an eye on the group of 'skilfully dressed communists' rather than take any action against a man who was still considered to be an 'exemplary employee of the RLM'.

In his position with the RLM, Schulze-Boysen was privy to a great deal of information about the level of military aid the Germans were providing to Franco and, at the same time, he was reading daily situation reports about the war published in the foreign press. It was clear that 'mission creep' was daily drawing in more and more German 'volunteer' aircrews which Schulze-Boysen viewed as an alarming development. He saw the war threatened to spread the conflict between authoritarianism and democracy beyond Spain's borders in a widening conflagration that would set capitalists against workers in a class war. Already there was evidence of grotesque massacres being carried out by both sides. What seemed important to Schulze-Boysen was to warn the German people about what was happening in Spain and make them aware of the dangers of escalation. With great prescience, he wrote to his parents describing his fears of a thirty-year war in which entire cities and cultures would 'go up in flames' and 'the most modern technical means' would be used to 'kill and destroy in ever more sophisticated ways'.[30]

There were many foreign journalists in Germany reporting on the Berlin Olympic Games in the summer of 1936 including Evan James who was a personal friend of Libertas. Schulze-Boysen was willing to pass on to James confidential information about the numbers and names of German pilots who had already died in Spain in the hope that he would publish it in the British press. That might force the Nazis to roll back their involvement and allow the civil war to peter out. James rebuffed the approach. Schulze-Boysen then turned to another means of getting the word out. The RLM had secret connections to Franco's forces and through them, Schulze-Boysen collected all the information he could find out about German forces in Spain. He copied photographs and documents from Spain detailing numbers and types of weapons, tanks and aircraft used by both sides. He also had access to the names of German agents infiltrated into the Republican International Brigades. All this he then passed on to his long-time friend and distant relation of Libertas, Georgine Gisela von Pöllnitz, who worked as a journalist at United Press. She placed them in an envelope and dropped them through the letterbox of the Soviet Embassy on Unter den Linden. Why they thought they could get away with this is puzzling. They might have guessed that the embassy was under intensive surveillance. First von Pöllnitz was arrested then the Gestapo came for Schulze-Boysen. After lengthy interrogation he was given a warning and released but von Pöllnitz was detained for several months before being released without charge. She became ill with pulmonary tuberculosis that she had contracted while in Gestapo custody and was taken to a sanatorium in Switzerland where she died on 14 September 1939. She was twenty-four years old.

Already, Libertas, in particular, was making a collection of names and addresses of citizens who had been arrested and thrown into concentration camps. Information about conditions inside these camps was known not from returning inmates who, by and large were constrained to keep a low profile to avoid being sent back, but from the guards who 'spoke freely . . . as if they had a need to speak [seeing] themselves as saviours of the fatherland [who deserved] honour and glory'.[31]

With promotion in the Ministry, Harro and Libertas moved into a spacious apartment at Altenburger Allee 19 at Neu-Westend near the Olympic Stadium. Schulze-Boysen now had access to information that, along with Walter Kuchenmeister, he used it to write a pamphlet *Der Stoßtrupp* ('The Shock Troop'), a savage indictments of the Nazi's plans for the occupation of Czechoslovakia. Fifty copies were made and mailed out, no more than two in any one mailbox, to teachers, doctors, lawyers, and others who might effectively spread opinions.

The working day was stretched once plans were afoot for the attack on Poland but Harro still found time to go out in the evenings to meet a group of friends centred around Heinrich Scheel who was also employed by the Luftwaffe. Hans Coppi, Helmut Roloff, Helmut Himpel and his fiancée Maria Terwiel were part of this social network with its common hatred of Nazism but one that really lacked any sort of plan of direct action. The military victory over France had the effect of boosting Hitler's popularity and consolidating the Nazi's grip on the German population which did nothing to make life easier for anyone planning resistance, but it did have the effect of binding this group closer together in its crusade. The network continued to grow, however, and one evening the Schulze-Boysens were introduced to Greta and her husband Adam Kuckhoff at the home of Herbert and Ingeborg Engelsings. Over the dinner table Herbert, the 'broad-shouldered [crime]writer with calm, dark eyes' and Greta, a translator who had worked on the English translation of Hitler's *Mein Kampf*, quickly revealed that they shared the same views of the Nazi regime as the Shulze-Boysens and all four became close friends.[32] It is through the Kuckhoffs that the Schulze-Boysens then got an invitation to dine with Mildred and Arvid Harnack. Arvid and Harro were not entirely strangers to each other. They had met briefly in 1935 when they recognised each other's political leanings but felt at the time that it was 'too dangerous' to pursue a friendship.[33]

Chapter 10

MILDRED FISH AND ARVID HARNACK

Und ich habe Deutschland auch so geliebt' (And I, too, so loved Germany)
The last words of Mildred Fish-Harnack before she was executed

Mildred 'Mili' Elizabeth Fish was born in Milwaukee, Wisconsin, on 16 September 1902, a time when three out of four Milwaukeeans were of German descent. One of four children, she was the daughter of William Cook and Georgina Fish, growing up learning to read, write, and speak both German and English. Her father was a teacher, and her mother was an activist for women's suffrage. She could trace her lineage back to one John Fish, a private in Captain Christopher Manchester's company of Rhode Island Minutemen. He was the great-grandson of Thomas Fish, who emigrated from England in 1642, becoming one of the earliest settlers and founders of the state of Rhode Island.[1]

After the death of her father, Mildred moved with her family to Chevy Chase, Maryland where she attended Western High School. An old school friend said that she was 'the most beautiful girl I ever saw', while another remembered 'a brilliant student, very self-assured [with a] swanlike neck . . . wearing long, straight hair [looking like] a sort of pre-Raphaelite beauty'.[2] The 'academically gifted, beautiful and brilliant' Mili later went on to George Washington University, famously referred to by Calvin Coolidge as 'hotbed of radicalism' where she studied humanities, journalism, and literature.[3] One of her professors, Ruth Wallerstein, described her as 'quite distinguished as a poet' while another, Warner Taylor, called her 'very aesthetic and a little on the radical side'.[4] After graduating she stayed on to teach and study for her master's degree in English while also working for the Wisconsin State Journal as a film and drama critic.

The 'blond, blue-eyed and tall'[5] Arvid Harnack, with 'wire-rimmed glasses and a sharply receding hairline', was a German economist and lawyer who came from a distinguished Baltic-German academic family and was studying at the same university on a Rockefeller fellowship after a brief spell at the London School of Economics.[6] When he saw Mildred, he was instantly beguiled by her beauty and introduced himself apologising for his poor English. Arvid was a man who took life seriously. In 1914, when he was thirteen, his father, Otto, in a fit of depression, committed suicide by drowning himself in the Neckar River and Arvid took on responsibility for helping to raise his younger brother, Falk and sisters, Inge and Angela. The family moved to Jena where their mother opened a studio teaching art. She joined the *Kunstverein* and exhibited her own work alongside members of the Bauhaus and the Dresden group *Die Brücke*. After the very first meeting between Arvid and Mildred, there followed a whirlwind romance. Intellectually they were well matched, amongst other things sharing a love of Goethe. They canoed and hiked around Lake Mendota with friends, they sipped bootleg wine and took part in student dramatics.[7] Arvid wrote to his mother, Clara:

> Spent a day of brilliant sunshine on Lake Mendota. Lots of flowers under the green trees and exotic, wonderful birds. On another Sunday we went to Devil's Lake. It's a crystal-clear lake between two high cliffs. We laid down on the highest point and looked down and across the wide countryside. The cliffs here are an exception the rest of Wisconsin is fairly level and flat. I read Faust with Mildred.[8]

Greta Lorke, who later married German writer Adam Kuckhoff, was also a German student who had been invited to the US on a stipend and became friendly with Arvid and Mildred. She later recalled the times they had together sailing ice boats and roasting pork chops over a wood fire on Lake Mendota and going off on long cross-country hikes. It seemed to her at the time that Mildred 'derived her notion of Germany entirely from her reading of the poetry, fairy tales, and histories of the Romantic period'.[9]

Two days after Mildred passed her Master's, on 7 August 1926, she and Arvid were married and she took the name Fish-Harnack, a bold and unusual move for the times (In Germany she would change it to Harnack-Fish). The couple honeymooned at Niagara Falls. In 1927, they took part in the protests against the executions of two Italian anarchists,

Nicola Sacco and Bartolomeo Vanzetti, convicted of murdering two men in the holdup of a payroll truck in South Braintree, Massachusetts. It became a profoundly radicalising experience for them and a foretaste of the show trials that would follow in both Nazi Germany and the Soviet Union.

When Arvid's fellowship ended, he returned to Jena in Germany and even though Mildred wrote to her mother-in-law saying that she and Arvid had 'become so much one person that when one of us is gone, the other feels a little broken and lost', she remained in Baltimore to complete her teaching contract at Goucher College.[10] In Germany, when Mildred met Arvid's mother in person she found someone deeply committed to Socialism, a cofounder and later chair of the International Women's League for Peace and Freedom but also someone who was excitable, impulsive, and unconventional. Mildred would often find hungry students, factory women with children sleeping in laundry baskets in the kitchen and Arvid's sisters were called on to volunteer in local orphanages.

The small Thuringian town of Jena, situated in the Saale valley amid pleasant hills and woods, conformed comfortably to Mildred's preconceptions about Germany. Its neoclassic buildings on the Market Square had seen both Goethe and Schiller strolling by and they carried plaques indicating that Hans Christian Anderson and August Wilhelm von Schlegel had lived there.

It was through Clara that Mildred developed a keen interest in modern art and would lead to her making the German translation of Irving Stone's fictional biography of Vincent van Gogh, *Lust for Life*, which was published in 1936. She began work on her doctoral thesis and lectured at universities in Jena and Giessen, while Arvid completed a second doctorate in Giessen with a thesis on the pre-Marxist workers movement in the USA. Moving to Berlin in 1930, she began working as an assistant lecturer in English and American literature at the University of Berlin introducing her students to her favourite English and American writers including Ralph Waldo Emerson, Walt Whitman, Thomas Hardy and George Bernard Shaw. She was so popular with students that in just a year and a half, enrolment in the class tripled.

In 1931, Arvid co-founded the *Wissenschaftliche Arbeitsgemeinschaft zum Studium der sowjetischen Planwirtschaft* (Scientific Working Community for the Study of the Soviet Planned Economy) that attracted scientists, intellectuals, and revolutionaries who came together to discuss communism as an economic solution for Germany's economic woes. In the following year he and Mildred travelled to the Soviet Union on a three-week study trip organised by the Soviet Embassy in Berlin. There they were introduced to progressive concepts such as maternity leave, equal pay, and birth-control education. There is no doubt that this was a trip carefully choreographed to provide an unrealistic, idealised view of the Soviet Union and to indoctrinate the visitors with the teachings of Soviet communism. It was at this time that Arvid Harnack agreed to become a Soviet intelligence source although he was not formally recruited as a spy until 1940.

On their return, Mildred encouraged her students to study Karl Marx's theories which resulted in her dismissal from the Friedrich-Wilhelm University of Berlin. Undaunted, Mildred took up a post teaching at the *Berliner Städtische Abendgymnasium für Erwachsene* where one of her students was Karl Behrens who became a close friend of the Harnacks and would go on to play a significant part in their lives.

Karl Behrens had joined the SA in 1929 and then went on to the NSDAP but in April 1931 he was expelled from the Party for having at one time being a supporter of Walther Stennes who later launched an abortive bid to unseat Hitler as leader in 1933. He joined the KPD and attended classes at the Berlin evening school where he met Mildred who taught English and later he joined the opposition discussion group around Mildred and her husband Arvid. Behrens worked as a designer at the AEG turbine factory and became one of Harnack's closest comrades in the resistance. He provided political, economic and military information to the Soviet intelligence service NKGB, which gave him the code name *Leuchtisti* ('Shining One'). In May 1942, he was drafted into the artillery but in mid-September, he was arrested in his unit on the Eastern Front in front of Leningrad because of his contacts with the Harnacks. He was brought to Berlin, sentenced by the Reich Military Court on 19 January 1943 after lengthy interrogations by the Gestapo, and beheaded in Berlin-Plötzensee Prison on 13 May 1943.

In 1933, after the Nazis had taken power in Germany, the newly appointed US Ambassador to Germany William Dodd arrived with his family in Berlin. Dodd's daughter Martha was initially greatly enamoured of the Nazis and admired the 'glowing and inspiring faith in Hitler, the good that was being done for the unemployed'[11] and this 'gifted, clever and educated woman [who] requires constant control over her behaviour' formed numerous relationships with leading members of the Party including Ernst Udet.[12] Ernst Hanfstaengl, one of Hitler's aides, was also one of Dodd's lovers and he tried to encourage a romantic relationship between Hitler and her. While Dodd found Hitler 'excessively gentle and modest in his manners', no romance ensued.[13]

In September 1933, she first met a young Soviet diplomat, Boris Vinogradov and they became lovers. After the Night of the Long Knives when Dodd became disillusioned with the Nazis, Vinograd was ordered to recruit her to the NKVD. She began providing Moscow with details of her father's reports to the State Department. Around this time, she came into contact with, and became a close friend of, Mildred Harnack through 'those now legendary tea parties which were such social events in Berlin in the 1930s'.[14] Martha later described those times as 'courageous tragic years of fulfilment and disappointment' which were 'the most significant of my life'.[15] With other American expatriates in Berlin, they formed a literary salon where anti-Nazi academics and intellectuals could express themselves freely but when the Gestapo took a keen interest in their work, they were forced to disband what Martha had called 'the last of the meagre remnants of free thought'. Together they worked to obtain visas for Jews and other Nazi political opponents, including the prominent publisher Max Tau, helping them to flee the country.

Mildred returned to the US on a book tour in 1937. Her family and old friends, shocked at the drastic change from her friendly and easy-going personality to one overly cautious, frightened, reserved, distant and subsumed with anxiety, urged her to stay in the US but she was determined to return to her husband and her political activism. It was generally assumed she had 'gone Nazi'.[16] On her return to Berlin, she began teaching at night school, where her students were mostly working class or unemployed. She recruited many of them to join a group called The Circle which included the writer Adam Kuckhoff, his wife Greta, occasionally the religious socialist and former Prussian Minister of Culture, Adolf Grimme, the entrepreneur Leo Skrzypczynski and others. The group published anti-Nazi leaflets, written by Mildred, and secretly left stacks of them in public places throughout the city.

Although an avid communist, Arvid was forced to join the Nazi Party in 1937 as a condition of retaining his government employment at the Reich Economics Ministry, but, in 1938, he established a relationship with US First Secretary Donald Heath, an intelligence officer in the Coordinator of Information, the predecessor of the Office of Strategic Services (OSS). He had met Heath by virtue of his role as deputy director of the American department of the German Trade Ministry and Mildred had come across Heath's wife through the American community in Berlin where Mildred was president of the American Women's Club of Berlin and the Berlin representative of the Daughters of the American Revolution. The two couples had become friends, spending weekends together going cross-country skiing in Grunewald.

Involved in almost all significant economic political activities of the regime, Arvid was able to pass confidential information to Heath, including operations of the German central bank, foreign trade statistics, Nazi debt, gold, and exchange policies, the financial results of IG Farben, or massive Nazi assets hidden in American banks, which could be confiscated by the United States.[17] He did this on the understanding that all information would be shared with the Soviet Union with whom he had been doing something similar since 1935 but had lost his main Soviet contact to Stalin's purges in 1937. That did not prevent him from acting on his own initiative by recruited a network of about sixty individuals to spy for Moscow.[18]

This physically and mentally demanding life required great self-discipline which Harnack maintained through what he called the 'roots of my strength' which were his family and a close relationship with nature closely connected to the work of Johan Wolfgang von Goethe. Minutes before his execution he would quote Goethe to the prison chaplain Harald Poelchau.[19]

On 17 September 1940, the Harnacks' flat on the exclusive Woyrschstrasse was visited by a man who introduced himself as Alexander Erdberg. This was, in fact, Deputy Head of the Foreign Intelligence Division of the 1 Division, Lieutenant of State Security Alexandr 'Sasha' Mikhailovich Korotkov. Under the Berlin NKVD *rezidentura* Amayak Kobulov, he had been assigned to reactivate moribund agents in Germany.[20]

Chapter 11

DIE ROTE KAPELLE

In the jargon of the German secret service, the head of a spy network was a *Kepellmeister*, a *chef d'orchestre* – an orchestra leader who directed and coordinated the playing of his instruments.¹

The good-looking Alexandr Korotkov, who called himself Alexander Erdberg, was in his early thirties with thick, light-brown hair and spoke in fluent German with a Viennese accent. Working as a GRU agent since 1927, Korotkov had been active all across Europe with special responsibility for assassinating Soviet traitors. ² In July 1940, he had arrived in Germany as part of Soviet exhibitions in Königsberg and Leipzig to re-establish communication with especially valuable sources. When Korotkov called on him, Harnack was alone in the flat since his wife was away for a few days. In a roundabout sort of way, Korotkov told Harnack that he had been sent by Harnack's old friend from the Soviet embassy, Alexander Hirschfeld, to see if he might be interested in resuming his dormant relationship with the GRU. Korotkov was wary of saying too much until he had made a judgement about Harnack's motivations for aiding and abetting a foreign power in time of war. It was a delicately balanced moment for both men. Unconvinced, Harnack demurred until Korotkov proposed a second meeting at the Soviet Embassy in Berlin which would establish his credentials. Harnack agreed.

In the meantime, Korotkov reported to Moscow that '[Harnack] considers it his duty to inform us about what his acquaintances tell him, not because he sees himself in the role of an agent with us as his chiefs, but rather first and foremost as representatives of the Soviet Union, of a country with whose ideals he feels connected and from which he awaits support'.³ Harnack was interested much more in getting support for an anti-fascist conspiracy rather than an acting as a Soviet agent but if that's what it took, he was more than willing to play along with Korotkov. For its part, Moscow baulked at the idea of playing second fiddle in Harnack's game but Korotkov assured his chiefs that it was this or nothing as far as Harnack was concerned and they had little choice but accept the situation, at least for the time being. Their forbearance later paid off when Harnack persuaded Schulze-Boysen to become part of the arrangement with Moscow.

Harnack was reassured about Korotkov's status and submitted his first intelligence report a week later, warning that Hitler was in the planning stages for an invasion of the Soviet Union. His first move would be the military occupation of Romania before advancing to the Leningrad-Black Sea line thereby creating a German vassal state, Harnack reported. The German invasion of Britain, he said, was postponed.[4] This was so far from what the Soviets expected that Moscow was very sceptical about Harnack's reliability but they saw him as a portal through which they could get a view of how far advanced internal opposition to Hitler had come. Arrangements were made for clandestine meetings between Harnack and Korotkov or one of Korotkov's agents, sometimes at the flat and sometimes at locations in the city. After a few weeks, when a more solid relationship had been built up, Harnack told Korotkov about the other sixty members of his group of dissidents that included state officials, engineers, and technical workers, he said. Their aim was to 'prepare cadres who would be able to take over command positions after a coup'.[5]

It was in December that Schulze-Boysen came into Korotkov's orbit. Moscow had urged Korotkov to contact Schulze-Boysen, who was given the code name *Starshina*, the Russian word for sergeant. The Luftwaffe employee was a prime target for Soviet espionage, but he had been transferred from Wilhelmstrasse in the centre of Berlin to a forest on the Havel River near Potsdam called Wildpark Werder, where the general staff of the Luftwaffe was housed, including Göring's command bunker which had taken on a number of experts on the Soviet Union. He was now the contact point for German Luftwaffe attachés from all across the globe. It was here in January 1941 that he first saw secret aerial photos of Leningrad and the nearby island Kotlin taken from six thousand feet by Luftwaffe reconnaissance aircraft flying out of Königsberg.

Every weekend he had come into Berlin, however, and made contact with Harnack to keep him informed about developments concerning war plans with the Soviet Union. Harnack made it clear to Schulze-Boysen that everything he was being told went to Moscow through Korotkov who, in turn, became anxious to meet Schulze-Boysen in person. When Harnack floated this idea to Schulze-Boysen he got a cool reception. It was one thing for an officer of the Luftwaffe to tell Harnack, a fellow German patriot, albeit one who was in contact with an agent of a foreign power, but quite another to actually come face to face with a spy working for a country with which Germany would soon be at war. The psychological hurdle was high but it forced Schulze-Boysen to ask the hard question of himself of how far he was prepared to go. He was not yet aware of the extent to which his principles could withstand the reality of treason. He would have to answer the ultimate question of who the traitor to the German state was, himself or Hitler.

At the same time, Schulze-Boysen had, along with Horst Heilmann, Mimi Terweil and Elisabeth Schumacher, started writing a pamphlet designed to persuade his fellow officers of the senselessness of an attack on Russia. The substance of the text compares Hitler's plans with Napoleon Bonaparte's failed invasion of Russia in 1812. Bonaparte's fundamental error had been his incorrect evaluation of the land and people he had been so convinced would fall under his onslaught.[6] Bonaparte had been born in Corsica and when the GRU saw a copy of the text they gave Harnack the codename 'Corsican'.

With war drums daily beating ever louder, Schulze-Boysen eventually agreed to meet Korotkov in his flat on 27 March 1941. Harnack had warned Korotkov that Schulze-Boysen required careful handling and should not be treated as a traitor to his country but as a German patriot. Korotkov attempted to take control of the agenda and establish a hierarchy within the relationship by telling Schulze-Boysen that it would be wise to stop sending out his leaflets. It was far too risky and there were much bigger opportunities to influence the course of events. The only real issue was the timing of a German attack on the Soviet Union. Schulze-Boysen insisted that he and his co-conspirators should be afforded respect for their stand against the Nazis and not treated as mere sources of intelligence. Some sort of understanding was arrived at which both sides could agree on and Schulze-Boysen then gave Korotkov a list of the main railway lines in the Soviet Union and the electric power stations of the Donetsk coalfield all of which would be attacked on the first days of the invasion. It was a serious violation of espionage protocols that Schulze-Boysen was allowed to continue with his internal resistance activities after he had agreed to work directly with Moscow as a source of military intelligence. Normally, active espionage groups would be kept small and remain in ignorance of other groups operating in the same environment so that if one is penetrated the damage would be contained.

Korotkov was duly impressed and reported to Moscow that Schulze-Boysen was 'a fierce man of inimitable enthusiasm and passion'. 'It is essential to activate the work with *Starshina* to the maximum extent,' they replied.[7] Three weeks later, Korotkov delivered a battery-powered portable radio transceiver mounted in a suitcase to Harnack. In the eventuality of war, it was to be used to communicate military intelligence directly to Moscow. A third network was established by Korotkov under Kuckhoff, codename Old Man, but kept strictly separate from Harnack and Schulze-Boysen for security reasons.

On 20 April, Schulze-Boysen met his wife Libertas who had come to Marquardt, a fishing village north of Potsdam with Elizabeth Schumacher. They were joined by Korotkov and agreed that Elizabeth would take charge of the radio since her husband, Kurt, codename Tenor, knew how to operate it. At the same time, Shulze-Boysen reported to Korotkov that agreement has been reached about who would be installed as heads of military-economic administration for various districts of Soviet territory after the occupation. These men had already received their conscription notice and were preparing to leave. Intelligence also included reports of intensified Luftwaffe reconnaissance flights taking off from Bucharest, Königsberg, and German-occupied Kirkenes in northern Norway with special attention being given to photographing the Soviet naval base at Kronstadt. Schulze-Boysen was receiving information direct from Erwin Gehrts, adjutant to the General of the Air Force at the headquarters of the Commander in Chief of the Army. Through Gehrts, Schulze Boysen learned about the number of divisions being relocated from France to Poland and the date of an invasion which turned out to be a month earlier than it actually took place. All this information went to Moscow via Harnack.

Then in early June, Schulze-Boysen reported that Göring was transferring his headquarters from Berlin to Romania and documents he had seen indicated that the Germans planned to capture the Red Army in pincer movement south from West Prussia and north from Romania. On 16 June Schulze-Boysen presented Korotkov with the Luftwaffe order of battle warning that 'All German military measures for the preparation of an armed attack on the Soviet Union have been fully completed and the blow can be expected to fall at any moment'.[8] When Stalin got this intelligence, he dismissed it as propaganda. 'Send your "informant" from the staff of the German Luftwaffe back to his whore of a mother. He's not an informer but rather a disinformer,' he wrote.[9]

On 22 June when the Germans launched Operation Barbarossa, the Soviet embassy in Berlin was surrounded by SS units and telephone lines were cut, There was no way to contact Moscow. Fearing an SS assault, the Russians proceeded to the top floor, where, behind steel doors and windows, they burned documents and code books in special quick-burning ovens. The families of Soviet diplomats were rounded up and taken to Gestapo headquarters then moved to an SS camp outside Berlin to await an exchange deal for German diplomatic personnel in Moscow. Ten days later, Korotkov and 1,500 of his fellow countrymen boarded a special train that took them to the Russo-Turkish border. He had in his pocket a memorandum from Harnack describing the strengths and weaknesses of the German armaments industry.

In Berlin, Schulze-Boysen sent a test signal and got a reply from Moscow so the link was established but Kurt Schumacher, who was the designated radio operator had been posted to Posen as a PoW camp guard. Hans Coppi, codename Small, 'a machinist, former deliveryman, house servant, and handy man',[10] stepped in to take over the role but quickly proved to be hopelessly inadequate. The rules for choosing dates and times to broadcast were complex and Coppi couldn't get the hang of call signs at all. While Harnack spent hours encoding messages, Coppi would send them out either at the wrong time or on the wrong wavelength. Night after night, Moscow listened in vain. Coppi eventually accidentally destroyed the transmitter by plugging it into the mains supply and blowing out the transformer.

Some intelligence continued to pass from Berlin to Moscow but it had to go first by courier to Brussels which was the hub of a network of Soviet spies operating all across Europe run by Leopold Trepper. This was a slow and dangerous process and Moscow was becoming frantic wondering why Berlin had gone silent. In desperation, the NKVD Chief of Foreign Intelligence, Pavel Fitin ordered Anatoly Markovich Gurevich to go to Berlin and find out why contact had been broken. Gurevich was in Brussels operating as part of the Soviet *Rote Kapelle* espionage network in the guise of Vincente Sierra, a South American language student, codename Kent. An instruction was sent to Brussels on 10 October 1941. It read,

KLS from RTX. 1010. 1725. 99 wds qbt.b from the director to Kent/Personal

Immediately go to Berlin to the three addresses indicated and determine the causes of the radio link failures. Stop. If interruption occurs again, undertake transmissions personally. Stop. Work [of] three Berlin groups and transmission of information of vital importance. Addresses: Neuwestend, Altenburger Allee 19, third right. Coro – Charlottenburg, Frederickstrasse 26a, Second left. Wolf. Friedenau, Kaiserstrasse 18, fourth left. Bauer. Send 'Eulenspiegel' back here. Password: Director. Stop. Report progress before October 20. New plan, repeat new, in force for three stations. Qtb ar. KLS from RTX[11]

This message was intercepted by an *Abwehr Funkabwehr* monitoring station at Cranz, a resort town on the Baltic seacoast north of the East Prussian city of Königsberg. The *Funkabwehr des Oberkommandos der Wehrmacht* (Radio Defence Corps) was an *Abwehr* radio counterintelligence organisation created in 1940 by Hans Kopp to monitor illicit radio broadcasts by using direction finding equipment. Its purpose was to discover the locations of radio transmitters used by secret agents and resistance groups who were communicating with other agents or sending intelligence from inside German-occupied territory to Germany's enemies. As early as 26 June, the Cranz monitoring station had picked up radio transmissions emanating from somewhere in Northern Europe and going to Moscow. These messages in an as yet unbroken code were forwarded to the *Funkabwehr* Radio Signals Security, headquartered on the Matthäikirchplatz only a few blocks from the Harnack apartment in Berlin. There was a flurry of excitement that got the attention of the director of the Reich Security Main Office, Reinhard Heydrich and his deputy Walter Schellenberg who set up a team of experts led by Harry Piepe to track down the source or sources of these messages. At first, all that could be deduced was that the signal had originated in North Germany, Belgium, Holland, or France. It would be many months before decoding of this message would reveal to Piepe the addresses of Schulze-Boysen, Harnack and Kuckhoff.

Gurevich had first met Schulze-Boysen in April 1939 when he had been sent to Berlin to establish a courier link between Berlin and Brussels. At that point he was using both Schulze-Boysen and Harnack as sources but neither at that time were agents of the GRU. At the end of October 1941, he duly went to Berlin and made contact with Schulze-Boysen, Harnack and Baur and giving them a new radio. Coppi tried again but his signals got no response from Moscow. They didn't know if it was an operational failure or if the radio simply wasn't working.

By 1942, the German advance into the Soviet Union had stalled. Schulze-Boysen and Harnack were more certain than ever that the Third Reich was doomed and applied themselves to establishing contacts with other opposition groups in Berlin factories and the Hamburg waterfront group led by Robert Abshagen, Franz Jacob, and Bernhard Bästlein. They even made contact with the White Rose students in Munich. Along with the neurologist John Rittmeister and a new friend John Graudenz, Schulze-Boysen printed a six-page pamphlet entitled *Die Sorge um Deutschlands Zukunft geht durch das Volk* (Distress about Germany's future runs through the nation). The pamphlet read:

> A final victory of National Socialist Germany is no longer possible. Every day that the war is prolonged brings only new, unspeakable suffering and victims. Each further day of war means that in the end a larger bill will have to be paid . . . Hitler will go under just as Napoleon went under.[12]

It was posted out to Catholic priests, Protestant pastors, judges, professors, and members of the diplomatic corps. Theya also managed to print about twenty issues of *Die innere Front* (The Home Front) distributed to foreign workers in the Reich. Kuckhoff and John Sieg wrote letters to soldiers on the Eastern Front hoping to incite passive resistance among Germans there. 'Can it be that difficult, Captain, when placed between one kind of death and another, to choose between the proud, honourable tradition of Prussia, which appeals to your conscience, and the base brutality of the SS rabble that has terrorized you into carrying out the "duty" of cowardly murdering Russian patriots?!', they wrote.[13] Naturally, the Gestapo came into possession of the *Die Sorge* pamphlet and Goebbels makes known his concerns but all investigations into the source of paper and envelopes comes to nothing. There were not even any fingerprints to work with.

Libertas collected documentary evidence of Nazi war crimes, such as newspaper clippings from party newspapers in which the Nazis boasted of their crimes, and she filed these away for future use. She and Kuckhoff were gathered evidence such as letters and reports of eyewitnesses, about the mass murder of Jews and civilians in the East. When perpetrators of these crimes requested copies of photographs of their atrocities Libertas started a card file linking names to incidents hoping to use it in future trials. All attempts at the time to pass this information to the Allies through their personal contacts in Switzerland and Sweden met with indifference.

It was increasingly hard to disguise the fact that the war in the East was not going well for the Germans with almost a million casualties. The *Das Sowjet-Paradies* (The Soviet Paradise) exhibition had toured many of the larger cities of the Reich and occupied countries to highlight what the catalogue described as the dreadful conditions of 'poverty, misery, depravity and need' in the Soviet Union under 'Jewish Bolshevist' rule and thereby justify the war against them. Goebbels had produced the exhibition complete with a collection of dilapidated shacks and other ramshackle buildings to illustrate the 'misery and hopelessness' of the lives of the farmers and workers and showing a society in which everything was falling down and the people were all robbers and criminals.[14]

From 8 May it had been at the Berliner Lustgarten, a former garden of the Berlin *Stadtschloss* (city palace) located between the Berlin Cathedral and the National Gallery. The exhibition stretched over nine thousand square meters and in one of the giant tents, visitors could see grim-looking men with daggers, knives, axes, and scythes who were meant to depict Soviet soldiers. At the centre of the exhibition was a purportedly true-to-life reproduction of a neighbourhood in 'Minsk, the City of Lies,' with dilapidated buildings and 'real objects secured and removed from the Soviet Union' that had been taken from that city and shipped to their present location. So-called *Schmutzwege* (paths of filth) depicted shabby hovels that lacked any trace of culture, and a grocery store with nothing but a few vodka bottles behind dusty panes of glass.[15] As propaganda went at the time, it was straight out of Goebbels' playbook.

On 16 June, a few days before the exhibition was due to close, Fritz Thiel and John Graudenz make plans to distribute stickers all across the city of Berlin to draw attention to the blatant propaganda aspect of the exhibition. The message on the stickers was short and to the point,

Permanent Exhibit
The NAZI PARADISE
War Hunger Lies Gestapo
How much longer?.

Some of their friends feared that such a protest would be a provocation to the authorities that could see reprisals against the community but, despite the low expectation of the stickers having any significant impact, Schulze-Boysen saw it as an important driver of momentum for their overall campaign and gave it his approval.

Harry Piepe, meanwhile, had not been idle. At midnight on 12 December 1941, his men had surrounded a house in the Ettrenebck district of Brussels which they had pinpointed as one source of the mysterious coded signals being sent to Moscow. Two hours later they burst into 101 Rue des Atrébates. Shots rang out. David Kamy (alias Anton Davilov), who had been operating the transmitter, tried to run but fell as a bullet struck him. Piepe recovered some charred scraps of paper from a fireplace that contained clues about how the messages had been encrypted.

By 30 June 1942, Piepe's more powerful detectors were now able to filter out even loud background 'noise' and homed in on a property at 12 Rue de Namur, occupied by a family called Kurt and Elizabeth Schumacher. Then, in the early hours of 30 June 1942, Piepe raided it. On the top floor they again found a transmitter, still warm, and a bundle of documents. Johannes Wenzel was captured as he tried to flee and was taken into custody.[16] He was quickly broken through interrogation and torture and gave up details of the codes he used and the identities of his collaborators. The 'tall, thin, cadaverous-looking' SS-Hauptsturmführer Karl Giering and his right-hand man, the 'short, plump' Willy Berg had taken over the investigation.[17] Clearly Heydrich felt that Piepe did not have the stomach for the kind of investigations that were now required to root out this 'cancer' of Soviet espionage that was growing in the Reich. Hitler himself was making more frequent references to the Soviet intelligence network and, no doubt, looking for more scapegoats to blame for the Wehrmacht's increasing military setbacks on the Eastern Front. It took the teams until July 1942 to actually decipher a single whole message and it landed on Giering's desk like a bombshell. Dated 10 October 1941, it was the message containing the addresses of three members of the Berlin group, Harro Schulze-Boysen, Arvid Harnack and Adam Kuckhoff.

The Gestapo set up a special commission with maximum *Geheime Reichssache* security classification to follow up on this intelligence. It was led by 39-year-old SS-Obersturmbannführer Friedrich Panzinger, who appointed SS-Hauptsturmführer Horst Kopkow to carry out the investigation. He in turn picked SS-Hauptsturmführer Johannes Strübing as his leading detective.[18] The three suspects were put under observation but these bohemians, one of them a Luftwaffe officer, were quite unlike any spies Kopkow and Strübing had come across before.

Horst Heilmann worked at the Radio Decryption Unit on Matthäikirchplatz where he saw a file about decoded Russian radio transmissions. The folder was labelled *Rote Kapelle*, a *Kappele* being the choir or orchestra of a royal or papal chapel or colloquially, any musical organisation.[19] A radio operator who tapped Morse code with his fingers was a 'pianist' in secret service jargon. A group of 'pianists' formed a 'band', and since the Morse code had come from Moscow, the 'band' was communist and therefore 'red'. The Brussels group under Treffer had already been given the name *Rote Kapelle* by the Gestapo and because of the 10 October message linking Brussels and Berlin, the Shulze-Boysen and Harnack groups were also included as part of that spy network but they were never really part of Trepper's operation. Heilmann tried to warn Schulze-Boysen by telephone but all he could do was leave a message asking him to call back.

The next day, 31 August 1942, Schulze-Boysen was arrested in his office by Kopkow and taken to Gestapo headquarters. He was photographed for their files still wearing his Luftwaffe uniform. No record exists of the interrogation that followed. Libertas, meanwhile, had been visiting friends in Bremen and when she returned to the apartment on Altenburger Allee she found that her husband had disappeared and she feared the worst. She contacted Heilmann who came over to the apartment and together they set about destroying anything that might be construed as evidence of wrongdoing. Arvid and Mildred Harnack, under Gestapo surveillance and unaware of Harro's arrest were enjoying a few days holiday at Priel on the Baltic coast where they too were arrested and brought back to Berlin.

The net closed in. Heilmann was arrested on 5 August and Libertas prepared to flee. She booked a berth on the sleeper train to Trier from where she hoped to cross over into Switzerland but at Wannsee, the last Berlin station, Gestapo board the train and arrested her. On 12 August, Adam Kuckhoff was arrested in Prague and his wife Greta in their apartment while their four-year-old son, Ule, was left with the caretaker. The Schumachers were taken on the same day as was Hans Coppi, on duty in the village of Schrimm, Coppi's seven-months pregnant wife Hilde, and John Graudenz in his apartment. Erika von Brockdorff, Oda Schottmüller, Hannelore and Fritz Thiel, Maria Terwiel, Helmut Himpel, Cato Bontjes van Beek and Heinz Strelow, Elfriede Paul and Walter Küchenmeister, Heinrich Scheel, were taken on 16 September and Helmut Roloff was caught a day later still in possession of the radio transmitter. More than 120 people in all were swept up in the operation, many with no more than a passing connection to any of the resistance groups.

Hitler and Göring were kept up to date with results of the investigations that revealed an astonishing range of espionage and resistance activities going all the way back to the Spanish Civil War. To avoid giving publicity to the internal resistance aspect of the activities, it was decided to focus on charging all the arrestees with treasonous acts on behalf of the Soviet Union. Goebbels wrote in his diary, 'The whole matter is highly embarrassing and for the Luftwaffe especially compromising. It will be investigated with vigour and with care, and one hopes at least that a large number of the carriers of the Bolshevist disease will be brought to light . . . To show leniency or hesitation in fighting this sabotage would be a crime against the very war effort itself.'[20]

Gestapo chief Heinrich Müller wanted a quick trial in the *Volksgerichtshof*, but Hitler handed over the whole prosecution to Göring who ordered that the case against his Luftwaffe officer be tried before the *Reichskriegsgericht* (RKG, Reich Court-Martial,) and that included women or civilians who had nothing to do with the military. The investigation itself was led by Kopkow, head of the Referat IV A 2 subdepartment and a specialist in sabotage with the baby-faced Colonel Dr. Manfred Roeder as head prosecutor. Hitler cautiously reserved the right to uphold or reject any decision the RKG came to. Harnack and Schulze-Boysen were tortured but John Sieg avoided extensive punishment by hanging himself in his cell on 15 October. Hilde Coppi gave birth to a son, Hans, in her cell on 27 November. She was allowed to take the newborn to visit the father one time but knew that she was no longer protected by the law shielding pregnant women from execution but it was postponed until August so that she could breastfeed her child. She wrote to her mother,

> You can imagine that I haven't had a pleasant time. It's lucky that little Hans is still with me. I have to pull myself together in his interest. Oh, Mama, the thought of being separated from my child almost drives me to despair. I don't think there can be a greater punishment for a mother than to be separated from her child.[21]

She was executed by guillotine in Plötzensee prison on 5 August 1943.

Roeder handed over the indictment to Dr Alexander Kraell, the chairman of the RKG's Second Judicial Panel. Göring was generous with bonuses 'for special achievement in an extraordinarily important investigative case'. Kopkow alone received 30,000 Reichsmarks. Three days before the court sat, a 'priority' memo, deemed 'essential to the war effort', was sent from the Reich Ministry of Justice to the commandant of Plötzensee prison. It required him to install a T-beam on the ceiling of the execution shed with eight movable meat hooks that slide on rollers.[22] On the morning of 15 December 1942 extra security was laid on for the trial before Kraell, another judge and three Wehrmacht officers. In the dock were Harro and Libertas Schulze-Boysen, Mildred and Arvid Harnack, Horst Heilmann, Elisabeth and Kurt Schumacher, Kurt Schulze, Herbert Gollnow, Hans Coppi, Erika von Brockdorff, John Graudenz. Mildred and Erika were given jail sentences of six and ten years respectively but the others received the death sentence. When this was communicated to Hitler at his *Wolfsschanze*, he rejected the jail terms and ordered that Mildred and Erika be sent to the guillotine.

Mildred spent her last days making translations of Goethe right up until the minutes before her execution. Arvid, too, had Goethe on his mind when he quoted Goethe's *Faust* in his last letter to his wife. On the day before the trial, Arvid Harnack also wrote to her, '

> If I have had the strength in the past few months to be calm and composed inside, and if I look forward to the things to come calmly and composed, I owe this above all to the fact that I feel connected to the good and beautiful in this world, and that I have the feeling that the poet Whitman sings about the whole earth. As far as people are concerned, it was those close to me and especially you who embodied both of these things for me.[23]

Chapter 12

THE VON SCHELIHA GROUP

[Scheliha] belonged to that group of people who were willing to take any risk to help those in danger.[1]

Ilse Frieda Gertrud Stöbe was one of the most controversial of the German opponents to Hitler's regime. A trained secretary and shorthand typist, she went on to work in the advertisement department of the Rudolf Mosse publishing house. When still only nineteen years old, her keen intelligence brought her to the attention of the Jewish author and journalist Theodor Wolff, the editor-in-chief of the *Berliner Tageblatt* newspaper, who employed her as his secretary and he encouraged her to become a journalist. In 1931 she began a relationship with the editor and KPD member Rudolf Herrnstadt who had been working for the GRU since 1929 under the code name 'Arbin'. Herrnstadt introduced Stöbe to the Soviet *resident* in Berlin, the Latvian Jewish communist and historian Yakov Bronin who recruited Stöbe as an agent for the GRU and gradually introduced her to intelligence work giving her the cover name 'Arnim'. It is doubtful if she was ever actually a member of the KPD. As of 2024, the Moscow Central Archive of the Ministry of Defence of the Russian Federation (ZAMO) files that might throw some light on her political views are still not available to Western researchers.

In early 1933, Stöbe lost her job when Wolff fled Germany after Hitler came to power and she became a freelance journalist travelling all across Europe. Living in Warsaw and working as a foreign correspondent for German and Swiss newspapers including the *Neue Zürcher Zeitung*, she met up again with Herrnstadt and became his mistress. Through Herrnstadt, she gained access to the circle of liberal, anti-Nazi German embassy staff around the ambassador Hans-Adolf von Moltke, the diplomat Rudolf von Scheliha and the press advisor Hans Graf Huyn. Herrnstadt maintained a network of informants, whose findings he passed on to Soviet military intelligence via the Soviet embassy but, as a Jew, he could not risk direct contact with his sources so he recruited Stöbe as a cutout this time giving her the cover name 'Alta'. There is some evidence to suggest that Scheliha, who held strongly anti-communist views, was under the impression that Herrnstadt was working for the British at that time. Scheliha was exchanging intelligence for money which he deposited in the bank, Julius Baer and Company of Zurich. On one occasion, he received $6,500 drawn on the Chase National Bank in New York and cleared through the Credit-Institut in Lyons. In 1939, $10,000 was transferred to the account of his sister, Renata Johanna von Scheliha at the Guaranty Trust Company of New York but most of the money Scheliha received from Moscow went on his rather lavish life-style which from a security aspect was distinctly unwise. The sort of intelligence that Stöbe was collecting from her sources, primarily Scheliha, included intelligence about the German-Polish situation, especially the outcome of conversations between the Polish Foreign Minister and the German Ambassador in Warsaw.

Stöbe became seriously ill at this time with venereal disease, believed to have been contracted as a result of rape while she was briefly imprisoned in Prague suspected of being a Gestapo spy, which left her with a painful debilitating medical condition. At the end of 1938, after consultation with Moscow, she accepted the post of cultural advisor in the women's department of the NSDAP foreign organisation in Warsaw giving her a chance to expand her circle of acquaintances but in August 1939, she left Warsaw along with the members of the German embassy in anticipation of a German-Polish conflict. By contrast, Herrnstadt went to the Soviet Union leaving Stöbe as Scheliha's handler in Berlin. Her contact with Herrnstadt had not gone unnoticed, however, and she was briefly investigated by the German police. Meanwhile, Scheliha had taken over the management of Subdivision XI 'Combating Enemy Atrocity Propaganda' in the *Auswärtiges Amt* Information Department, where he attended the daily briefings to the chiefs of departments giving him access to a great deal of important information. Shortly afterwards he was able to get Stöbe a job in the press section of the *Auswärtiges Amt* which gave her official ties to representatives of the Soviet news agency Tass. Intelligence now passed from Scheliha through Stöbe to Tass and then to the Soviet Commercial Attaché at the Berlin Embassy.

It was here that Stöbe met and moved in to live with the journalist Carl Helfrich. An attractive young woman, Stöbe earned a reputation for insubordination, often joking in the office about the badly written texts by her head of department. Her illness meant that she was hospitalised for a brief spell but then she lost her job after reorganisation on 1 January 1941 as part of numerous dismissals aimed at consolidating the influence of the NSDAP in the *Auswärtiges Amt*. Denied official accreditation as a bona fide journalist by the Nazis, Stöbe worked in the advertising department of the Lingner Works in Dresden which allowed her to travel on business trips to Prague and Preßburg. She was still able to get intelligence from Scheliha, who still thought she was working for the British. At the same time, Scheliha had clandestine contacts with a journalist of Jewish origin, Immanuel Birnbaum, who emigrated to Sweden. It was to him that he passed on much confidential information about terror in occupied Poland.

In his role at the he department in the Information Department and through contacts he had made while at the Warsaw embassy, Scheliha had access to information about victims of the Nazi atrocities in Poland and he was able to intervene on behalf of many through the *Reichssicherheitshauptamt* (RSHA, Reich Security Main Office). It is known he enabled Prince Olgierd Czartoryski's escape to Switzerland[2] and saved Prince Ksawery Druckiemu-Lubecki's life by enabling him to work as an agricultural expert in Germany.[3] Thanks to him also, Princess Teresa Sapieha-Różańska née Lubomirska was able to leave in January 1940 and go to Italy. Countess Elisabeth von Oppersdorf, who had many family connections in Poland, wrote in 1980 that Scheliha 'helped many Polish families, including mine'.[4] It is known also that Scheliha arranged for the secret export of a significant quantity of valuables and jewellery belonging to the Polish aristocracy to Switzerland but this did not go entirely unnoticed by officials in the *Auswärtiges Amt* courier office.

In the summer of 1941, the Wehrmacht occupied Lviv and slaughter of the civilian population began. Scheliha did what he could to save a number of prominent figures by placing them under special police protection ostensibly to allow them to write an account of crimes committed by Red Army units under the Soviet occupation of eastern Poland from 1939 to 1941. The idea was to then use these texts for propaganda purposes both in Germany and abroad. The RSHA was quick to approve. Among this group of men was Andrzej Szeptycki, the Greek-Catholic Archbishop of Lviv and Halicz, who hid around 200 Jewish children in the monasteries under his jurisdiction, including 21 in his own cathedral. Through him also, Scheliha was able to convey covert information about German crimes in the occupied territories to the Vatican. The list of Scheliha's contacts also included the prominent art historian, Professor Mieczysław Gębarowicz from Lviv University, and Professor Franciszek Groer. Scheliha's whose involvement in assisting the Polish aristocracy was confirmed after the war by many diplomats who had encountered him earlier. For example, the ambassador of the Federal Republic of Germany in Portugal, Herbert Schafarczyk, who came from Chorzów, confirmed that 'many representatives of Polish aristocratic circles asked him for help, and he always tried not to refuse it'. Also hailing from Głuchów Górny near Trzebnica, the diplomat and distinguished dissident of the Third Reich, Albrecht von Kessel, claimed that Scheliha 'persistently and at great risk to his own safety rescued representatives of the Polish aristocracy from reprisals by the Gestapo and SS'.[5]

On 20 January 1942, SS-Obergruppenführer Reinhard Heydrich hosted the Wannsee Conference to establish the foundations for the extermination of Jews living in the area administered by the Third Reich. Without knowing what was on the agenda, Scheliha had been involved in the preparation process for this meeting but afterwards, when he found out what was being planned, he contacted an acquaintance from his Warsaw days who had been a representative of the League of Nations in Gdańsk, the Swiss Carl Burckhard. It is believed that it was through Scheliha that the world first became aware of what was about to happen.

When the Soviet embassy in Berlin had been closed at the beginning of July 1941, Stöbe was left stranded from her Moscow handlers and Herrnstadt with all lines of information cut off. Previously there had been several attempts by Moscow to train Stöbe in the use of radio technology and encryption techniques but they ran out of time when the Germans launched their invasion on 22 June 1941. The invasion made life very dangerous for Stöbe and Helfrich who changed address without informing Moscow. Despite this attempt to hide from the authorities, Stöbe came under suspicion after the *Abwehr* and the Gestapo had intercepted a radio signal sent from Brussel's to Moscow that contained her name, albeit distorted, her alias, her old address and telephone number. They were contained in orders to re-establish contact with Stöbe at all costs. This was the message that had exposed Schulze-Boysen. She was now caught up the massive operation to uncover the whole *Rote Kapelle* organisation.

In July 1942, Hitler personally authorised Scheliha's promotion to the highest official rank in the *Auswärtiges Amt*, Legationsrat der I Klasse, which entitled him to serve as an ambassador but, much to the annoyance of the Gestapo, who wanted rid of him, he chose not to take up the invitation of the German ambassador in Turkey, Franz von Papen, to join his embassy. For a long time, Scheliha had been a thorn in the side of the Gestapo with his constant and intrusive demands for explanations regarding the reasons behind terrorist acts in Poland and warnings about the international consequences of such actions.

The OKW and Gestapo became aware of Stöbe's activities through the successful decoding of a Brussels agent's radio communications with Moscow. As other names were deciphered at the same time, a special commission was formed in the Reich Main Security Office to uncover what was obviously a huge Berlin resistance organisation.

On the strength of the decoded message and with no further evidence, Stöbe and Helfrich were arrested in Hamburg on 12 September 1942. Nothing could be proved until a Soviet agent, Erna Eifler, who had been parachuted into Germany was captured and identified Stöbe as a person she was ordered to make contact with. When another Soviet agent was arrested, a receipt for a money transfer to Rudolf von Scheliha was found in his possession. Scheliha was arrested on 29 October. A short time later, Ilse Stöbe admitted to spying for the Soviet Union and using Scheliha to do so.

The investigation against Scheliha was conducted by the fanatical Nazi Manfred Roeder but the documents that were supposed to prove Scheliha's alleged acceptance of GRU money could not be verified as genuine and the only incriminating material against him was his own testimony coerced through torture. In court, the judge Alexander Kraell, despite having no substantial evidence of Scheliha's collaboration with Soviet intelligence, found him and Stöbe, who was tried alongside him, guilty as charged and sentenced them both to death. They were murdered in Plötzensee prison on 22 December 1942, Stöbe by guillotine and Scheliha by hanging. Stöbe's mother was also arrested and sent to Ravensbrück concentration camp, where she died in 1943.

Chapter 13

HERBERT BAUM AND THE JEWISH RESISTANCE

Be a good citizen – think for yourself, Love your country, a good German is not afraid to say 'no'.[1]

In 1933, German Jews faced a choice between accepting degradation and persecution or, where it was possible, emigration. Those who stayed and opted to defy the Nazi regime had a choice between *Widerstand*, resistance as part of antifascist groups, or *Nonkonformität*, opposition through nonconformist behaviour. In an effort to protect Jewish communities, Leo Baeck and Otto Hirsch formed the *Reichsvertretung der Juden in Deutschland* (National Representative Organisation of Jews in Germany). Up until *Reichskristallnacht* many Jews, along with other Germans, had expected the Nazi regime to buckle and allow some sort of normality to return but after the night of 9–10 November 1938 all such notions were obliterated. A coordinated wave of anti-Semitic violence saw more than 1,000 synagogues burned or otherwise damaged, about 7,500 Jewish businesses ransacked, 91 Jews murdered, and Jewish hospitals, homes, schools, and cemeteries vandalised. Some 30,000 Jewish males aged 16 to 60 were arrested. For Jews, flight now became an imperative but for most that was impossible, In full view of the German people, forced labour and ghettoisation quickly followed with little or no public protest.

Few outside the Jewish community offered them a route to resistance. Social conservatives and clerical elites joined forces with the National Socialists in calling for a 'traditional solution' to the 'Jewish question'.[2] By and large, the Jews did not have access to the Goerdeler bourgeoise resistance of dignitaries, bureaucrats and military elites. Only the left-wing movements offered a way in but that was strictly on the basis of political allegiance to the communist cause and not because of their Jewishness.

By the age of fourteen, Herbert 'Hebbi' Baum was already an active member of different left-wing and Jewish youth organisations, and then in 1931, when he was twenty, he became a member of the *Kommunistischer Jugendverband Deutschlands* (KJVD, Young Communist League of Germany). When the Nazis came to power in 1933, Baum and his wife Marianne (née Cohen) together with their friends Martin and Sala Kochmann began organising clandestine meetings of young Jewish people to discuss ways of opposing the regime and so came into contact with Berlin communists such as Robert Uhrig. Baum was instructed by the leadership of the Communist youth organisation to contact Jewish youth movements and organisations and recruit them to resistance. In consequence, Baum joined the *Ring-Bund Deutsch-Jüdischer Jugend* (German-Jewish youth group) at the beginning of 1934 and from then he assumed leadership of the Communist youth organisation in the southwestern sub-district of Berlin.

Baum's principal allegiance was to the KPD but his group accommodated a variety of political viewpoints and it operated independently of any dictates from Moscow or the exiled German communist leadership. Baum excelled as an organiser, combining personal charisma with political passion. An acquaintance of his from the 1920s recalled, 'In his calm style he always pleaded for justice.... [He spoke] in such a persuasive and simple manner, that everyone not only understood him, but also agreed with him. He had everything that a natural-born leader should possess.'[3] Baum coordinated a network of small groups engaged in covert forms of resistance such as surreptitiously dropping leaflets around Berlin, scrawling anti-Hitler graffiti on walls, and seeking allies among the forced labourers in the factories where they worked. Baum came up with a novel method to distribute the leaflets. Explosives with detonators and fuses were placed in tin cans then a metal plate was put on top of the can with leaflets stacked on top of that. These cans were placed on rooftops and when they exploded the leaflets were scattered onto the streets. The main activities of the Baum groups, however, were semi-formal *Heimabende* (home evenings) when they would discuss novels, political texts, and music. These evenings helped to bond the groups and maintain morale as well as act as a way of attracting new members.

At the 'Brussels Congress' of the KPD which took place in Moscow in October 1935 the Jewish members were barred from communist underground cells to protect both them and the cells themselves and the Jewish youth organisations began to serve as a recruiting pool for the Jewish Communist group which was taking shape. The Herber Baum Group is often regarded as the 'example par excellence' of German-Jewish resistance but it operated not only outside the orbit of other resistance groups but also was at odds with the wider Jewish community whose leadership disapproved of its actions for security reasons.[4] Baum's group grew to contain around 100 members but the inner core consisted of around 30 members mostly from lower middle-class backgrounds, many of whom worked for the Siemens organisation.

In 1940 Baum and several of his closest comrades were rounded up to become forced labour at the Siemens Elmo-Werke plant. Baum was elected as representative of the Jewish workers and coordinated resistance activities such as producing a monthly newsletter called *der Ausweg* (The Way Out), sabotaging production at the factory and establishing indirect contact with the Robert Uhrig organisation, a large communist-led resistance network that was based in Berlin's factories.[5] After the German invasion of the Soviet Union the Uhrig Group had around 100 active members who went round Berlin putting up posters urging workers to sabotage production at industrial-military industries such as *Deutsche Waffen und Munitionfabrik*. They also produced a monthly newssheet called *Informationdienst* (Information Service) publicising German war crimes and giving updates on German military setbacks in the Soviet Union. A Gestapo round-up in February 1942 saw 200 people associated with the group rounded up with 100 being executed. Uhrig was executed by guillotine on 21 August 1944 in Brandenburg-Görden penitentiary.

Baum and his colleagues decided to hold a memorial gathering for Rudi Arndt in Berlin's large Jewish cemetery, the Weissensee. This was a particularly risky venture, as it involved a congregation of approximately fifty people at a time when any sort of a crowd would arouse police suspicion. Arndt had been a Jewish communist and leader of the underground resistance inside the Buchenwald concentration camp. According to reports, he had 'encouraged his fellow prisoners to write poems and songs' and 'made the greatest efforts to combat the degradation of humanity'. He had even got permission to assemble a string quartet, which performed works by Mozart, Haydn, and Beethoven.[6] At around this time, Baum began a collaboration with a group of a dozen young Jewish men and women run by Heinz Joachim who also worked at the Siemens Elmo-Werke.

When the German attack on the Soviet Union was running into trouble in early 1942, Baum, with misplaced optimism, wrote a letter to communist officials saying that he was on the verge of creating a 'mass movement [that would] transform the imperialist war into a "civil war"'.[7] On 18 May 1942, his group cooperated with the Hans Fruck, who ran a small group of communist youths, and a group led by Joachim Franke and Werner Steinbrinck. Together they organised an arson attack on the *Das Sowjet-Paradies* anti-communist and anti-Semitic propaganda exhibition. The objective of the attack by the Baum group was to send out a message to the German people that not everyone was taken in by the propaganda but the plotters had failed to appreciate that Goebbels was fully in control of the country's media and no word of the attack found its way to the outside world until the following year. Of course, there was word-of-mouth dissemination but that was hardly significant under the circumstances. Incendiary bombs were set and detonated but the resulting fires were soon extinguished. Damage was minimal and the exhibition was reopened the following day.

At noon on 22 May, Herbert and Marianne Baum, Gerhard Meyer, and Heinz Rotholz were arrested at their workplace while Joachim Franke, Werner Steinbrinck, and all the members of their group were arrested also. Nine days later, the Gestapo arrested a number of Jews and incarcerated them in the internment camp at the Lewetzowstrasse Synagogue. The next day, 154 of them were taken to the SS camp in Lichterfelde and shot immediately upon arrival. Ninety-six other Jews were taken out of the evening roll call that same day and also shot. In line with *Sippenhaft,* the concept that family members share responsibility for criminal acts, family members of the Jews who had been shot in Lichterfelde were sent to Theresienstadt in various transports. Two hundred and fifty other Jews from Berlin were deported to Sachsenhausen. Some were shot there, and others sent to Auschwitz.

On 11 June the Gestapo informed the state prosecutor that Herbert Baum had been declared a suicide, although it is likely that he had been tortured to death in the three weeks after his arrest. At least three other members of Baum's groups died in police custody and altogether thirty-two members and supporters of Baum's groups were executed in Plötzensee prison or otherwise murdered by the German authorities over the next year and a half. Sixteen of those executed were no more than twenty-three years old. Three of the youngest women were sent to Auschwitz and perished there.

Chapter 14

THE WHITE ROSE

When, ten years ago we learned – first in the form of a rumour and later reliably confirmed – of the bold attempt of the Scholls and their friends to touch the conscience of university students, we recognized and stated: This cry of the German soul will echo through history. Death cannot now, nor could it then, compel this outcry to silence. Their words, sent fluttering on sheets of paper through the hall of the University of Munich, were and have remained a beacon.

Extract from the Address by President Heuss of the Federal Republic of Germany to the Students of Berlin and Munich on the Occasion of the Memorial Ceremony Held on 22 February 1953.[1]

The earliest friendships between people who would become the White Rose group of resistance was between Alexander Schmorell and Christoph Probst who met in 1935 at the *Neue Realgymnasium* in Munich and developed an 'unbreakable' bond. The friendship group grew to include the artistically gifted Otto 'Otl' Aicher and Werner Scholl and Scholl's sister Elizabeth. All five shared strong anti-Nazi views inspired by conservative Christian principles enshrined in the works of St. Augustine of Hippo, St. Thomas Aquinas, Blaise Pascal and Cardinal John Henry Newman.[2] In the autumn of 1941, Aicher introduced Scholl's younger brother and sister, Hans and Sophie, to Professor Carl Muth editor of the banned Catholic newspaper *Hochland* and a vibrant discussion group was formed meeting almost daily to talk about religion and philosophy.

Hans Scholl had been active in the *Jungenschaft*, a cultural organisation which was one of the few remnants of the *Bündische Jugend* long since disbanded by the Gestapo. It was essentially a harmless group of young people exploring their world and developing their minds in a free and questioning way doing many of the things that the *Hitlerjugend* did, such as camping, hiking and singing but without the militarisation and propaganda. Then suddenly the *Jungenschaft* was also brutally shut down and many young people given their first taste of prison life. All at once the chasm between their ideals and the reality of life under the Nazis yawned before them. Hans turned to literature for guidance and in 1940, having grown into a 'tall, dark fellow, with brown eyes and enormous intensity', he had started a university but also drafted into the war in France as half-soldier and half-student.[3]

Another member of the friendship group was Heinz Brenner who copied the sermons of Bishop Galen condemning the confiscation of a number of convents and monasteries by the Gestapo and distributed the leaflets among his friends in the spring of 1942. Franz Josef Müller and Heinrich Guter helped by putting the leaflets in envelopes and Susanne Hirzel helped to distribute them. Another medical student, Traute Lafrenz had a passionate but brief relationship with Hans but afterwards they remained friends and the six students now formed what was an inner circle of four male and two female activists. Around this core there grew a wider grouping of friends some of whom were much older than the main body of students such as the architect Manfred Eickenmeyer who had a practice in in Schwabing and Josef Söhngen who was a bookseller. A friend of Hans Scholl's father, Eugen Grimminger, provided money to finance their own pamphlets the first of which came out in June and July 1942 written by Hans Scholl and Schmorell. Around one hundred were produced on a typewriter and duplicating machine. Soon afterwards, both men were drafted for medical training on the Eastern Front. The male students were obliged to study medicine and alternate their time between study and time spent on active service on or near the front. Graf, Schmorell and Hans Scholl were thus exposed to the brutal reality of war in the Soviet Union.

On the day that Sophie Scholl left home to enrol as a student at the University of Munich in 1942 her sister, Inge recalled 'It was beautiful to see her dark, smooth, shiny hair hang down to her shoulders. With her large brown eyes she looked upon the world critically but with lively interest. Hers was still a child's face, with delicate features. In it there was something akin to the nervous curiosity of a young animal and at the same time an expression of great seriousness.'[4] In Munich, she moved into lodgings at Muth's house. In this way, she was introduced to Muth's literary circle of friends including the writers Theodor Haecker and Werner Bergengruen.

Like her siblings, Sophie had joined the *Bund Deutscher Mädel* as soon as she was old enough and was caught up in the 'drumbeat and song'. 'We felt we belonged to a large, well-organised body that honoured and embraced everyone', she wrote, and her enthusiasm saw her made a group leader. It was not long before she began to question the ideals of the movement, however, especially the marginalisation of Jewish girls, and turned to her brother Hans and his friends who were actively exploring philosophical and religious ideas in books such as *Sternstunden der Menschheit* by Stefan Zweig that had been banned by the Nazis. Drawn to the beauty and calm of the natural world, Sophie wrote in a school essay, 'I can never look at a limpid stream without at least dangling my feet in it; in the same way, I cannot walk past a meadow in May . . . I lie in the grass, quite still, my arms spread, my knees raised, and am happy'. Later she wrote to her boyfriend Fritz Hartnagel who was a serving officer on the Eastern Front, 'If I had time, I'd stretch out beside the Iller, swim, laze, and try to think of nothing but the beauty around me'.[5] Inevitably, the glaring disparity between her maturing emotions and the disaster occurring all around her, especially after the outbreak of war, gave her a sense of hopelessness but at the same time she told Fritz that it was 'cowardly to turn your back on [politics]'.

A few weeks after her arrival in Munich, the first leaflet of the White Rose appeared at the university. Up until this point, Sophie had been quite unaware of student opposition to the war and certainly did not know that her brother was involved in it. In all, four badly typed single-spaced leaflets, each a précis of concentrated rage, printed on cheap duplicating paper were circulated between 27 June and 12 July 1942 appealing to the students political responsibility and to convince the readers especially of their moral duty to resist. They were entitled 'Leaflets of the White Rose'. Written in an intellectual and philosophical style they were clearly aimed at the students and did not address the working classes. The first leaflet began:

> Nothing is so unworthy of a civilized nation as allowing itself to be 'governed' without opposition by an irresponsible clique that has yielded to base instinct. It is certain that today every honest German is ashamed of his government. Who among us has any conception of the dimensions of shame that will befall us and our children when one day the veil has fallen from our eyes and the most horrible of crimes – crimes that infinitely outdistance every human measure – reach the light of day?

It went on to quote Schiller and Goethe and urged recipients to make as many copies as they could and pass them on to others. These leaflets were the cause of much excitement among the students calling on them to examine their consciences and resist totalitarianism. In the days that followed, more leaflets appeared at brief intervals. Like the first, the second leaflet was written by Hans Scholl and Alexander Schmorell and contained the following.

> Now it is our task to find one another again, to spread information from person to person, to keep a steady purpose, and to allow ourselves no rest until the last man is persuaded of the urgent need of his support in the struggle against this system.
> ...
> Since the conquest of Poland three hundred thousand Jews have been murdered in that country in a bestial manner. Here we see the most terrible crime committed against the dignity of man, a crime that has no counterpart in human history.
> ...
> Why tell you these things, since you are fully aware of them – or if not of these, then of other equally grave crimes committed by this frightful sub-humanity?
> ...
> The German people slumber on in their dull, stupid sleep and thereby encourage these fascist criminals; they give them the opportunity to carry on their depredations.
> ...
> Everyone is guilty, guilty, guilty! It is not too late, however, to do away with this most reprehensible of all miscarriages of government, to avoid being burdened with even greater guilt.
> ...
> Up until the outbreak of the war, the larger part of the German people was blindfolded; the Nazis did not show themselves in their true aspect. But now, now that we have recognized them for what they are, it must be the sole and first duty, the holiest duty of every German, to destroy these beasts.[6]

And the third,

> The family is as old as man himself, and out of this initial bond man, endowed with reason, created for himself a state founded on justice, whose highest law was the common good. The state should reflect the divine order, and the highest of all utopias, the *civitas dei*, is the model it should ultimately resemble.
> ...

Every human being has the right to a just state, a state that safeguards the freedom of the individual as well as the good of the whole.

...

Man should be free and independent, while fulfilling his natural duty of living and working together with his fellow citizens, and strive to achieve earthly happiness through self-reliance and self-motivation.

...

Why do you allow these men in power to rob you step by step, both openly and in secret, of one of your rights after another, until one day nothing, nothing at all will be left but a mechanised state system presided over by criminals and drunkards? Is your spirit already so crushed by abuse that you forget it is your right – or rather, your moral duty – to eradicate this system?

...

Many, perhaps most, of the readers of these leaflets cannot see clearly how they can mount an effective opposition. They cannot see any avenues open to them. We want to try to show them that everyone is in a position to contribute to the overthrow of this system. Solitary withdrawal, like embittered hermits, cannot prepare the ground for the overthrow of this 'government' or bring about the revolution at the earliest possible moment. No, it can only be done through the cooperation of many convinced, energetic people – people who agree on the means they must use to attain their goal. We have few choices as to these means. The only one available is passive resistance. The meaning and the goal of passive resistance is to bring down National Socialism, and in this struggle we can't shrink from any means, any act, whatever its nature. At every point we must oppose National Socialism, wherever it is open to attack. We must bring this monster of a state to an end soon. A victory for fascist Germany in this war would have inconceivable and terrible consequences.

...

Sabotage armament industries, sabotage every assembly, rally, ceremony, and organisation sponsored by the National Socialist Party. Obstruct the smooth functioning of the war machine (a machine designed for war that is then used solely to shore up and perpetuate the National Socialist Party and its dictatorship). Sabotage in every scientific and intellectual field involved in continuing this war – whether it be universities, technical colleges, laboratories, research stations, or technical agencies. Sabotage all cultural institutions that could enhance the 'prestige' of the fascists among the people. Sabotage all branches of the arts that have even the slightest dependence on National Socialism or serve it in any way. Sabotage all publications, all newspapers, that are in the pay of the 'government' and that defend its ideology and help disseminate the brown lie.[7]

The fourth leaflet saw the world in religious terms as a battleground between good and evil.

> Who has counted the dead – Hitler or Goebbels? Neither of them! In Russia thousands are lost daily. It is the time of the harvest, and the reaper cuts into the ripe grain with wide strokes. Mourning enters the country cottages, and there is no one to dry the tears of the mothers. Yet Hitler feeds lies to those people whose most precious belongings he has stolen and whom he has driven to a meaningless death. Every word that comes out of Hitler's mouth is a lie.
>
> ...
>
> Man is free, but without God he is defenceless against evil. He is like a rudderless ship, at the mercy of the storm, an infant without his mother, a cloud dissolving into thin air.
>
> ...
>
> We are trying to facilitate a renewal of the severely wounded German spirit from within. This rebirth must be preceded, however, by a clear recognition of all the guilt with which the German people have burdened themselves,
>
> ...
>
> For Hitler and his followers, no punishment on this earth can be commensurate with their crimes. But out of love for coming generations we must make an example after the conclusion of the war, so that no one will have the slightest urge to attempt such actions ever again. And do not forget the petty scoundrels in this regime; note their names, so that none will go free! Having played their part in these abominable crimes, they should not be able to rally to another flag at the last minute and then act as if nothing had happened!
>
> ...
>
> We will not be silent. We are your bad conscience. The White Rose will not leave you in peace![8]

Christof 'Christl' Probst had served two years in the Luftwaffe before resuming his medical studies in 1939. A man of deep Christian faith, he was by no means a born revolutionary, but he was tormented by news of the Nazi euthanasia programmes for mentally and physically handicapped people. He was no less affected by persecution of the Jews and the growing number of reports of mass crimes committed in the concentration camps and on the Eastern Front. He married Herta Dohrn in August 1941 and started a family so when Sophie Scholl, Willi Graf and Traute Lafrenz joined the circle later in the summer term of 1942, they agreed that he would be kept out of everything. He would not agree, however, and was determined to be involved in the distribution of leaflets.

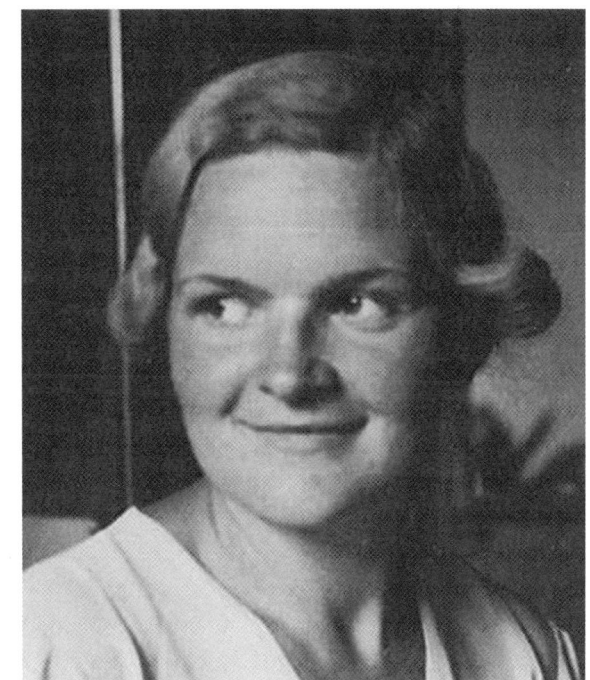

Erika Gräfin von Brockdorff, executed by guillotine on 13 May 1943

Eva Maria Buch, executed by guillotine on 5 August 1943

Hans Coppi, executed by hanging on 22 December 1942

Hilda Coppi, executed by guillotine on 5 August 1943

Arvid Harnack, executed by hanging on 22 December 1942

Mildred Fish Harnack, executed by guillotine on 16 February 1943

Harro and Libertas Schulze-Boysen, Harro, executed by hanging on 22 December 1942, Libertas executed by guillotine on the same day.

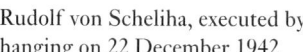

Rudolf von Scheliha, executed by hanging on 22 December 1942

The lone bomber Johann Georg Elser

Erwin Gehrts, executed by guillotine on 10 February 1943

Friedrich Rehmer, executed by hanging on 13 May 1943

Sophie Scholl, executed by guillotine on 22 February 1943

Christof Probst, executed by guillotine on 22 February 1943

Poster for the 1943 'Soviet Paradise' exhibition

Swing Youth resistance group showing off their style

Claus von Stauffenberg (left) with Hitler at Wolf's Lair in July 1944 only days before he planted the bomb in an attempt to kill him. The look of Stauffenberg's face speaks volumes.

Wolfs Lair after the explosion of 20 July 1944

The execution building Plötzensee prison

The Guillotine at Plötzensee prison

Roland Freisler, head of the Volksgerichtshof (People's Court)

Alexander Schmorell's family had strong links to the Soviet Union. Still referred to sometimes by his Russian nickname 'Shurik', he had come to Germany as an infant, brought by his parents from that country and his family had done a great deal to help emigrants and dissidents over the years. To see what was happening in the Soviet Union was a deeply traumatic experience for this 'tall, lean, brown-haired man with an ironic gleam in his grey eyes' and whose 'light, casual way made people around him want to smile'.[9] In November, he wrote to a Russian friend, 'Now that I've been to Russia, everything here seems alien and strange to me. My days are filled with thinking of you and of Russia because my heart, my soul, my thoughts, I left them all behind in Russia.'[10] The students returned to Munich for the winter term but before that they take some leave and go to Chemnitz where they meet Falk Harnack an ex-Munich University student whose brother Arvid has been imprisoned in Berlin for being a member of the *Rote Kapelle* resistance group.

One of the most important unifying ideals of the group of friends was their exploration of philosophical ideas about humanity and its place in the universe. All revelled in the beauty and delights of existence which made the reality of what their world was turning into intolerable. Willi Graf was typical of their approach with his careful thought and deliberate speech that gave him the 'impression of being precise, genuine, and wholly reliable'.[11] None of them could have had any illusions about how little their actions could change the course of history yet each was driven by an urgent need to bear witness to their Christian faith and do whatever they could to atone for what they saw as the sins of the German people.

In January and February 1943, a fifth and sixth leaflets were produced and distributed by the thousand in Regensburg, Salzburg, Linz, Vienna, Frankfurt, Freiburg and Hamburg. The fifth leaflet, written by Willi Graf and Kurt Huber was an appeal to the entire population in a clear, political language and entitled 'Leaflets of the Resistance Movement in Germany. Appeal to all Germans!' It was intended to suggest that there was already a large, interconnected opposition against the Nazi dictatorship across Germany.

> The war is nearing its inevitable end.
> ...
> It has become a mathematical certainty that Hitler is leading the German people into an abyss. Hitler cannot win the war
> ...
> Are we to be forever the nation which is hated and rejected by all mankind?
> ...

> Prussian militarism must never come to power again. Only in a generous, open cooperation among the peoples of Europe can the groundwork be laid for genuine reconstruction. All centralized power, like that exercised by the Prussian state in Germany and Europe, must be eliminated. The coming Germany must be federalistic. At this juncture only a sound federal system can imbue a weakened Europe with new life. The working class must be liberated from its degraded conditions of slavery by a reasonable form of socialism.
>
> ...
>
> Freedom of speech, freedom of religion, the protection of individual citizens from the arbitrary will of criminal regimes of violence – these will be the bases of the New Europe. Support the resistance. Distribute the leaflets![12]

The sixth and final leaflet was written by Kurt Huber and was entitled 'Fellow Students! It was directed specifically at Munich students. Willi Graf wrote in his diary, 'We are truly getting to work now, getting the ball rolling.'

> Our people are deeply shaken by the fall of our men at Stalingrad. Three hundred and thirty thousand German men were senselessly and irresponsibly driven to their deaths by the brilliant strategy of our World War I corporal.
>
> ...
>
> The day of reckoning has come – the reckoning of German youth with the most abominable tyrant our people have ever been forced to endure. In the name of German youth, we demand Adolf Hitler's state restore our personal freedom, the most precious treasure that we have, out of which he has swindled us in the most wretched way.
>
> ...
>
> There is only one slogan for us: fight against the Party! Get out of all Party organisations, which are used to keep our mouths shut and hold us in political bondage! Get out of the lecture halls run by SS corporals and sergeants and Party sycophants! We want genuine learning and real freedom of expression. No threat can intimidate us, not even the closure of universities and colleges. This struggle is for each and every one of us, for our future, our freedom, and our honour under a regime that will be more conscious of its moral responsibility.
>
> ...
>
> The name of Germany will remain forever stained with shame if German youth do not finally arise, fight back, and atone, smash our tormentors, and set up a new Europe of the spirit.
>
> ...
>
> Our people stand ready to rebel against the National Socialist enslavement of Europe in an impassioned uprising of freedom and honour.[13]

Hans Scholl, Alexander Schmorell and Willi Graf experimented with other ways of expressing their opposition as well by painting slogans of freedom on walls across Munich during three nights in February 1943. In black tar coal, they wrote 'Freedom', 'Mass murderer Hitler' and 'Down with Hitler' in large letters on the entrance to the university and on buildings around the central areas of Marienplatz and Viktualienmarkt. These graffiti were immediately removed by the Gestapo.

A seventh leaflet was drafted but before it could be copied, Hans and Sophie Scholl were arrested while distributing the sixth leaflet in the grounds of Munich University. For weeks the Gestapo had been intensifying their efforts to locate the source of the leaflets and had created a special investigative commission. They did not make any immediate connection between the leaflets and the graffiti but the university was put under increased surveillance by Oswald Schäfer, director of the Gestapo's Munich office. On the late morning of 18 February 1943 round 11 a.m. the Scholl siblings were spotted by the caretaker Jakob Schmid leaving copies of the sixth leaflet outside lecture rooms and were reported to the Gestapo who came and arrested them. Willi Graf and his sister Anneliese were arrested that evening but Schmorell, who had witnessed the Scholl arrests, went into hiding.

The Scholls were interviewed separately, Sophie by Robert Mohr and Hans by Anton Mahler. A copy of the draft of a seventh leaflet had been found in Hans's pocket. Hoping to divest himself of it during the melee of the arrest, he had ripped it to shreds but the pieces had been reconstructed. He had merely found it, Hans said. For seventeen hours they were questioned but maintained their innocence until a search of Hans' rooms uncovered a quantity of stamps and a copy of a letter in handwriting that matched that on the draft leaflet he had tried to destroy. The letter was written by Christoph Probst. Eventually both Sophie and Hans confessed to distributing the leaflets but did not implicate any others. The Gestapo, however, confident that they had now solved the mystery of the leaflets arrested friends of the Scholls and where they could not be found, as in the case of Schmorell, put up wanted posters all over southern Germany offering a reward for information about his whereabouts. Schmorell had hidden in the flat of a friend, Lilo Ramdohr, who had no connection at all with the White Rose group. From there he planned to make his way to hide in a Soviet PoW camp near Innsbruck and from there take one of the Alpine passes into Switzerland. Unaware that the Scholls had been taken, Christoph Probst was arrested as he turned up for his weekly pay envelope.

The trial was set for Monday 22 February at the *Volksgerichtshof* but before that the accused were allowed to write to their parents. The letters were never delivered, however, and used in evidence at the trail. When they were taken from their cells, Sophie had left behind a sheet of paper on which she had written '*Freiheit*'. In his cell, Hans had written a quote from Goethe, '*Allen Gewalten zum Trotz sich erhalten*'.[14] Family members of the accused had not been officially told about the arrests and none were present in court. When the trial opened and the charges were read out, the prosecution demanded the death sentence. Himmler had taken a personal interest and was keen to make an example of the three accused to deter others. The Munich gauleiter wanted the three students hanged publicly on the Marienplatz, the central square of Munich or in front of their university but Himmler thought that might be just a little bit too provocative and, even before the trial had begun ordered that executions would take place both secretly and quickly. No witnesses were called and the presiding judge Freisler ranted and raved, in his usual ferocious, maniacal manner but the accused remained calm. Before giving his judgement, Freisler gave each defendant a chance to speak. The Scholls refused but Probst pleaded for clemency in the name of his wife and three young children.

Before Freisler retired, ostensibly to consider his verdict which was never in doubt, Hans and Sophie's parents arrived at the courthouse but were denied entry. When the verdict of guilty was handed down and the accused were led from court, Robert Scholl, the father, managed to shake hands with each of them and Hans was able to say a few works to him, 'Stay strong, no compromise'.[15] Pleas for clemency were shrugged aside. Probst received last communion in his cell. Hans and Sophie talked with a Protestant chaplain and sang a few psalms.

The Scholls' parents went away and planned to continue the appeal process but only three hours after the trial had ended, Sophie was the first to be taken into the execution chamber at the Munich-Stadelheim prison where the guillotine stood. Hans followed and cried out 'Long live freedom' before the blade fell. The next day posters were put up all over the city and newspapers declared that three *Einzelgänger* (troublemakers) who had defied 'the spirit of the German people in a shameless manner', had been tried and executed for high treason. 'At this time of heroic struggle on the part of the German people, these despicable criminals deserve a speedy and dishonourable death', reported the *Münchner Neueste Nachrichten*.[16]

With threats of tough sanctions against the Munich University student fraternity, a meeting was called to show solidarity with the Nazi regime. Hundreds of students protested against the traitors who had lived in their midst. When he appeared, the caretaker, Jakob Schmid, received a tumultuous ovation. He would later be arrested and imprisoned by the Americans, claiming that he had only done his duty. There were still students who privately refused to toe the line, however. Although Lisa Grote later said, 'When the Scholls were killed, our courage was broken', within days new graffiti appeared on the walls of university buildings, 'Scholl lives! You can break the body, but never the spirit!'[17]

One by one, friends of the Scholls were picked up by the Gestapo, then on 24 February Munich was struck by a fierce RAF bombing raid. Taking shelter in a bunker, Schmorell was recognised and the Gestapo were quickly called to arrest him. The second trial for high treason against fourteen defendants of the resistance group took place on 19 April 1943. The *Volksgerichtshof* pronounces death sentences on Alexander Schmorell, Willi Graf, and Kurt Huber.

The Gestapo spared Graf's life in the hope of extracting the names of other White Rose collaborators from him but Graf gave nothing away. He was eventually guillotined on 12 October 1943. Eleven more White Rose activists were subsequently rounded up, including eight from a Hamburg affiliate. All of these died, whether by execution or by suicide or in a concentration camp. Many others were sent to prison.

The White Rose leaflets were smuggled out of Germany into Sweden and Switzerland. Once they reached the West, the leaflets of the White Rose were reprinted in their tens of thousands and dropped from Allied aircraft over the cities of Germany.

Chapter 15

THE KREISAU CIRCLE

> Am I to learn this and still sit at my table in a heated room and drink tea? Don't. I thus make myself also guilty? What shall I say when I am asked, 'And what did you do during that time?' Since Saturday the Berlin Jews are being rounded up. Then they are sent off with what they can carry ... How can anyone know these things and walk around free?
> Helmuth von Moltke, 21 October 1941[1]

Helmuth James Graf von Moltke, as his name suggests, was a Prussian aristocrat, a descendant of Teutonic Knights and a member of the German branch of the Knights of St. John of Jerusalem (Hospitallers). His was one of the great families of Germany. He was the great-grand-nephew of Helmuth von Moltke the Elder, the famous Prussian general of the Franco-Prussian War, from whom he inherited the Kreisau estate in Prussian Silesia. He was, however, a most un-Prussian example of Junkers aristocracy. Like others in his privileged position, he had been active in the voluntary work camps all through the 1920s where young people of all classes experienced a certain simplicity of life and moral guidance through religion that cultivated a sense of community. For Moltke this enhanced his sense of duty and responsibility that came with his inheritance and also brought home to him the artificiality of barriers between peoples most blatantly evinced in national borders. During his formative years he witnessed large sections of the German people alienated from the state through economic deprivation and political upheaval. It was the youth whom he saw as vital to restoring a sense of community through cultural values they shared with other young people, regardless of nationality or race, throughout the continent. Later he studied law and political sciences in Breslau, Vienna, Heidelberg, and Berlin before taking over the management of the family estate, which had become run down, in 1929. On the estate, which comprised around 1,200 acres of arable and 400 acres of pasture, he introduced radical new ideas such as dividing relatively unused sections into independent lots to be managed by the peasants themselves. This was naturally frowned upon by other large landowners who saw it as a dangerous move towards socialism.

In 1931, he married another lawyer, Freya Deichmann, who shared his political outlook. Both were early opponents of the Nazis. On the day that Hitler was sworn in, the couple were dining at their Berlin apartment at 10 Derfflingerstrasse. Their guests took comfort in the prospect of the NSDAP government failing like all the rest had since 1919, but Moltke saw it as the beginning of 'a catastrophe of the worst kind'.[2] In 1935, he turned down the chance to become a judge which would have required him to join the NSDAP and he went into partnership with the international law specialist Karl von Lewinski and started a private law practice in Berlin specialising in international law instead. Through this he was able to help many victims of the Nazis to emigrate, and he, himself, travelled abroad building up contacts with foreign governments.

In 1939 he was drafted into the *Abwehr* to gather information of military-political importance from military attachés and foreign newspapers and advising on questions of the international laws of war. A year later at around the time of the German invasion of France and the Low Countries, along with Peter Yorck von Wartenburg he became co-leader of a loosely formed group of intellectuals, civil servants, social activists and clergymen which gave it a broad spectrum of social, political, and economic views covering the aristocracy, the *Abwehr*, the *Auswärtiges Amt*, the law, trade unionists and the church. The significance of this grouping was the wide range of backgrounds, philosophies and beliefs of its members. Because early participants were primarily members of the high nobility it became known as the *Grafenkreis*.[3]

Yorck worked alongside Goerdeler at the Reich Price Commission and was familiar with his anti-Nazi views. Like Moltke, Yorck was landed gentry and like Moltke he was a lawyer. The first grouping that met in Berlin included Eduard Waetjen, an attorney, Horst von Einsiedel, and Carl Dietrich von Trotha. The objective was to bring together as widely diverse group of highly independent personalities as possible to discuss ideas about what a new Germany and a new Europe might look like in a politically united continent after the Nazis had gone. While discussions were led by a specialist in the field, the group as a whole did not have any clear leaders. The order of the day was compromise which was a vital part of the political process because, so they believed, if the members could not do that then there was little point in holding meetings at all. Politics without compromise was what had got the country into such a mess in the first place.

For Moltke and Yorck, religion was not something just to be discussed at dinner parties or acknowledged once a week on Sundays. It was a creed unreservedly accepted by which they lived their lives, and it played a big part in the substance of their discussions about the future of Germany and about how people were expected to behave. The moral code of a reborn Europe would be one based on the teachings of Christianity. They developed a plan for the constitution of a future, democratic Germany and prepared concepts regarding the punishment of war criminals and compensation for those countries attacked and occupied by the Nazi Germany and there was by no means always agreement.

Acutely aware of the risks they were taking, the twenty or so, mostly young, members met in small groups of three or four at a time. Larger meetings would have attracted too much attention in Berlin. It would be a little more secure when they started holding meetings at the Kreisau estate deep in the countryside but in the meantime the small meetings each explored a particular subject such as cultural, social, economic or foreign policy and generally, for security reasons, invitees were not aware of the identity of others in the circle. Only Moltke and Yorck saw the whole picture and it was they who formulated the agenda for the later meetings at Kreisau.

While anti-Nazi opposition within the military was fundamentally reshaped after 1941 under the leadership of Henning von Tresckow, chief of staff of the Army Group Centre, the civilian resistance like the Kreisau Circle began to develop comprehensive reform plans for a post-National Socialist government. To foreign observers it must have been strange to see how much time and energy Goerdeler and the Kreisau circle devoted to the elaboration of constitutional and social-political principles instead of concentrating their efforts pragmatically on the overthrow of the system. This can be partly explained by neither group wanting a return to the Weimar constitution with what they saw as its over-democratisation of the state.

The real significance of the Kreisau Circle was its unique blend of 'Christianity and socialism, its stress on the value of the individual, its preference for a decentralised, organically structured state, its distrust of mass democracy, political parties and labour unions and the creation of a large European community'.[4] The number of people involved grew to include Adam von Trott zu Solz whom Moltke had met at

All Souls College in Oxford in February 1937. Although the two men had quite different temperaments, Moltke was quiet, thoughtful and down-to-earth while Trott was intellectual, impulsive and energetic, they had much in common. Trott was widely travelled and worked for the *Auswärtiges Amt* as their China specialist which gave him ample scope to continue to travel. On a visit to the US in 1940, he had some influence in arranging a peace mission to Europe by Sumner Welles of the State Department.

Goerdeler had based his philosophy on an order of justice established by God and a respect for His commandments, freedom, and human dignity and, indeed, the Kreisau Circle was equally strongly motivated by religion. It was also in the Kreisau Circle that the belief was held that the nation stood on the threshold of a critical secular turning point moving away from an erroneous line of development involving the loss of personal attachments, the decay of the Christian and natural law bases of society, and a trend toward atomisation and mass culture. It was also in sympathy with the views of Fritz-Dietlof von der Schulenburg, who would later become part of the inner circle of conspirators around von Stauffenberg, and who was convinced that only the violent overthrow of the Nazi regime could prevent a social revolution that would open the floodgates of communism and destroy the basis for all meaningful political activity.[5]

Schulenburg prided himself on being part of the state's military and professional civil service elite beyond which was only 'the mob'. He nevertheless took a patriarchal approach whereby he believed that he had a duty to act for the good of all of the people. His political outlook was undoubtedly progressive but he took a clear stance against communism. In February 1932, he joined the NSDAP, which he saw as 'the incarnation of the faith and will of the German people'. Here he gained influence as the prototype of a new kind of member, combining left-wing politics and old Prussian traditions.[6] After holding a number of posts including Vice President of the Berlin Police, however, Schulenberg was expelled from the NSDAP in 1940 having been classified as 'unreliable'. He signed up for the military and served on the Eastern Front where he was awarded the Iron Cross but also saw at first hand the atrocities being committed by the *Einsatzgruppen*. Transferred to a role in administration he began attending meetings of the Kreisau Circle and later become a close confidant of Stauffenberg.

In 1942, Moltke made several unsuccessful attempts to negotiate with the British government by arranging for Dietrich Bonhoeffer and Hans Schönfeld to meet the British Bishop George Bell in Stockholm. The idea was to find out what the attitude of Britain would be to dealing with Germany if Hitler was eliminated. The trouble was that Bell was already considered a 'pestilent priest' by the British government for his very vocal opposition to the British policy of bombing civilian areas. Unsurprisingly all entreaties were bluntly rebuffed.

When Kreisau Circle meetings were held in the country some of the more prominent members such as Mierendorff and Hans Bernd von Haeften, who were under constant Gestapo surveillance, could not leave the city for fear of their absence being noticed. For those who made it to the peace and quiet of the Silesian countryside at Krzyżowa, there was good food, drink, and laughter far from the air raids that plagued the cities. Still the meetings were restricted to just a few people at any one time except for three particular occasions when they met in a larger groupings. These were essential to provide an expanded forum when many more voices could be heard and a programme with wide support could be agreed on.

The first large meeting in Krzyżowa was held between 22–25 May 1942 and included Helmuth and Freya von Moltke, Peter and Marion Yorck von Wartenburg, Theodor Steltzer, Augustin Rösch, Hans Peters, Adolf Reichwein, Harald Poelchau, Hans Lukaschek, Asta von Moltke (Helmuth's sister) and Irene Yorck von Wartenburg (Peter's sister). All travelled by rail but on different trains. At these times, Freya von Moltke recalled that the house was 'full of children'.[7] None of the Kreisau meetings were purely working meetings, she wrote, in between sessions they took the walks, sometimes into Graditz on a Sunday when the group would split up to worship separately according to their religion.

The topics for discussion were clearly set out and for each topic there were discussion leaders. Relatively uncontentious topics were chosen for the first weekend so that if any word of discussions got out the meetings could have been justified without becoming a matter of treason. The topics were the role of Christianity in society, relations between the state and the Church, and problems related to the upbringing of children, secondary education and universities. Details of the meetings were then distributed in Berlin, Munich and Stuttgart to members who had not been present. From the start and all through its existence, the Kreisau Circle was clearly not a conspiracy. While the main topics concerned the future of Germany after a war it was expected to lose, there was no talk of coup or putsch.

Over the months, policies were formulated covering a range of issues. One that Moltke had grown up with in Silesia was the coexistence of ethnic groups which, over the course of discussions led to a new concept of how different countries could coexist by rejecting outmoded attitudes of nationality. One of the fundamental issues was how such a collapse of society had occurred as to allow the rise of Hitler and the Nazis and what measures could be taken to ensure that it did not happen again. Was it a freak accident or evidence of some 'sickness originating in age-old roots'?[8] Socialist in the group wanted to talk about the plight of the industrial working masses alienate from their natural world through technology and also how to create a new relationship between them and the capitalist economy. It was fundamental to their world view that natural sources of wealth should serve the common good.[9] Religion played an especially prominent role in discussions about how man could reestablish contact with his spiritual self and create a harmonious community that was not blinkered by a drive for material wealth. How man could challenge the 'totalitarian claim of the state on the citizen with its elimination of his religious and moral responsibilities'.[10] Freedom of conscience, the dignity of the individual, the sanctity of family life and the crucial importance of community were the essential foundations of the new society. Close correlation between Goerdeler and Moltke is evident by their joint commitment to 'religion and education [and] the proper relationship between responsibility and rights' but Moltke would 'have nothing to do with [Goerdeler's] dubious methods of conspiracy'.[11]

The success of that first meeting encouraged Moltke to organise a second, bigger one soon afterwards on 16–18 October 1942. For the second time the economist Einsiedel was there along with Haubach, Helmuth James and Freya von Moltke, Peter and Marion Yorck von Wartenburg, Theodor Steltzer and Hans Peters. New guests were the theologian Eugen Gerstenmaier from Wurttemberg and the Jesuit Father Alfred Delp. Leuschner was represented by Hermann Maas, a former youth leader but Maas was not considered to be a member in his own right. The topics this time were of crucial importance for the future post-Nazi Germany such as the reconstruction of the civic society and the political shape of the state and economy. Special emphasis was laid on discussions about how to shape society and the structures of the state in such a way as to ensure that extremist groups never again seize power. All this added a clear risk of consequences if news of the meeting leaked through informants either working on the estate or in the local town. There was a palpable tension present at this second weekend and the air of relaxation and optimism was less pronounced as there permeated the gathering a feeling that a conspiracy was brewing. Talks went on late into the night.

The third meeting of the Kreisau Circle in Krzyżowa took place between 12–14 June 1943. Amongst the guests this time were the

Yorcks, Trott, Gerstenmeier, Maass and Father Delp with Paulus van Husen, a state-employed lawyer, attending for the first time. Against the background of the defeat of the German army near Stalingrad, the extensive agenda included discussions about how to deal with the perpetrators of the war crimes being committed on the Eastern Front. For them it was important that the German people should face up to the enormity of what was taking place and take responsibility for the prosecutions so that they were not seen as a victor's revenge over the vanquished. The main emphasis, however, was on foreign policy and the post-war economic policy.

That was the last large-scale meeting at Kreisau, the next was in Berlin on 9 August 1943 when two documents were produced, 'Basic Principles for the New Order' and 'Directions to the Regional Commissioners' with instructions about how to maintain order in the event of a collapse of society, and to act against disintegration. In summary, the documents categorically stated that man stood above the state. It was held that conscience and dignity was still to be found in the hearts of men and each man was an individual responsible for himself. On the political level, the power of the state should be curbed by the formation of provincial governments having no more than five million citizens. As for the bigger European picture, Moltke wrote in 1942 that post-war Europe should be less about frontiers and soldiers and more about 'how the image of man can be re-established in the hearts of citizens'. A new European order was called for to curb the influence of nation states whose political ambitions would inevitably lead to another war.

The creation of these two documents was essentially the culmination of the discussion stage establishing a social and political programme for the foundation of a post-Hitler Europe. Concrete measures were now required to put the theory into practice and this called for qualified men to assume responsibility for implementing the programme and governing the various regions although it was accepted that the military would make the first move by removing Hitler and Himmler. Moltke exerted his efforts toward establishing common basic principles and a common program for the inner circle. Until his arrest, he expended an enormous amount of energy trying to bring about the necessary compromises and agreements, but he consistently overestimated the degree of intellectual agreement among his followers. Moltke and Yorck looked to members of the opposition group associated with Goerdeler, hoping that there would be a sufficiently robust administration to take control once the military had done the dirty work. This meant that there would have to be a certain level of cooperation with the Wehrmacht and agreement with them on who would lead the new government. There had always been an unbridgeable distance between Moltke and Julius Leber but the Kreisau group as a whole favoured Leber, who had been privy to all discussions and resolutions, for the role even though he had kept his distance from them until Mierendorff was killed in a bombing raid in December 1943. Both Moltke and Yorck made strenuous efforts to persuade Leber to consider accepting the role but before they could get far with discussions disaster struck.

On 19 January 1944, under circumstances that had nothing to do with the Kreisau Circle, Moltke was arrested for warning an acquaintance, who had a habit of openly criticising the Nazi regime, that he was about to be arrested. He spent some weeks in the notorious basement of Gestapo headquarters at Prinz-Albrecht-Strasse before being sent to a small prison that belonged to the women's concentration camp Ravensbrück near Furstenberg in Mecklenburg. Ger van Roon's 1967 groundbreaking study *Neuordnung im Widerstand* contended that all activities of the Kreisau Circle came to a halt after Moltke's arrest left a gaping hole at the centre of its structure but more recent research has challenged that view.

Meetings continued to be held in Yorck's small house at Hortensienstrasse 50 in Berlin and it was he who assumed the role of *Geschäftsführer*. A central core of members including Trott, Gerstenmaier, von Haeften, Reichwein, Haubach and Leber continued to meet frequently while others, especially the Jesuits, attended only sporadically when they could get to Berlin. It was Yorck also who became increasingly involved with his cousin Claus von Stauffenberg whose own plans to remove Hitler were in the process of gestation and who had effectively replaced Goerdeler as the main driving force of the resistance. Up to this point, Yorck had not been one of those clamouring for Hitler's assassination, although, like some others in the Circle, he had urged military leaders, whenever he could, to overthrow the regime. The act of killing, even a hated dictator was anathema to him and an affront to his religious beliefs. He had simply expected the Nazi regime to collapse under the weight of one military disaster after another, but Stauffenberg was persuading him that precipitate action was the only was to save Germany. In the absence of Moltke, who had grown utterly frustrated with military procrastination and feared that, even if a coup succeeded, the conspirators would go down in history as reviled stab-in-the-back traitors, members of the Kreisau Circle were now being slowly but inexorably drawn into the conspiracy to assassinate Hitler.

Yorck and Stauffenberg became close confidants and together laid the foundation for what would be cooperation between the military and civil administration post-coup. In his diplomatic role, Trott was able to travel abroad and maintain contact with representatives of foreign governments. It was his role to ascertain the views of Britain and the US over what strategy they would adopt if a new German government emerged to replace the Nazis. It was no surprise that there was little enthusiasm from any of the Allied governments for any serious discussion about anything except total and unconditional German surrender. No peace talks would be acceptable without the participation of the Soviet Union and, whatever happened, nothing now would avoid the complete military occupation of Germany at some point. Nevertheless, discussions within the Kreisau Circle went on about who would take on the main government roles. Haeften was seen as Foreign Minister. Paulus van Husen agreed to become Interior Minister. Leber, who was touted as a new Chancellor, became more closely involved and was 'stepping very much into the foreground'.[12] So much so that Stauffenberg also agreed to endorse Leber.

Whilst not put forward for a government post, Reichwein played an equally important part during the early months of 1944 by liaising with the communists to persuade them to take part in any future administration to ensure close cooperation between all political forces after the change of government. It was part of the Kreisau philosophy that the participation of the communists was essential to counteract conservative influence. Reichwein successfully arranged for Leber to meet members of the Berlin Communist Party Central Committee. This was not entirely welcome news to many who long suspected that the Berlin communists had been significantly infiltrated by Gestapo informers and the least contact between them and the communists would end in disaster. In the event, Leber pulled out of the meeting at the last minute but Reichwein urged Yorck to let him go in his place.

The meeting took place on the evening of 3 July 1944, but Reichwein failed to return afterwards and very quickly it was clear that Leber had disappeared also. The obvious conclusion was that they had been taken by the Gestapo and would soon be persuaded to tell all they knew. It was a time of high tension. Stauffenberg's assassination plans were brought forward and delegates were chosen to represent the German opposition in negotiations with the Allies. Stauffenberg expected to be invited to a conference to be held at Hitler's *Wolfschanze* headquarters on 20 July 1944.

Chapter 16

HITLER AND HIS GENERALS

> Let's get straight to the point, I am committing high treason with every means at my disposal.
> Lieutenant Colonel Claus, Count Schenk von Stauffenberg to Lieutenant Urban Thiersch[1]

Up until 1918, the Prussian army had been controlled by the wealthy Junker landowning aristocracy of north-east Germany and had great influence over German foreign and domestic policy. This powerful minority ensured that the conservative Prussian army tradition had always been one of total loyalty to the monarchy, but this was tempered by a military culture that valued freedom of expression and the exercise of independent judgement. The qualities of a Prussian military officer were measured according to how well they kept a cool head under pressure and their ability to apply rationality and ingenuity to the solution of problems they faced. Of great importance to the Junkers was a moral code committed to tradition, humanity and political responsibility, which was instilled in the military. These were characteristics quite at odds with the fanatical, emotional character of the Nazi regime which was at the root of the tensions that would eventually arise between them.

The Nazis knew how important the military was to the German state, even though it had been humiliated and eviscerated at Versailles, and understood perfectly well that Junkers military traditions presented challenges to their ultimate control of Germany. Hitler had acknowledged this at Potsdam on 21 March 1933 when he paid homage to President von Hindenburg who, in turn, legitimised the reconciliation of Prussian tradition with National Socialism.[2] His clearly stated aim to cast off the manacles of Versailles and restore the

German armed forces to their pre-war eminence was welcomed by the *Reichswehr* and was an important reason why the generals initially supported the NSDAP regime but when this was achieved it had unwelcome consequences for them. After 1935, the officer ranks were increasingly filled by young men who were more inclined towards Nazi doctrine and Prussian traditions began to lose their relevance.

When the Gestapo murdered generals Schleicher and Bredow at Göring's instigation during the Night of the Long Knives, there was barely a murmur of disapproval from the Army High Command who had been glad to see the back of Röhm. Hitler took this as a sign that the generals were malleable and encouraged him to come out boldly and declare 'In that hour of need I was responsible for the fate of the German nation', thus placing himself at the forefront of the German state. In this moment the *Reichswehr* became complicit in Hitler's crimes and would find it increasingly difficult to regain the moral high ground.[3] For some army officers, however, it was the beginning of their path to resistance.

This political resistance crystallised in 1938 after the Anschluss and before the annexation of Czechoslovakia around the Chief of the General Staff, General Ludwig Beck. When the German 8th Army had crossed the Austrian border on the morning of 12 March 1938 and Hitler had appeared before a rapturous crowd in the Heldenplatz in Vienna three days later, it all seemed a natural culmination of what had long been desired by large majorities of both countries but when Hitler turned his attention to Czechoslovakia it was a different issue altogether. Although that country had a large German population, especially in the Sudetenland, the country, as a whole rejected any sort of amalgamation into the German Reich and its government urged its allies, Britain and France, to oppose, with force if necessary, any German move in that direction but Hitler showed no inclination to scale back his public belligerent rhetoric and privately ordered his armed forces to prepare an invasion plan.

Beck had become increasingly concerned at the rise of the SS that was beginning to look like Hitler's private army and would inevitably, at some point, come into conflict with the regular army, increasingly seen as outmoded and too much under the influence of the less-than-enthusiastic Nazi supporters in the Prussian Junker class. He waited anxiously to see if he could work out to what extent the hostility to the army was official party policy or whether it would calm down and the General Staff could reassert its dominant position within the state. He got his answer with the dismissal of Fritsch, Blomberg and Neurath in early 1938. Then when, at a conference in the Reich Chancellery on 28 May 1938, Hitler told his generals that he planned to 'crush' Czechoslovakia, an act that he admitted could well lead to war in the West, Beck called it a 'policy of force and perfidy'.[4] 'If something is not quickly done,' he told the new Army chief Brauchitsch, 'one can only see the fate of the Wehrmacht [and of Germany] . . . in the blackest of colours'.[5]

Ludwig August Theodor Beck was, above all, a military man who had a deep knowledge of the science and history of war but he came from a family that was immersed in literature and music. From his parents he inherited both intellectual curiosity and a strong ethical background which sustained him during all his years in the military. A determined, almost defiant, youngster, he received a classical education at the *Humantischen Gymnasium* in Wiesbaden then went on to join the 15th Prussian Field Artillery Regiment at the age of 19. Selected for the *Kriegsakademie* he made friends with men who would later achieve high positions in the Wehrmacht, such as Fritsch and Bock. At the end of the First World War, Beck had favoured retaining the monarchy and wrote a letter in which he stressed that the role of military officers is not to undermine political leaders but to 'embody the state', a statement which characterised a political philosophy he held onto throughout his life.[6] On 1 October 1922, he was made Chief of Staff of the 4th Division in Dresden, where he came to know Captain Hans Oster, Major Erwin von Witzleben, Major Erich Fellgiebel, and Captain Friedrich Olbricht all of whom would become members of the resistance to Hitler.

After an incident in 1929 in which he defended three of his young officers against charges of treason brought by Reichsminister Wilhelm Groener. Beck condemned the political activities of the men on grounds of law and discipline, but he supported their view that the army needed more of a 'national spirit'. He was almost thrown out of the army for what was seen as his lack of support for the Nazis and survived only through the support of General Kurt Freiherr von Hammerstein-Equord, Chief of the Truppenamt.

He was not entirely opposed to the Nazis, however, and he does not appear to have expressed reservations about other aspects of National Socialism. On the contrary, he fully endorsed Hitler's ambition to revise the terms of the Versailles treaty pertaining to the permitted size of the German Army and looked forward to a military and political symbiosis that would create a German army fully equipped to meet the demand of modern warfare. In 1934 he was perfectly willing to consider an attack against Czechoslovakia but he would later change his mind in 1938 when such a move threatened to launch Germany into a wider European war on two fronts. By 1933, Beck had been promoted to Generalleutnant and was named Chief of the General Staff. He saw this as an opportunity to bring about a joint political and military understanding whereby the army and the government would stand side by side as the two pillars of state and dictate internal policy together. It was Beck's slow realisation that Hitler would totally reject any concept of power sharing, however, that took him irrevocably onto the path of resistance.

Strategically, Beck believed it essential that Germany should once again achieve dominance in the affairs of Central Europe and that German army should be strong enough to conduct a two-front defensive war, possibly with Czechoslovakia and France. In 1933 he had been a powerful advocate of rapid rearmament, despite having no concept of the economic implications of such a move, but only a year later he was voicing misgivings about the consequences that rearmament might trigger. He found much agreement for this view within the *Auswärtiges Amt* and the diplomatic corps. As Chief of Staff, however, he was obliged to prepare the armed forces to defend the country in what was rapidly becoming an unstable political environment privately recognising that it was the rearmament of Germany that was shaking the fragile foundations of peace on the continent. A military alliance between France and the Soviet Union in 1935 sent shockwaves through the German military in 1935 and when the Soviets concluded a similar agreement with the Czechs in 1936 it was clear that threats were building.

As a first step to regaining its former status, Germany would have to occupy Czechoslovakia and on 2 May 1935, Blomberg issued a directive for the three services to prepare an operation code-named *Schulung* (training) under the greatest secrecy using peacetime organisation and equipment, 'without regard for the current insufficient state of armaments' and with minimal efforts for defensive holding action.[7] This was clearly a blueprint for a 'sudden strike' and invasion of Czechoslovakia to seize its defence industry and fortifications. Beck would later come to reject the whole idea in 1938 when faced with the prospect of attacking the Czech's formidable border defences and provoking retaliation by Britain and France into a war that Germany could not win. Hitler was 'endangering the unity of the German people . . . with his wishful thinking . . . and shattering lack of foundation', he wrote.[8]

When the rise of SA Chief of Staff Ernst Röhm with his three-million-strong militia had threatened to relegate the German army to a subordinate role in the state, Beck welcomed Hitler's brutal crushing of Röhm's private army but was less enthusiastic about the way that Hitler used the crisis to murder other opponents of his regime, including some in the military. Far from clearing the air, however, the elimination of Röhm allowed Himmler's SS to fill the power vacuum and mount a new challenge to the prestige and power of the army. Hitler tried to maintain a balance of power between the SS and the army both of which he needed if his plans were to come to fruition but it was the army that he needed to keep in check and bend to his will. He was frustrated by the traditional military who he saw as far too cautious and 'sterile [and]imprisoned in the coils of their technical knowledge' and particularly exasperated with Beck whom he had deprived of the traditional privilege of direct access to the leaders of state.[9] When Brauchitsch joined in the public humiliation of Beck, it was only a matter of time until he would be forced out. It was too much for a man whose character and personality set him apart as a man who showed respect for others and who had the ability to inspire unity. This 'perfect type of senior Prussian officer' whose eyes 'would occasionally light up with the charm of human warmth' impressed with his 'clear mind . . . and humanity'.[10] Beck's Prussian background made it impossible for him to accept the democratic concept of subordination of the military to political leadership. On 20 October 1938, Beck wrote to Hitler's adjutant Colonel Hossbach bemoaning the fact that 'in five years, excepting five minutes during the Austrian affair, I never had a chance to present to the Fuhrer my views on territorial defence [or] conduct of war . . . and I have never, not even indirectly, been asked by [Hitler] for my views'.[11]

If *Schulung* really was a practical preparation for war, Beck would not countenance it. The Czech crisis had to be settled by negotiation. He considered resigning but instead made an appeal in writing to generals in the OKW to follow their conscience, recognise their responsibility to the German people and urge Hitler to turn away from war. On 29 July he urgently called on Brauchitsch to lead a 'forceful, stern and brutal collective protest' in which senior commanders would resign if Hitler persisted with his plans for war.[12]

Brauchitsch responded by calling a meeting of senior commanders on 4 August to discuss the consequences of military action against Czechoslovakia. Beck appealed to their concepts of duty as defined by Clausewitz's doctrine of the relation between political and military leadership. He urged Brauchitsch to 'halt the war preparations [and] postpone his proposed solution of the Czech question by force until the military conditions for it have changed radically'.[13] He implored Brauchitsch to 'act according to [his] professional and political conscience' where his knowledge, responsibility and conscience 'forbid the execution of an order' but all to no avail.[14] The meeting ended with most generals present giving muted support for Beck's views but when it came to action, Brauchitsch would not agree to openly show support for Beck who saw that without his commander-in-chief his case was hopeless, the others would not follow. Isolated, Beck tendered his resignation as Chief of Staff on 10 August 1938 and was reassigned as commander of the First Army on the western frontier. Although he knew that he would be closely watched now, he began making contacts behind the scenes for an opposition movement to the Nazi regime.

Hitler said of Beck that he was the only man he feared and was relieved to see him go. He knew now that the generals, led by the meek Brauchitsch, who was already compromised by having received substantial assistance from the Nazis in relation to financing his divorce proceedings, would not stand against him.

Beck's successor, Halder was no less antagonistic towards the Nazis but after the Munich Agreement of September 1938, his enthusiasm for a coup had faded. By 1939, Halder had a whole list of reasons why he could not be associated with any move to oust Hitler. For a start it violated tradition and furthermore there was no obvious successor. Beneath it all, however, were his doubts that the officer corps would support him if he called on them to revolt. He was left in a position where he fundamentally opposed war but was every day fully involved with preparations for one. Within the *Abwehr*, however, a simmering mood of rebellion persisted but the Oster conspiracy of September 1938 had failed and much energy within the conspiracy dissipated with it. When Hitler made it clear that his ambitions for conquest were far from satisfied and on 3 April 1939 ordered the OKW to prepare for an attack against Poland, a mood of rebellion was reignited but there was little time to act before the attack took place on 1 September 1939.

Poland fell within weeks and Germany found itself in a state of war with Britain and France, albeit at a distance and with little actual engagement, but the euphoria of a stunning military victory was tempered within the OKW by two factors. The first was the evidence of SS terror that had been unleashed against the Polish intelligentsia and the Jews. Of course it was no surprise that Himmler had extended his terror campaign to Poland but it was the sheer scale of the atrocities that were committed during those first few weeks of occupation that shocked and horrified the Wehrmacht generals. Then there was the simple fact that Germany was now at war with two nations that were significantly more powerful, both militarily and economically, than

Poland and as early as October, Hitler was already making plans for 'the final military defeat of the West'.

The three Army Group commanders in the west, Wilhelm Ritter von Leeb, Gerd von Rundstedt and Fedor von Bock protested in the strongest terms saying that their forces were nowhere near ready to take on the Western armies. Fearing a catastrophe if Hitler went ahead with his plan, Halder kept two armoured divisions in reserve and ordered Lieutenant-Colonel Grosscurth to formulate a plan for a coup. Lieutenant-General Karl-Heinrich von Stülpnagel and Oster, with whom he had plotted in the 1938 conspiracy, met Beck who, in turn, kept closely in touch with Goerdeler and the diplomats Ernst Heinrich Freiherr von Weizsäcker and Ulrich von Hassel. At the *Auswärtiges Amt* Erich Kordt drew up a memorandum outlining the 'threatening catastrophe' that would follow at attack in the West. 'Never was Germany closer to chaos', he wrote, and 'once the furore of war is let loose, it cannot be coaxed back by reason'.[15]

Oster was again at the heart of planning. Beck and Goerdeler were kept informed. On 5 November 1939 Brauchitsch and Halder tried to dissuade Hitler from issuing an attack order timed for seven days hence but Hitler dismissed them furiously with an insult aimed at the 'defeatist' OKW. Brauchitsch was subdued by Hitler's rant and seemed to lose heart for insurrection. Beck remained committed and Oster made arrangements to procure explosives for a bomb but fate stepped in three days later when another, quite separate bomb plot almost took Hitler's life at the Bürgerbräukellar in Munich.

Johann Georg Elser had long been hostile to Nazism and plotted all alone to put an end to Hitler's rule. An *Einzelgänger* or 'lone wolf' with no known friends, he had witnessed Hitler's speech on the previous year's anniversary of the 1923 coup attempt and was appalled by Nazi's attack on human dignity and the mesmeric hold Hitler had over his audience. Along with many Germans he feared that war was coming closer with Hitler's every reckless gamble and throw of the political dice and the increasing persecution of vulnerable minorities within Germany filled him with disgust. There grew within him a conviction that he must act somehow to give expression to his opposition to all that he saw around him. Right behind where Hitler made his annual speech was a load-bearing support for the balcony and heavy roof above. It did not take much imagination to see what would happen if that pillar was suddenly removed. It was not necessary to smash through Hitler's formidable security cordon that accompanied him everywhere on his now infrequent public engagements.

Elser collected material to construct a time-bomb and moved to live in Munich permanently in August 1939. He started visiting the bierkeller every day for his evening meal and hid in a cloakroom when the place was locked up for the night. Each night he would work on excavating a hole in the main columns holding up the roof where he planned to place the bomb then in the morning he would sneak out again when the building was opened up. He installed the bomb on the night of 2/3 November and activated the timing mechanism to detonate three days later. Then he left Munich to go to Konstanz with a view to crossing the border into Switzerland.

On the evening of 8 November, there were some 1,500 people in the bierkeller to hear Hitler make his annual speech. The audience consisted mostly of many veterans of the original Putsch dressed in their old uniforms, fuelled by Bavarian ale and roused by martial music. Hitler was deep into planning for the invasion of France and had wanted to avoid the trip to Munich altogether but had been persuaded that it would be seen as disrespectful not only to the audience but to the Nazi movement as a whole if he did not go. He went but insisted on having his personal train ready for a swift overnight return to Berlin immediately afterwards. Eager to get back to Berlin as soon as possible, Hitler started his speech half an hour early and finished at 21.07 hrs, a whole hour before it would have finished had it followed precedent.

A mere thirteen minutes after he had stood down from the podium and left the room the bomb exploded bringing down the whole roof. The pillar had been torn apart by the blast, and where Hitler had stood the entire ceiling had crashed onto the lectern and onto the surrounding rows of chairs and beer tables. The falling masonry, roof girders and wooden beams killed three people instantly and buried dozens, five of whom died after being admitted to hospital. Elser was arrested on the Swiss border. He spent the war in various prisons and was eventually executed in the Dachau concentration camp at some time in April 1945.

The bomb inevitably banished any thought of attacking France, which was a relief for the generals but for the Oster conspirators it was a major setback. They were further disheartened and chastened on 23 November when Hitler addressed the General Staff and roundly condemned his critics over a period of several hours. He called his audience an 'antiquated upper class', that had failed the German people in 1918 and was failing them again with its prophecies of catastrophe. All who stood against him would be destroyed, Hitler vowed. Only one member of the General Staff, Heinz Guderian, protested at the insults. Brauchitsch tendered his resignation which was contemptuously brushed aside.

By January 1940, Beck was again broaching the subject of a coup with Halder. More attempts were made to re-establish contact with British government officials who seemed a little more interested in what the German dissidents had to say but that was too little too late to encourage Halder who now stood firmly against any coup attempt believing that it would take a significant military defeat for Germany before the rank and file would support it. Brauchitsch had been cowed and humiliated by Hitler's criticism and was now in no mood to entertain any talk of insurrection. He even cloaked his loss of self-esteem by threatening to expose the plotters as traitors. When *Fall Gelb* was launched on 10 May 1940 and succeeded beyond all expectations, it dealt a body blow to the conspirators. It would be even more difficult now to persuade sufficient German officers to support an insurrection. Any lingering hope that Brauchitsch would throw his weight behind the rebellion was crushed when he was relieved of his post on 19 December 1941 and there was further disappointment when Beck failed to persuade Witzleben in Paris and Falkenhausen in Brussels, to commit their troops to support him. For a time in early 1942, it looked as if Field Marshal Günther von Kluge's Army Group Centre would come on board but nothing came of it.

After the German military setbacks of 1942 culminating in the unmitigated disaster of Stalingrad, there were fresh rumblings of discontent in the German army. One was centred around General of the Infantry Friedrich Olbricht in the OKH in Berlin and the other was in Army Group Centre on the Eastern Front where Major Henning von Tresckow was on the Operations staff. Both men would go on to play critical roles in the Stauffenberg plot. The latest in a family line of military officers with a devout Protestant tradition, Henning von Tresckow, travelled widely as a broker on the Stock Exchange before graduating from military college in 1936 and going on to join the German General Staff. He gained a reputation as 'a soldier of quite considerable stature . . . far above the average' with an 'almost inexhaustible capacity for work'.[16] For him, the Nazi's determination to revise the Versailles Treaty and a general dissatisfaction with Weimar politics were major factors in his early support for the NSDAP and offset any misgivings he may have had about their social policies but it was the Night of the Long Knives with the murders of General von Schleicher, Schleicher's wife and his friend and collaborator General von Bredow that brought the Nazi regime into focus for him. That focus sharpened significantly after the *Reichskristallnacht* which, for him, was 'a personal humiliation and a degradation of civilization' but it was the SS slaughter of civilians in the occupied lands of Eastern Europe that accompanied the Wehrmacht advance after 1941 that finally persuaded him to act.[17] 'You and I, also, will be counted amongst the guilty', he told one of his officers.[18]

Between 1941 and 1943, Tresckow gathered about him a trusted group of conspirators all committed to the overthrow of Hitler. Prominent among them was the 'disciplined, sober and serious' one-legged Colonel Berndt von Kleist.[19] Colonel Georg Schulze-Buettger, admired for his calm and intellectual judgement, who had at one time been adjutant to Beck, was another. Others included the 'witty and eloquent' Colonel Freiherr Rudolf-Christoph von Gersdorff, a particularly valuable ally, Lieutenant-Colonel Alexander von Voss, a relation of Stülpnagel, and Fabian von Schlabrendorff who had already been involved with the Oster conspiracy of 1938. The primary motivation for resistance was the witnessing, or in some cases involvement with, SS massacres in occupied Soviet Union lands. Killing enemy combatants was part of their duty in war but wholesale butchery of civilians by SS *Einsatzgruppen* was completely contrary to the laws of war and beyond their understanding. Tresckow had become aware in May 1941, before the launch of Operation Barbarossa, that an order had gone out giving the military immunity to punishment for extra-judicious executions of civilians but the reality of what was happening came as a visceral shock. It was a complete loss of honour if the order could not be rescinded. For him there was no option but resist despite the consequences and he warned all who joined him that they were putting on the 'shirt of Nessus', meaning that their actions would bring upon their heads a misfortune from which there was no escape. It was clear to Tresckow that, because of the soldiers' oath of allegiance, it was impossible to win support for a wider movement within the military to stop the war while Hitler remained alive. For him personally, however, neither Prussian 'honour' nor Christian morality stood in the way of permanently eliminating Hitler whose many deceitful and criminal actions, he believed, had nullified the oath.

Tresckow's first plan to assassinate the *Führer* was on 4 August 1941 when Hitler visited Army Group Centre for a conference with Field Marshal Fedor von Bock. He planned to simply shoot Hitler as he entered Bock's headquarters but security was so tight that he was not able to get close enough to carry out the deed. It did, however, alert him to the fact of how very difficult it would be to carry out any plan that required an assassin to get physically close to Hitler and was a valuable precursor to later assassination attempts.[20]

Hitler's personal security arrangements had made him virtually inaccessible. Whether at the Mauerwald in East Prussia or on the

Obersalzberg, he was virtually cut off from the outside world. He had the 'instincts of an animal of prey for his own safety', honed by an ability to sense hostility in those few who had access to him.[21] All his movements were made under the strictest secrecy. His Achilles Heel, however, was the daily lunchtime briefing conference when a variety of military experts were allowed in depending on the situation. Here, a single assassin might find himself in close proximity to the *Führer* but, naturally, all weapons were surrendered before entry to the conference room.

Friedrich Olbricht was from a family with an intellectual rather than a military tradition. A good ten years older than most of the conspirators, he was ever willing to step back and play a secondary role with no consideration of rank. Considered 'affable and approachable [with] a quick wit and lively personality',[22] he had been a firm supporter of the Weimar constitution and in 1933, 'primarily motivated by religious and patriotic considerations' and was 'outraged, that such a dilettante [Hitler] with such an unsavoury past could become chancellor of the German Reich'.[23] In 1940, he was appointed Chief of the *Allgemeines Heeresamt* (General Army Office) in the OKH. He was furthermore made Chief of the Armed Forces Reserve Office (*Wehrersatzamt*) at the OKW. He would later appoint Stauffenberg as his Chief of Staff and introduce him to the wider conspiracy. At that time, Stauffenberg was reluctant to join the resistance because he believed that all efforts should be directed towards a military victory rather than changing the government. He saw no prospect of change until the Wehrmacht suffered the sort of defeats on the Eastern Front that would guarantee to make the war unwinnable.

By 1941, both Olbricht and Tresckow were on Beck's list of officers willing to act against Hitler and had already made contact with Stülpnagel, General Alexander von Falkenhausen and Goerdeler. By the winter of that year Olbricht and Tresckow were among the first to formulate a conspiracy under the codename Valkyrie. *Unternehmen Walküre* (Operation Valkyrie) was a German contingency plan that had been issued to the *Territorialheer* (Territorial Reserve Army of Germany) to be implemented in the event of an emergency such as uprisings of forced labourers or the death of Hitler resulting in a general breakdown of national civil order. It was designed to restore order or in the latter case, oversee a smooth transfer of power to the new leader. The emergency plan was modified to utilise the existing chain of command within the Replacement Army to effect a controlled take-over by making it appear as if it was the SS who were staging the coup. SS leaders would be arrested *en masse* across the country. One of the most active members of the conspiracy, General Erich Fellgiebel, the Chief of Signal Troops, would isolate Hitler's *Wolfsschanze* headquarters giving time for the conspirators to set up the new government without interference from the Nazi leaders.[24]

Membership of the post-Hitler government was drawn up on paper, and drafts of radio announcements were written. The *Territorialheer* would provide a body of armed troops without which they could not hope to carry out their coup and with modifications *Unternehmen Walküre* would create the ideal conditions to implement it. It was Olbricht who had first suggested using a modified version of *Unternehmen Walküre* as a template for their coup attempt and then he sent Tresckow to Berlin to assure Beck, that if he and his fellow conspirators were willing to stage a coup, Army Group Centre would carry out the assassination.[25]

In January 1943, Olbricht was in Berlin working out the logistics of a coup including assigning fellow officers to secure key locations in Berlin and kill Nazi leaders who resisted. Beck met with Goerdeler, Popitz, Professor Jens Jessen, Hassel, Schulenburg, Trott, Moltke and Gerstenmaier at the house of Peter Yorck on 8 January. It was not an easy meeting. Beck found Moltke arrogant and mildly contemptuous of the military. There were also significant differences between Goerdeler and the Kreisau Circle who suspected him of wanting a return to Weimar government whereas Yorck and others wanted a clean break and a new start for Germany but there was broad agreement on the need for swift action against Hitler. The broad range of aspirations and the level of disagreement over fundamental issues is perhaps an indication of the chaos that may well have followed a successful coup. Tresckow, however, left the meeting with a clear sense of purpose and felt that he had all the support he needed to proceed with all haste although it was clear by now that he would have to bear the main burden of carrying out the 'dirty work' himself.

After his failed plot of 4 August, he realised that it would have to be some sort of timed explosive device and so he had set about acquiring the knowledge and materials and started experimenting in the summer of 1942 with various types of explosives. Gersdorff was in charge of a sabotage section and he was able to procure a quantity of a new British high-impact plastic explosive, one that could be shaped to fit any container. This material had been dropped throughout Europe by the RAF to assist the anti-Nazi movement in German-occupied areas. It had its advantages and drawbacks. It could be moulded to any shape making it easy to conceal and its chemical time fuses were much quieter than the German equivalent but could not be set to explode until about fifteen minutes after the chemical fuse was set. Having said that the timing device was much more accurate but the time delay varied dramatically depending on the ambient temperature. Tests carried out along the Dnieper river near Smolensk showed that cooler temperatures slowed the timing process.

By February 1943, Canaris, Dohnanyi and Lahousen were in Smolensk making final preparations for the coup and Tresckow was working out how to implement them but Kluge, whilst not opposing them, refused to come out openly in support. It was Kluge, however, who was inadvertently central to the plot although he was not privy to its details. He had made known to Berlin that he had reservations about Hitler's plan *Unternehmen Zitadelle* for an offensive against the Kursk salient and that prompted Hitler to come out to Army Group Centre headquarters at Smolensk on 13 March 1943 to discuss it with him. The plotters knew that Hitler would be heavily guarded but it would be in an environment that his security people would not be familiar with and that might be an advantage. Tresckow envisaged three possible scenarios. The first was for Lieutenant-Colonel Georg von Boeselager to take a group of his cavalry officers and ambush Hitler's party during his trip from the airport through the woods to Army Group Centre headquarters but this was discounted because there was no confirmation which of several roads Hitler could take. The second option was for an assassin to burst into the dining area and shoot Hitler but that would require precision because it was known that Hitler wore a bulletproof vest under his uniform. The chances of that working were slim. It was the third option that Tresckow chose but these first two ideas would prove useful references when Stauffenberg's 1944 plot was hatched.

Hitler flew in a special Focke-Wulf Fw 200 Condor long-range aircraft with a heavily armed section that could be detached from the rest of the plane and parachuted to safety in the case of an emergency and it was here that Hitler sat.[26] For his chosen option, Tresckow planned to place a time-bomb in this very place but how to put it there was the problem. This was compounded by the fact that he knew that there were always two identical Condor aircraft when Hitler flew, and it was impossible to know beforehand which of the two he and his entourage would choose to fly in. Tresckow's plan was simple and ingenious.

He approached Colonel Heinz Brandt, a member of Hitler's entourage, and asked him if he would do him the favour of taking back to Berlin a small parcel containing two bottles of brandy for General Helmuth Stieff of the High Command at Headquarters. Stieff was an explosives expert and had been recruited to the conspiracy by Tresckow early in 1943. Brandt was happy to oblige and it was agreed that Schlabrendorff would take the package to the airport when Hitler left. On the way there Schlabrendorff prepared the time fuse so that acid started eating away at a thin metal filament in one of the bottles. The other bottle was packed with the explosive that would be ignited when the filament broke while aircraft was somewhere over Minsk. At the same time, a code word 'Flash' was sent to Olbricht in Berlin to say that the operation was under way. Two hours after Hitler's aircraft had taken off, however, it landed safely in Berlin. The device had failed to explode.

Schlabrendorff quickly bought two bottles of brandy and phoned Brandt to hold off on delivering the parcel to Stieff saying that he had packed the wrong bottles. He would bring the correct ones personally to Berlin within hours. Then, having retrieved the bomb package from Stieff, Schlabrendorff very cautiously examined it. The wire had been eaten through and the firing pin had been released but the explosive had obviously not ignited. The only reason that has been put forward to explain this is that possibly the temperature inside the aircraft was below the point where the explosive remained in an active state.[27]

Nothing daunted, Tresckow planned to use a similar bomb in another assassination attempt on Hitler when he visited an exhibition of captured Soviet weaponry at the Zeughaus in Berlin. Gersdorff, who worked for the Intelligence section of Army Group Centre would be present as part of Hitler's party and he volunteered to carry a bomb and sacrifice himself by exploding it close to the *Führer*. All went to plan and Schlabrendorff delivered the bomb to Gersdorff at the Hotel Eden on the night on 20 March. The next day Gersdorff, with a small bomb in each coat pocket, left Hitler's party as they were looking at exhibits and went into a toilet where he set the fuses of the bombs with a fifteen-minute delay but when he returned to the room Hitler was just leaving, having curtailed his visit abruptly. Gersdorff had to rush off to a place where he could remove the fuse before it triggered the explosive.

Refusing to be discouraged by yet another failure, Tresckow used these experiences to take on board four important lessons that would be applied on 20 July 1944. To ensure maximum support within the Wehrmacht, it was important to make a move when the war was not going in Germany's favour and morale was low. This would become increasingly likely after Stalingrad. Secondly, any assassin required direct access to Hitler to penetrate his security cordon. Also, any assassination attempt would have to take place in Hitler's own headquarters where his security detail would be more comfortable and possibly, as a result, less diligent. The fourth and final lesson was that the method of assassination could only be a bomb. Tresckow and Olbricht became the main architects of the plot because they were seasoned members of the military resistance who applied the lessons they learned from prior experience but they would also bear a significant portion of blame for its failure.

In April 1943, the Gestapo uncovered documents showing that *Abwehr* personnel had been helping Jews to escape the country. Josef Müller, Pastor Dietrich Bonhoeffer, Dohnányi and his wife Christel were all arrested. Dohnányi managed to get a message out to Beck telling him to destroy any incriminating evidence linking him to the resistance, but Beck insisted that they should be preserved for historical evidence of the internal struggle against Nazism. Beck was actually seriously ill in hospital at the time undergoing one of his many operations for intestinal cancer. Oster was removed from his duties and placed under house arrest. When it seemed as if the conspiracy was in disarray, Stauffenberg stepped up to take a leading role not only in the assassination of Hitler but also in the subsequent implementation of Valkyrie.

The German military situation in the Autumn of 1943 was deteriorating rapidly. The Chief of Wehrmacht Operations, General Afred Jodl described it as 'difficult' and said that further crises could be expected. On the Eastern Front the German offensive at Kursk had collapsed almost as soon as it started with Soviet forces taking Orel and Kharkov in August then Smolensk a few weeks later. There was strong Soviet pressure on the Army Group Centre near Nevel and in the south towards Kiev. Allied forces were in control of southern Italy. The U-Boats in the Atlantic were bring picked off as a result of new radar techniques and no longer the held the Allied convoys to ransom. German cities and industrial areas were being pounded by Allied bombers. There would be only one outcome to the war but Hitler refused to listen to sound advice and one military setback followed another. These were the very conditions that Tresckow had outlined as conducive to insurrection within the German armed forces. Despite this, Jodl went on to express his 'profound confidence' on 7 November and called upon the German armed forces to 'suppress faint-heartedness' and join him in a spirit of 'confidence from which alone victory can grow'. He reiterated his own 'confidence and faith in [Hitler]' to achieve victory without which 'the history of the world would have lost its meaning'.[28]

At the beginning of October 1943, Stauffenberg took up his post as the Chief of Staff to General Olbricht in the *Allgemeines Heeresamt* in Berlin. The main function of this office was to provide the reserves of men and material needed at the battle front which became increasingly difficult task with internal squabbles over priorities between various ministers and army groups. Stauffenberg cut a dramatic figure as a result of injuries he had sustained on 7 April earlier in the year. He had been in a column of vehicles in Mezzouna, Tunisia, when it was strafed by an RAF P-40 Kittyhawk fighter bomber. Severely wounded, he spent three months in a Munich hospital in Munich. For weeks it was expected that he would not survive but he eventually emerged having lost his left eye, the whole of his right hand, and two fingers on his left hand.

He had been born at his family's ancestral seat and grew up devoted to poetry and music. It was something of a surprise, therefore when he joined the *Reichswehr* where this 'tall, slim and agile' man progressed quickly through staff college impressing all around with his great charm, self-confidence and competence.[29] He was fascinated by Hitler as a man whom he saw as one who could inspire huge numbers of people to act, often against their own self-interest, by adopting contemporary ideas, simplifying them and making them politically effective. He was not blind to the obvious baseness of Hitler's character, however, but applauded his stand against communism. He felt that there was a chance that Hitler could lead Germany in a political rebirth ushering in a stronger and socially renewed country. What admiration he might have had for the *Führer*, however, did not last beyond *Reichkristallnacht* and the realisation that his ultimate aim was war.

As early as the winter of 1938/39 Stauffenberg had been in contact with Beck and Schulenberg and had begun to visualise an alternative future for his country built on National Socialist ideals but without the perversions evident in National Socialist practice but even at this stage, he had no illusions about how hard it would be to persuade fellow officers to show enthusiasm for opposition to the regime. Hitler's victories over Poland and France did nothing to ameliorate Stauffenberg's concerns and, indeed, made it even more likely that those unacceptable aspects of Hitler's rule would continue to take Germany down a road to ruin. The great victory parade planned for the Arc de Triomphe and the Tuileries in Paris at the end of June 1940 was a case in point when the occupation would begin with a humiliation for the French population exacerbating the resentment and shame felt after the crushing military defeat. Such hubris was not conducive to resigned acceptance of German jackboots on the Champs Élysée. Later the Nazi policies in Soviet Russia, he felt, were simply 'sowing hatred which would one day be avenged on our children'.[30]

The catastrophe of Operation Barbarossa was, for Stauffenberg, only one of a series of military blunders that demanded a realignment of the command structure that, by 1941 had Hitler right at the top with few limits on his powers. Stauffenberg approached commanders to try and persuade them to make at least some gesture of constraint. There was no lack of support for reining in Hitler's control of operations and many urged Stauffenberg to lead such a movement but, much to Stauffenberg's irritation, none showed much enthusiasm to get involved beyond offering to put themselves fully at his disposal after a successful coup d'état.[31] In particular it was the higher-ranking officers, many of whom had become deeply involved in the crimes of the regime, who prevaricated that angered him most. The lower ranks he did not necessarily hold accountable for sticking to their duty.

By early 1943, Stauffenberg's outspoken criticism of Hitler was beginning to have repercussions, and he was relieved to get a posting to Tunis, but it was here that he almost died after being wounded in action. By the time he had left hospital he had learned to write using only his thumb and remaining two fingers and could dress himself with the help of his teeth. He declined having a false limb fitted saying that he didn't have time for that.

Six months after sustaining his life-threatening injuries, Stauffenberg took up his post as Chief of Staff to Olbricht in the Reserve Army Office in Berlin. Olbricht's secretary, Anni Lerche later said that he never showed bitterness over his disability and, when speaking, retained his former self-possession and infectious, sparkling liveliness although his demeanour was, at other times, heavy and menacing. Another one of his contemporaries remembered someone who had the look of a 'poet . . . young but intensely serious'. In a city now pounded nightly by allied bombers, he gathered around him a small, close group of collaborators who shared his determination to act but discussions were, in the main, restricted to general tactics and he kept the full details of exactly what he and Beck were planning to a very small number. Any one of the group who came under the least suspicion was quietly sidelined.

Nothing in writing from Stauffenberg or Tresckow concerning details or motivations of the plotters or organisation of the attempted coup survives and all close collaborators were executed. Gestapo files of interrogations shed little light on the matter but there are copies of written orders and appeals to the German people issued by the plotters on 20 July concerning measures to be taken the moment that Hitler's death was announced. There is also a draft of a memorandum written or dictated by Stauffenberg stating his arguments for action. If the present course continues, he said, defeat and destruction are the inevitable consequences. He went on to say that National Socialist ideals, largely correct, had been corrupted by selfish leaders. The treatment of Soviet prisoners who were left to starve to death and the mobilisation of the civilian population for slave labour were stains on the honour of the German nation that could not be eradicated.

Stauffenberg's closest collaborator was his brother Berthold who worked at the *Oberkommando der Marine* (OKM, Naval High Command) in Berlin but his real mentor was Tresckow until Tresckow was transferred to the Eastern Front in October 1943. Olbricht provided the necessary cover under which Stauffenberg plotted but also made a positive contribution by sifting through his many contacts to identify potential accomplices, even working to persuade commander of the Replacement Army, Colonel-General Friedrich 'Fritz' Fromm to join the conspiracy. The tall, corpulent Fromm, however, was more concerned with enjoying the social benefits of his rank and resisted Olbrecht's overtures but, like many others, made it clear that he would be happy to give his full support for the coup *post facto*.

Detailed plans were drawn up for the execution of Valkyrie once Hitler had been removed. General Orders were written ready for distribution. These covered:
- The systematic military occupation of postal and Wehrmacht communication and broadcasting centres.
- The arrest of all senior government administrators.
- Arrest of all concentration camps commanders and disarming of all guards.
- Arrest of all SS leaders who offered resistance.
- Occupation of all SD and Gestapo centres.
- Political officers appointed to each military district.
- No arbitrary or revengeful action to be taken.

Fromm was reluctant to put his name to these documents and was not pressed to do so.

Martial Law was to be imposed with the following regulations:
- Only Wehrmacht, police and specially authorised guards units can bear arms.
- All marches, demonstrations, assemblies and distribution of leaflets is strictly forbidden.
- Transport service to continue uninterrupted.
- A new Commissioner of the Labour Front will be appointed.
- Civil servants are to remain at their posts with all leave cancelled.
- All orders issued by the Nazi party are invalid.
- All assets of the Nazi Party are to be confiscated.
- Drumhead Courts Martial are to be set up.

All that was needed now was a successful strike to eliminate the *Führer* but Stauffenberg was acutely aware that the method envisaged, i.e. a bomb, exploded at one of Hitler conferences, would inevitably kill a number of high ranking military leaders too and this can only have presented him with the most difficult moral challenge. Towards the end of 1943, it had been decided that modifications were required to uniforms issued to soldiers on the Eastern Front but the new designs had to be agreed with Hitler so it was arranged for a young front-line officer to attend one of the lunchtime conferences at the *Wolfsschanze* on 16 November and demonstrate the new winter uniform. Schulenberg suggested to Stauffenberg that he approach his young friend Captain Axel von dem Bussche-Streithorst who had been traumatised after witnessing the systematic mass execution of some 3,000 Jews in Ukraine. The 23-year-old blond-haired and blue-eyed battalion commander agreed immediately to ally himself with the cause and offered to sacrifice himself in a suicide attack against Hitler.[32] A plan was hatched to arm and detonate a modified landmine hidden in his uniform and rigged with a hand-grenade detonator with a five-second fuse. When introduced to Hitler, Bussche would arm the bomb and fling his arms around the *Führer* and grip him tightly. Unfortunately, on the night before the demonstration, the railway carriage containing the new uniforms was destroyed in an air raid on Berlin and the demonstration was cancelled. Bussche returned to his unit on the Eastern Front. He volunteered to attempt the assassination again in February 1944 when new uniforms would be available but before that could happen, he was seriously wounded by Soviet shrapnel and his right leg was amputated.

International contacts were canvassed to support a coup. Moltke twice went to Istanbul in July and December 1943. Canaris contrived to cloak the visits as part of official *Abwehr* business but in reality they were to meet members of OSS, US intelligence. Through them a message was conveyed to Washington outlining the current state of opposition. Moltke said that there were two factions, pro-Western and pro-Eastern. In the Luftwaffe, especially, there was a 'strong and traditional conviction of a community of interests' between Germany and the Soviet Union that had stemmed from the illegal military cooperation during the late 1920s and early 1930s. In a reference to the Schulze-Boysen spy ring, Luftwaffe officers, he said, had 'for a long time been in direct communication, including regular wireless contact, with the Soviet government'.[33] The pro-Western faction was smaller but contained a larger proportion of 'key men in the military and civil service hierarchy' as well as church leaders, trade union leaders and industrialists.

Moltke conveyed to the Allies an acceptance that 'unequivocal military defeat and occupation of Germany [was] regarded as a moral and political necessity for the future of the nation'. Demands for unconditional German surrender in the west were entirely justified but it was essential to hold off the Soviets beyond a line from Tilsit to Lemberg and in pursuance of this aim, Germany would provide military cooperation with the US and Britain 'on the largest possible scale'. Bolshevisation of Germany, he said was the 'deadliest imminent danger' to the whole of Europe. The pro-Western conspirators would ensure that an anti-Nazi government would take over all non-military administrative tasks in the country but they were not prepared to become involved in any collaboration with 'limited aims'.[34] Colonel William J. Donovan, the director of OSS responded by telling his agents that they were not authorised to enter into any sort of negotiations whatsoever based on Moltke's proposal but they were to 'keep open the channels of contact'.[35]

At the same time, Berthold von Stauffenberg was in Stockholm negotiating a German-Swedish agreement for maritime shipping through Göteborg and using this as an opportunity to revive a contact with the Wallenberg brothers first established by Goerdeler in 1937. There is some evidence that is opened a channel of communication between the plotters and the British government but Claus von Stauffenberg's assertion to Goerdeler that he had a 'direct line to Churchill' seems to have been something of an exaggeration. When Trott later met the British diplomat David MacEwan in Stockholm he warned that if the Allies would not drop their demand for unconditional surrender, then cooperation between them and the German opposition was 'impossible politically and psychologically'.[36]

Next up was Otto John, a corporate lawyer with Lufthansa who did work for the *Abwehr*. His position allowed him much scope for travel so it was not thought unusual for him to travel to Madrid at the end of 1943 but once there he made contact with the American Embassy to apprise them of the state of the opposition movement in Germany. Unfortunately, he got a muted response. Returning to Berlin in January, he met Stauffenberg at Haeften's house where he was given the task of opening a line of communications to the US and British commanders General Eisenhower and Field Marshal Bernard Montgomery. John had made some progress but in March 1944 he could only report that the Americans were not prepared to modify their demands for unconditional surrender and would not countenance a rift with their

Soviet allies. The fate of Eastern Europe under Soviet occupation was not a principal consideration for them.

By April 1944, Beck was a mere shadow of his former physical self after returning to active duty subsequent to undergoing several operations for cancer but his 'dynamic will-power was unbroken'.[37] He sent two emissaries, Gisevius and a Berlin lawyer, Eduard Waetjens, to Bern for a meeting with US President Franklin Roosevelt's Special Representative Allen Dulles. They proposed that US and British troops would be allowed to enter Germany unopposed once Hitler was removed from power and they, along with the Wehrmacht, would oppose any further advance by the Red Army but Dulles told them that the US was not willing to turn against the Soviets. Nothing but unconditional German surrender on all fronts would be acceptable, he said.

There is evidence to suggest that, almost in desperation, Stauffenberg and Hassell agreed to Trott trying to make contact with the Soviets through the KPD members Anton Seafkow and Franz Jacob. They had apparently reached the conclusion that failure to find any common ground with the Western Allies meant that they had no choice but try to reach some sort of agreement with the Soviets. It may be, however, that they simply wanted to use such an approach as a way of persuading the Western Allies to negotiate with them. Waetjens, who was in touch with Dulles, told him that some members of the Kreisau Circle, such as Moltke and Trott, were inclined towards negotiating with the Soviets whom Trott believed were not nearly as bad as propaganda portrayed them.

Gourdeler kept up his correspondence with senior commanders at the fighting front while Stauffenberg made contact with Moltke's Kreisau Circle but they had never met personally until the autumn of 1943. Overall Gourdeler gained a favourable impression of Stauffenberg but was not impressed by what he called his wrongheaded wish to involve himself in politics of the left. It was only on 12 July 1944 that Gisevius actually met Stauffenberg when he returned from Zurich. Like Gourdeler, Gisevius had his doubts about Stauffenberg. Like some other conspirators Gisevius was irritated by Stauffenberg joining the conspiracy at a late date and seeming to take over the reins. Neither did he meet with equanimity Stauffenberg's proposed aim of establishing a 'workers and peasants' regime in Germany. He later told Dulles that Stauffenberg favoured a pro-Soviet policy. The Soviets, he said, would need German resources and would therefore offer some sort of future, albeit one under total communist control, whereas the Western Allies would probably want to strip Germany of all economic potential and condemn it to a purely agrarian economy.[38] Dulles was of the opinion that the actions of Western policy makers were uniting all Germans to resist to the bitter end'.[39]

Notwithstanding the Allies' obduracy during negotiations, the conspirators were not dismayed because at no time had their actions been contingent on allied assurances and they were still not in July 1944. Should an attempt succeed in eliminating Hitler it would be a complete leap in the dark in terms of what would follow. It was irrational in the extreme but as Tresckow put it, 'The assassination must be attempted at any cost. Even should that fail, the attempt to seize power in the capital must be undertaken. We must prove to the world and to future generations that the men of the German resistance movement dared to take the decisive step and to hazard their lives upon it.'[40]

Meanwhile there was a huge rise in the number of arrests and executions for political 'crimes' which imposed severe stress on the conspirators. Moltke, Otto Kiep and Oster's man Ludwig Gehre had been arrested. Canaris had been relieved of his post and Himmler had uttered bloodcurdling threats against Gourdeler and Beck. There was even a Reuter's report to the effect that the German resistance movement had a German General Staff officer who had been chosen to carry out an assassination attempts against Hitler.[41] There were some who wanted to call the whole thing off and there was a small but significant gap appearing in the conspirator's ranks where the civilian side suspected that the military were losing the will to continue. This may well have been because Stauffenberg was saying little about his plans to those outside his immediate circle fearing that further arrests would lead to discovery of the plot.

Meetings of conspirators continued but Stauffenberg was relying more and more on the younger members of the conspiracy who were more in tune with his own political ambitions for the sort of Germany society that would follow a successful coup. It was felt that Gourdeler, already being hunted down by the Gestapo, was too committed to restoring the old system with its outmoded economic doctrine and over-reliance on support from industrialists. The thorny issue of what sort of appeal to make to the Allies also exposed differences. Kaiser would later say, however, that the resistance 'never lost the strong bonds and the feeling of collective commitment towards Germany'.[42]

Stauffenberg was promoted to colonel and appointed Chief of Staff to Fromm after Guderian and Himmler had shaken up the military command to bring in new blood. At Stauffenberg's suggestion his replacement as Chief of Staff to Olbricht was Colonel Albrecht Ritter Werz von Quirnheim, another dedicated conspirator. Stauffenberg's promotion now gave him direct access to Hitler with whom he had his first meeting on 7 June 1944, the day after the Allied D-Day landings had commenced in Normandy. His experience of seeing how the generals behaved in Hitler's presence appalled him. Many known to be staunch opponents of the Nazi regime who had been sober and objective before the conference, became meek and compliant when they came face-to-face with the *Führer*. In contrast, he found himself to be quite unaffected by Hitler's dominant personality.

The plotters were keenly aware that the maintenance of a coherent defence on all three military fronts was now vital to ensure a strong negotiating position after a successful coup but Hitler was endangering this with poor decisions which the generals were unable or unwilling to countermand. It was clear that the final defeat of Germany was close and what small chance of negotiations with the Allies was disappearing fast. Serious doubts were raised about whether it was already too late to launch a revolt. The violent removal of Hitler at this stage could result in a total and immediate military collapse and history would forever condemn the conspiracy as a second *Dolchstoßlegende* (stab in the back myth) reminiscent of the accusations levelled against the German politicians for betraying the military in 1918. Beck conceded that the inevitability of a defeated and an occupied Germany could not be averted by a coup at this late stage but he still believed that the removal of Hitler could avoid further destruction and loss of life and possibly halt the Soviet advance in the east. Despite the negative responses from the Western Powers, there was still a chance that if Hitler could be removed there might be a change of heart when the focus could be shifted towards stopping the Soviets. Schlabrendorff urged Stauffenberg to meet Field Marshal Erwin Rommel, General Inspector of the Western Defences, who was known to support Hitler's removal although not his assassination, to bring the war in the west to an end immediately. Stauffenberg agreed that they had to act. Failure to do so, he said, would be to succumb to disgrace and paralysing tyranny.[43]

News of the arrest of Trott and Haubach on 5 July was followed by reports that the Gestapo had picked up Leber. Two days later, Rundstedt was replaced as commander of forces on the western front by Kluge, Tresckow despatched Boeselager to plead with Kluge to withdraw his forces so that the Eastern Front could be reinforced. Kluge refused to consider the idea commenting that his forces would be unlikely to hold out much longer in any case. On 8 July, the Army Group Centre collapsed and the Red Army advanced as far as the Vistula. Army Group North was facing isolation. Beck expected Soviet armour to reach the German border within days. Rommel had a meeting with Kluge in which they agreed to tell Hitler that the Western Front was close to collapse but did not agree on what to do if Hitler, as was expected, refused to 'draw the proper conclusions'.

Through Colonel Wessel Freiherr von Freytag-Loringhoven, Tresckow again obtained explosive similar to that used in the failed brandy-bottle plot and they were now in Stauffenberg's possession. On 11 July Stauffenberg was summoned to Berchtesgaden to report to Hitler on the current military situation. His plan was to use the bomb, but Stauffenberg held back because Hermann Göring and Heinrich Himmler, also considered crucial targets, were not present as expected. The next opportunity arose on 15 July when Stauffenberg and Fromm were called to report to Hitler at the *Wolfsschanze*. Two hours before the conference was due to start, Olbricht issued the 'Internal Unrest' code signal to Berlin to set Valkyrie in motion and units set out in full marching order. Stauffenberg carried into the meeting a briefcase containing two kilograms of explosive but before he was able to find an excuse to leave the room and set the fuse, Hitler suddenly left the conference. Stauffenberg rushed to inform Berlin and recalled the troops.

The German forces were coming under extreme pressure on all fronts. On 17 July, the Soviets launched a major offensive against the southern sector of the Eastern Front making significant advances. In the west, St, Lô and Caen fell and Rommel was seriously injured when his car was strafed by an aircraft and crashed into a tree. He was unconscious and was not expected to live. The Gestapo issued a warrant for Goerdeler's arrest. With two failed attempts behind him Stauffenberg became even more determined to press ahead with another one despite Beck's growing pessimism. There were so many variables that the prospects of success, never high at the best of times, were becoming vanishingly small but the conspirators were united in their determination to keep trying. There was still a shared belief that a failed coup was better than no coup at all. The important thing was that history would record their determination to put their lives at risk for, as Berthold von Claussenberg put it 'our country and our children'.[44]

Another opportunity opened up when Stauffenberg was ordered to attend a conference with Hitler on 20 July to report on progress with newly established Volksgrenadier Divisions. At a meeting on 19 July, an officer described Stauffenberg as good humoured, calm, relaxed and showing no signs of nervousness.[45] On that day, messages were passed by word of mouth to everyone closely involved in the plot. Passing through Dahlem on his way home that night, Stauffenberg stopped his car outside a church and went in. He returned after a short while and spent the rest of the evening with his brother Berthold.

Chapter 17

20 JULY 1944

> In the end one can do no more than die for the cause.
> Ulrich Wilhelm Count Schwerin-Schwanenfeld[1]

In the early morning of 20 July 1944, Stauffenberg, together with Haeften, flew from Rangsdorf airfield in Berlin to Rastenburg in East Prussia. The pilot of the aircraft was instructed to wait and be ready to take off again at some time just after noon. After half an hour's drive through dense woodland, the two men passed through a gate giving access to a road crossing an extensive minefield and a ring of fortifications. Some two kilometres further along they passed another gate into a compound surrounded by electric fencing and barbed wire then after a further kilometre they arrived at the gloomy collection of concrete encrusted huts and bunkers that was the *Wolfsschanze*.

After taking breakfast, Stauffenberg reported to Keitel's office at noon. While they were waiting to be summoned to the conference room, Stauffenberg and Haeften went into the guest sitting room and were observed by one of the staff, W. Vogel, to be whispering together seemed to be working on an object that he couldn't identify. They were still in there when Keitel called for them to accompany him to the meeting. The same staff member went to fetch them and found them still huddled together. A loud voice then called out for Stauffenberg to come immediately and he emerged from the sitting room carrying his briefcase seeming quite heavy hanging from his three fingers. When Vogel suggested that he to carry the briefcase for him, Stauffenberg declined the offer.

It took them three minutes to walk to the conference room where Stauffenberg informed the sergeant manning a telephone booth that he was expecting an urgent call from Berlin and was to be informed as soon as it came through. When Stauffenberg and Keitel entered the room, Hitler acknowledged them and shook Stauffenberg's hand. Neither Göring nor Himmler were at the conference, which was unusual in those days. Heusinger reported on the situation in the east and Hitler leaned over the table to study the map.

A few minutes later Keitel noticed that Stauffenberg was no longer in the room. He had quietly excused himself saying that he had to inquire about the phone call he was expecting. He was, in fact, already getting into a car with Haeften when the bomb exploded at 12.42 hrs. He had left his briefcase containing the bomb close to where Hitler stood but someone moved it away and rested it up against one of the stout oak table supports. Although the explosion splintered the table into small fragments, the table and its support had absorbed and deflected enough of the blast to prevent it from causing Hitler any serious harm. It did, however, kill one conference members who was close to the bomb and had not been shielded by the table leg and blew two others several metres through a window. Three others died later from their injuries. Survivors staggered from the burning building. Seriously injured were being carried out. Hitler, face blackened so that he was unrecognisable and his uniform in tatters, emerged supported by Keitel and an ADC. For Hitler it was just another sign of the divine providence that protected him. He survived with a sprained right elbow, several bruises and a punctured eardrum.

According to the logbook of the first checkpoint, the car in which Stauffenberg and Haeften were travelling was stopped at 12.44 hrs but allowed to pass through. The guards at the next gate refused to let them pass, however, and Stauffenberg telephoned the camp commandant's ADC. He manged to persuade him to authorise the opening of the gate and the car sped towards the airport, both men convinced that Hitler was dead. On the way, Haeften threw a package containing one kilogram of unused explosive and two fuses out of the car window. They boarded the plane and were airborne enroute to Rangsdorf at 13.15 hrs. For two and a half hours they were out of touch with events. Because Staufenberg had become such a central and pivotal figure both during the assassination and its aftermath, few steps were taken to activate Valkyrie during these crucial moments which may not have been such a fatal flaw in the plan had the assassination been successful.

When they landed, Haeften called Olbricht to say that Hitler was dead. Olbricht then issued orders to General Joachim von Kortzfleish, the Wehrmacht commandant of Berlin who was not aware of the plot, to alert all units under his command. Lieutenant-Colonel Bernardis ordered troops to occupy the broadcasting stations at

Königswursterhausen and Zeesen. Guards sealed off all entrances to the *Allgemeines Heeresamt* situated in the Bendler Block at Bendlerstrasse 13. Olbricht had then gone to inform Fromm and asked him to issue orders to Military District commanders to initiate *Unternehmen Walküre*, the official operation to supress an uprising, but Fromm refused to do anything until he had official confirmation that Hitler was actually dead. He phoned the *Wolfschanze* at 16.10 hrs and was put through to Keitel who told him that there had been an explosion but the *Führer* was alive and only slightly injured. Keitel also inquired if Fromm had any idea where his Chief of Staff was.

Beck and other conspirators arrived at the Bendler Block closely followed by Stauffenberg and Haeften at 16.30 hrs. Stauffenberg gave Olbricht his version of events and said that Hitler could not have survived the blast. The whole building had been completely wrecked with Hitler inside it, he said. When told of the call to Keitel, he said that Keitel was just playing for time. He urged Olbricht to press ahead with Valkyrie. Beck said that whatever the truth of the matter they must act as if Hitler was indeed dead. If he wasn't, it was vital that the conspirators broadcast their appeals to the German people before Hitler could speak. Olbricht confirmed that coded signals had been sent out to military commanders which caused Fromm to leap up and demand to know who had issued the orders. Convinced by Keitel's assurances that Hitler had survived the blast, he had become desperate to distance himself from the conspiracy. He told Stauffenberg that the best Stauffenberg could do was go away and shoot himself. Olbricht interposed and urged Fromm not to rescind the orders. There followed a farcical scene when Fromm tried to have Stauffenberg, Haeften and Olbricht arrested. Olbricht responded by saying that it was Fromm who would be arrested if tried to stop them. Olbricht and Fromm came together in a scuffle until Olbricht drew his pistol and had Fromm put under guard.

Half an hour later two SS officers and two plainclothes policemen turned up with orders from Gestapo chief Ernst Kaltenbrunner to question Stauffenberg about why he had left the *Wolfschanze* so precipitously. Stauffenberg had all four men placed under arrest. Kortzfleish was next to arrive demanding to see Fromm. He had been told that Hitler was still alive and he refused to carry our orders to alert his troops. Not even Beck could persuade him so Kortzfleish, too, was arrested and General von Thüngen took over his command and confirmed the orders. The government quarter was sealed off by three companies of the Guard Battalion. Beck got through to Army group North headquarters and formally ordered an immediate withdrawal from its current hopeless position as far as the Dvina but he was ignored.

By now there was a clear distinction between the military and civilian sections of the conspiracy. While Olbricht and Stauffenberg were totally absorbed in trying to progress Valkyrie, Gisevius, Yorck, Schulenburg and others were tensely standing around unable to take political actions until the military situation was clarified. Witzleben arrived at the Bendler Block at 19.30 hrs and got into a furious argument with Beck that went on for some time as Stauffenberg and Schwerin looked on in silence. Conflicting messages abounded. Keitel issued instructions that all orders emanating from the Bendler Block were to be ignored. Witzleben left the building after an hour declaring that he would have nothing more to do with the whole thing.

Then at 21.00 hrs, the radio announced that Hitler would speak and that Himmler had been appointed as commander-in-chief of the Reserve Army. Any orders emanating from Witzleben, were to be ignored. The Guards Battalion surrounding the Bendler Block started to withdraw. Other troops that had started moving into position as part of Valkyrie were also returning to their barracks. Stauffenberg tried to assert some control but he could see that the plot was unravelling. A general state of confusion and acute tension developed. Officers who had been part of the conspiracy gathered together in the building and reasserted their obedience to the *Führer*. They ordered up a lorry load of machine guns from Spandau. A group of them burst into Olbricht's room and detained him there. Suddenly shots were heard and people started running along the corridors. Fromm appeared, flanked by armed men, and entered the room where Hoepner, Olbricht, Stauffenberg, Beck, Mertz von Quirnheim and Haeften were. He ordered them to surrender their weapons. Hoepner said that he was not involved in the coup and wanted an opportunity to defend himself. Fromm spoke briefly to him in private and ordered that he be taken away and held separately. Beck tried to talk to Fromm but Fromm told him to be quiet at which Beck took his revolver and tried to shoot himself in the head but he only grazed his temple and slumped into a chair where he was disarmed. Fromm turned to the others. 'If you have letters to write', he said, 'you have a few moments to do so'.[2] He left and returned a few minutes later telling the four detainees that he had just conducted a summary court martial that passed a death sentence on them. Beck asked to be given another pistol and went into a small side room. There he once again tried to shoot himself in the head but again the bullet did not kill him. Fromm ordered one of his officers to finish him off but he could not do it and it was left to a sergeant to deliver the coup de grâce.

Stauffenberg told Fromm that he accepted full responsibility for the conspiracy but Fromm silently stood to one side in a gesture inviting the men to leave the room under escort.

A few minutes after midnight, ten NCOs under the command of Lieutenant Schady assembled in the courtyard lit by the headlights of an army truck. Stauffenberg, Haeften, Olbricht and Mertz were lined up. Stauffenberg was the only one to speak. '*Es lebe das heilige Deutschland!* [Long live sacred Germany!]' he said just before all four were shot. Fromm sent a flash signal to all authorities 'Attempted Putsch by irresponsible generals bloodily crushed. All ring-leaders shot.'[3]

Inside the Bendler Block, Berthold Stauffenberg, Schulenburg, Yorck, Schwerin and Gerstenmaier were placed under arrest. A search of the building revealed a number of other plotters but several, including Otto John, managed to avoid detection and escaped. Then an hour later, a detachment of SS troops under the commend of Hauptsturmführer Otto Skorzeny entered the building, rounded up all the detainees in a room and forced them to listen to Hitler's broadcast before being driven away in handcuffs to Gestapo headquarters at Prinz-Albrecht Strasse. The bodies of Beck, Stauffenberg, Haeften, Olbricht and Hoepner were taken away and buried in the old churchyard of the Matthäus Church in Schöneberg. The next day, Himmler had the bodies exhumed and cremated with their ashes scattered in nearby fields.

When the Gestapo began its investigations they hardly knew where to begin and so made sweeping arrests of more than 600 people. They set up a special commission with a staff of over 400 in eleven sections and launched a full-scale operation called *Gewitteraktion* (Thunderstorm). Investigations soon unveiled a much wider network of resistance. Not satisfied with hunting down and executing anyone even vaguely implicated in the conspiracy, the Nazis revived the ancient custom of *Sippenhaftung*. Derived from Germanic law of the Middle Ages, this declared that a family or clan shares the responsibility for a crime or act committed by one of its members. Whilst it had originally taken the form of fines or confiscations, the Nazis took it to its limits by arresting and even murdering family members. Himmler said on 3 August 1944 'treasonous blood will be exterminated . . . The family Graf Stauffenberg will be exterminated down to its last member.'[4] The wives and children of Claus and Berthold Stauffenberg were arrested, as were cousins, uncles, aunts and even in-laws. The same applied to families of other leading conspirators. All arrestees were put in prisons or concentration camps and moved from place to place as the Soviets advanced in the east. Himmler also used the occasion of that speech to describe the bomb plot as 'only the ultimate manifestation of a long trend [of incompetence and sabotage] of the Officer Corps of the German Army' which had been going on since 1918.[5]

Fromm, who might have hoped that his actions on the day might have saved him, went to see Goebbels, hoping to be the first to proclaim the end of the conspiracy and also hoping to speak directly to Hitler but he was arrested. He pleaded with Goebbels but fell under immediate suspicion for his peremptory execution of the four conspirators. He was later accused of having violated regulations of martial law by executing the conspirators on 20 July. That was hardly a capital crime so when he came to trial he was charged with and convicted of 'cowardice before the enemy' and shot by firing squad on 12 March 1945.

A search of Goerdeler's lodgings in Askanischer Platz uncovered documents including draft appeals and proclamations intended for broadcast after the coup. Diaries contained coded, but easily identified, names of people who were quickly arrested. The Gestapo prison cells were filling up. While in custody, many conspirators were subjected to what was euphemistically called 'intensified interrogation' which Heydrich had authorised in 'important cases' where a suspect might give up 'information concerning hostility to state and nation' if this information cannot be obtained by ordinary investigation methods.[6] Some of the hunted committed suicide and others tried to evade detection but few succeeded. Otto John, using his Luftwaffe connections, was one of those who fled the country to Madrid and eventually to London where he started working for British Intelligence.

The first group of 20 July conspirators to be brought before the *Volksgerichtshof* on 7 and 8 August 1944, Field Marshal von Witzleben, General Hoepner, Brigadier General Stieff, 1st Lieutenant von Hagen, Major General von Hase, Lieutenant Colonel Bernardis, Captain Klausing and 1st Lieutenant Graf Yorck von Wartenburg, were all charged with treason and high treason. Showing obvious signs of brutal treatment, they were dressed in shabby ill-fitting clothes, often having to grip their baggy trousers to hold them up. Photographs of court proceedings show each of the men with calm disposition and obvious contempt for Freisler. When the defendants tried to speak, Freisler shouted them down but witnesses attest that Witzleben, during a pause in Freisler's fanatical, inarticulate, wild rant, was heard to say, 'You can hand us over to the hangman [but] in three months' time the indignant and tormented people will call you to account and drag you through the streets alive.'[7] Freisler must have regretted asking Haeften why he had criminally broken faith with Hitler when

Haeften replied that it was because Hitler was 'a great executor of evil'. All eight accused were hanged in a particularly cruel and barbaric way on 8 August at Plötzensee Prison.

From the start of proceedings against the conspirators, Hitler decreed that executions would be by hanging rather than by firing squad as had been traditional for military personnel. The hangman and his accomplices were usually drunk. A movie camera recorded the deaths so that Hitler could later see how his enemies had died. The naked victims were brought in one at a time. They had a noose on a short rope placed around their necks then they were lifted up so that the other end of the rope looped around one of a series of butcher's hooks fastened to a metal beam that straddled the room. Rather than experiencing a sudden drop that would have broken their necks and killed them outright, the victims were simply left to dangle with their feet inches from the ground in a slow strangulation. In some instances to intensify the agony, Hitler specified that instead of a rope, a thin hemp cord, sometimes referred to as a 'piano wire' was used. Occasionally, the victim, still alive, would be taken down after a short while and revived. Then when fully conscious they would be once again lifted up and suspended to be strangled again. This process would be repeated several times until the victim was dead.

When others came to trial, they continued to treat proceedings with disdain. Fellgiebel told Freisler that he had better hurry with the hangings or else he would be hanged before the men on trial. The lawyer, Joseph Wirmer told the irascible judge that he looked forward to meeting him in hell. Proceedings got so out of hand that Freisler was even reported to Martin Bormann, at this time Hitler's secretary, for acting in an undignified manner. Trials continued right through until the last weeks before the end of the war. When Schlabrendorff was put on trial on 3 February 1945, proceedings were interrupted by an air raid and the court retired to the air raid shelter. Freisler returned to the court to retrieve some documents just as it was hit by a bomb. The ceiling collapsed on him, and he was pulled out alive but died a short while later.

POSTSCRIPT

Schreibt un farshreibt [write and record]
Simon Dubnov[1]

None of the protagonists mentioned here can have ever had more than a faint hope of success of toppling the Nazi regime. The chances of resistance in the context of total domination of social and political landscape were minimal. All protest was little more than a gesture, 'a cry in the wilderness' which made it all the more heroic given the certainty of brutal punishment if caught balanced against the paucity of any tangible result from a given action. Remarkably, however, it was broadly based and much more widespread than might have been expected given the circumstances. While the more prominent activists came from identifiable social groups, the rank and file were composed of all elements of German society from aristocratic to communist, from military to religious.

Fabian von Schlabrendorff said that resistance began 'as the reaction of individuals with religious and moral convictions' to the abominations of Nazism and even in small groups, the resisters, said Helmuth von Molkte, lacked unity and suffered from the isolation that was essential for security reasons.[2] What motivated the resistance, more often than not a *Waldgänger*, a lone voice, or small grouping 'in the face of utter hopelessness' was the importance of bearing witness to record the crimes of the regime and make their own individual statements and say 'not in my name!' Dietrich Bonhoeffer advocated 'free and responsible action' rather than allow oneself to become a 'silent witness of evil deeds'. In his farewell letter, written in prison as he awaited execution, Gourdeler wrote, 'I ask the world to accept our Martyrdom as penance for the German people'.[3]

Appendix 1

SHULZE-BOYSEN / HARNACK GROUP MEMBERS

Members of the Shulze-Boysen Group
Harro Schulze-Boysen, born 2 September 1909, arrested 31 August 1942, killed 22 December 1942 Plötzensee prison, Berlin.
Libertas Schulze-Boysen, born 20 November 1913, arrested 8 September 1942, killed 22 December 1942 Plötzensee prison, Berlin, beheaded.
Robert Barth, parachute agent, killed 23 November 1945.
Arnold Bauer
Carl Baumann, artist, released.
Cato Bontjes van Beek, born 14 November 1920, arrested 20 September 1942, killed 5 August 1943 Plötzensee prison, Berlin.
Jan Bontjes van Beek, sculptor.
Hanna (Johanna Elisabeth Hochleitner-Köllchen) Berger, teacher, director, theatre director
Liane Berkowitz, arrested 26 September 1942, killed 5 August 1943 Plötzensee prison, Berlin
Karl Böhme, clerk, arrested 16 September 1942, killed 29 October 1943 Halle Penitentiary, committed suicide while in detention.
Margaret Böhme, executed by the Gestapo.
Elsa Boysen.
Erika Gräfin von Brockdorf, Labour Ministry employee, arrested 16 September 1942, killed 13 May 1943 Plötzensee prison, Berlin.
Cay-Hugo Graf von Brockdorf, sculptor, killed on active duty 28 March 1945.
Eva Maria Buch, student, arrested 11 October 1942, killed 5 August 1943 Plötzensee prison, Berlin, wife of Adam Buch.

Leo (Hugo) Buschmann, President of the Eternit AG, a construction materials company.
Fritz Cremer, sculptor.
Werner Dissel, beheaded.
Erwin Gehrts, Colonel in the Luftwaffe, born 18 April 1890, arrested 9 October 1942, killed 10 February 1943 Plötzensee prison, Berlin.
John Graudenz, journalist, photographer, sales representative, born 12 November 1884, arrested 12 September 1942, killed 22 December 1942 Plötzensee prison, Berlin, murdered during interrogation.
Toni Graudenz, 3 years in prison.
Ernst Happach, executed by guillotine.
Horst Heilmann, cipher section of *Abwehr*, born 15 April 1923, arrested 5 September 1942, killed 22 December 1942 Plötzensee prison, Berlin.
Bruno Hempel, 2 years in prison.
Hans Henninger, Air Ministry employee, born 10 March 1904, executed by guillotine.
Hans Helmut Himpel, dentist, arrested 17 September 1942, died in Sachsenhausen concentration camp
Walter Hoffmann, toolmaker, 1 year in prison.
Albert Hößler, Bruno, parachute agent, born 11 October 1910, arrested; September 1942, executed by guillotine.
Max Hübner, politician, killed 10 February 1943 Plötzensee prison, Berlin
Walter Husemann, codename Akim, journalist/schoolmaster, born; 2 December 1909, arrested 19 September 1942, killed 13 May 1943 Plötzensee prison, Berlin
Marta Husemann, actress, executed by guillotine.
Else Imme, sales clerk, born 24 September 1885, arrested October 1942, killed 5 August 1943 Plötzensee prison, Berlin, executed by hanging.
Anna Krauss (Krause), fortune teller, born 27 October 1884, arrested; 14 September 1942, killed 5 August 1943 Plötzensee prison, Berlin.
Werner Krauss (Kraus), 5 years in prison.
Walter Küchenmeister, writer/ technician, born; 9 January 1897, arrested 16 September 1942, killed 13 May 1943 Plötzensee prison, Berlin
Hans Lautenschläger, commercial employee and union official, 5 years in prison.
Helmut Marquandt, put in concentration camp.
Marcel Meilland, businessman, released.
Gisela von Pöllnitz, journalist, mistress of Hans Helmut Himpel, executed by guillotine.
Friedrich 'Fritz' Rehmer, soldier, born 2 June 1921, arrested 29 November 1942, killed 13 May 1943 Plötzensee prison, Berlin.

Herbert Richter-Luckian, architect, killed 8 May 1944 Brandenburg-Görden penitentiary. sentenced by Soviet military court.
John Friedrich Karl Rittmeister, psychoanalyst and neurologist, born 21 August 1898, arrested; 26 September 1942, killed 13 May 1943 Plötzensee prison, Berlin, husband of Hanna Berger.
Eva Rittmeister, paediatric nurse, office clerk, 3 years in prison.
Helmut Roloff (Rohloff), pianist, 2 years in prison.
Philipp Schaeffer, librarian/orientalist, librarian and sinologist, born 16 November 1894, arrested 2 October 1942, killed 13 May 1943 Plötzensee prison, Berlin
Ilse Schaeffer, ran the Coro group, code name Strahlmann, 3 years in prison
Heinrich Scheel, student/historian, 5 years in prison.
Paul Scholz, Construction contractor, 3 years in prison.
Oda Schottmüller, dancer and sculptor, born 9 February 1905, arrested 16 September 1942, killed 5 August 1943 Plötzensee prison, Berlin
Hermann Schulz, schoolteacher, born 10 September 1890, arrested 10 October 1942, killed 10 November 1942.
Kurt Schulze, postal worker, born 28 ecember 1894, arrested; 16 September 1942, killed 22 Deceember 1942 Plötzensee prison, Berlin, executed by hanging.
Elisabeth Schumacher, graphic designer, born 28 April 1904, arrested 12 September 1042, killed 22 December 1942 Plötzensee prison, Berlin.
Kurt Schumacher, sculptor, born 6 May 1905, arrested 12 September 1942, killed 22 December 1942 Plötzensee prison, Berlin.
Alexander Spoerle, writer, film and radio author.
Heinz Strehlow, journalist, born 15 July 1915, arrested October 1942, killed 13 May 1943 Plötzensee prison, Berlin, executed by guillotine.
Hans Sussmann, historian and politician, executed without trial at Sachsenhausen concentration camp in 1945.
Maria 'Mimi' Terwiel, sectretary, born 7 June 1910, arrested 17 September 1942, killed 5 August 1943 Plötzensee prison, Berlin, executed by hanging.
Fritz Thiel, mechanic, born 17 August 1942, arrested 16 September 1942, killed 13 May 1943 Plötzensee prison, Berlin.
Hannelore Thiel, arrested 16 September 1942, 6 years in prison.
Erhard Tohmfor, chemist and engineer, born 10 February 1909, arrested November 1942, killed 13 May 1943 Plötzensee prison, Berlin.
Alfred Traxi, cipher clerk, born 30 October 1912, arrested; 5 September 1942, committed suicide while in detention.
Albert Voigts, patent engineer, born 4 June 1904, arrested October 1942, killed 30 June 1943

Günter Weisenborn, writer, playwright and drama critic, 10 years in prison.
Stanislaus Wesolek, metalworker, born 10 September 1878, arrested 18 October 1942, killed 5 August 1943 Plötzensee prison, Berlin.
Johannes Wesolek, radio technician, 6 years in prison.
Walter Wesolek, technician.

Members of the Harnack Group
Bernhard Bästlein, KPD Hamburg.
Karl Behrens, tool designer at AEG, born 18 November 1909, arrested 16 September 1942, killed 13 May 1943 Plötzensee prison, Berlin (code names Beamer, Shining One).
Clara Behrens, wife of Karl, a secretary at OKH.
Elly Lotte Bergtel-Schleiff, librarian, 8 years in prison.
F. Buch.
Hilde Coppi, clerk, born, arrested 12 September 1942, killed 5 August 1943 Plötzensee prison, Berlin.
Frieda Coppi, tailor, killed 12 September 1942, by *sippenhaft*, mother of Hans.
Martha Dodd, writer.
Otto Donner, chief of the Research Office of War Economics.
Jutta Dubinsky, 8 years in prison.
Viktor Dubinsky, student/soldier, born 28 December 1912, 5 years in prison.
Adolf Grimme, former Culture Minister, killed 13 May 1943 Plötzensee prison, Berlin, executed by hanging.
Arvid Harnack, scientific expert in the Reich Economic Ministry, born 24 May 1901, arrested 7 September 1942, killed 22 December 1942 Plötzensee prison, Berlin.
Mildred Fish Harnack, translator, born 16 September 1902, arrested 7 September 1942, killed 16 January 1943 Plötzensee prison, Berlin.
Wolfgang Havermann, naval lieutenant/lawyer, killed 22 December 1942 Plötzensee prison, Berlin, executed by hanging (code name Italian).
Greta Margarete Kuckhoff, 10 years in prison.
Friedrich Lens, professor of economics.
Josef Römer, lawyer, killed 25 September 1944 Brandenburg-Görden penitentiary.
Hans Rupp, head economist for I. G. Farben (code name Turk).
Anton Saefkow, killed 18 September 1944 Brandenburg-Görden penitentiary.
Lotte Schleif, librarian, murdered at the Tegel shooting range.

Rose Schlösinger, secretary at the Foreign Office, born 5 October 1907, arrested 18 September 1942, killed 5 August 1943 Plötzensee prison, Berlin, executed by guillotine.
Rose Schösinger, typist.
John Sieg, journalist/railway worker, born 3 February 1903, arrested 11 October 1942, killed 15 October 1942, committed suicide while in Gestapo detention.
Leo Skrzypczynski, industrialist, put in concentration camp (code name Teacher).
Wolfgang Thieß, clerk, born 30 October 1911, arrested 21 October 1942, killed 9 September 1943 Plötzensee prison, Berlin
Wilhelm Utech, (codename worker).
Egmont Zechlin.

Members of both Schulze-Boysen and Harnack Groups

Hans Coppi, errand boy/student, born 25 January 1916, arrested 12 September 1942, killed 22 December 1942.
Ursula Goetze, student/typist, born 29 March 1916, killed 5 August 1943 Plötzensee prison, Berlin.
Herbert (Hans) Gollnow, officer in the Luftwaffe, born 13 July 1911, arrested 19 October 1942, killed 12 February 1943.
Wilhelm Guddorf, journalist and writer, born 20 February 1902, arrested 15 October 1942, killed 13 May 1943 Plötzensee prison, Berlin.
Ruthilde Hahne, sculptor, 4 years in prison.
Carl Helfrick, journalist in the Foreign Office, put in a concentration camp.
Krystana Iwanowa Janewa, Soviet agent.
Adam Kuckhoff, film producer/writer, born 30 August 1887, arrested 12 September 1942, killed 5 August 1943. Plötzensee prison, Berlin
Ina (Ender) Lautenschläger, courier, 6 years in prison.
Elfriede Paul, physician, released from prison to serve on the Eastern Front where he was killed on 24 September 1943.
Paul Thomas, code name Armless.
Edwin Tietjens, a wealthy White Russian emigrant, psychologist and author (code name Albanian).
Richard Weissensteiner, welder and technical draftsman, born 6 February 1907, arrested 16 September 1942, killed 13 May 1943 Plötzensee prison, Berlin.
Frida Wesolek, housewife, born 3 September 1887, arrested 18 October 1942, killed 5 August 1943 Plötzensee prison, Berlin.
Baron Wohlzogen-Neuhaus, worked in the technical department of the OKW (code name Greek).

Appendix 2

MEMBERS OF THE UHRIG GROUP

Bernhard Almstadt, killed 6 November 1944 Brandenburg-Görden penitentiary.
Walter Budeus, killed 21 August 1944.
Charlotte Eisenblätter, secretary, killed 25 August 1944 Plötzensee prison, Berlin.
Karl Frank, Cabinetmaker and politician, killed 21 August 1944 Brandenburg-Görden penitentiary.
Franz Mett, Miner and metal-worker, killed 21 August 1944 Brandenburg-Görden penitentiary.
Karl Müller, locksmith who worked at the AEG turbine factory in Berlin, killed 21 March 1945.
Willy Sachse, mechanic, sailor and writer, killed 21 August 1944 Brandenburg-Görden penitentiary.
Felix Tucholla, locksmith, killed 8 September 1943 Plötzensee prison, Berlin, executed by guillotine
Käthe Tucholla, athlete and gymnast, killed 28 September 1943 Plötzensee prison, Berlin, executed by guillotine.
Robert Uhrig, toolmaker, killed 21 August 1944 Brandenburg-Görden penitentiary.

Appendix 3

MEMBERS OF THE VON SCHELIHA GROUP

Gerhard Kegel, diplomat, father of Cato Bontjes van Beek.
Heinrich Koenen, engineer, born 29 October 1942, 5 years in prison.
Rudolf von Scheliha, diplomat who worked at the German Foreign Office, killed 22 December 1942 Plötzensee prison, Berlin.
Ilse Frieda Gertrude Stöbe, journalist/foreign office employee, born 12 September 1942, killed 22 December 1942 Plötzensee prison, Berlin, executed by guillotine.

Appendix 4

MEMBERS OF THE BAUM GROUP

Herbert Baum, died in prison on 11 June 1942.
Marianne Baum, executed in Berlin-Plötzensee on 18 August 1942.
Heinz Birnbaum, executed in Berlin-Plötzensee on 4 March 1943.
Alfred Eisenstadter.
Edith Fraenkel, murdered in Auschwitz concentration camp.
Felix Heymann.
Alice Hirsch, murdered in Auschwitz concentration camp.
Hella Hirsch, executed in Berlin-Plötzensee on 4 March 1943.
Charlotte Holzer, survived the war.
Marianne Joachim, executed in Berlin-Plötzensee on 4 March 1943.
Martin Kochmann.
Sala Kochmann, executed in Berlin-Plötzensee on 18 August 1942.
Hildegard Löwy, executed in Berlin-Plötzensee on 4 March 1943.
Gerd Meyer.
Hanni Meyer, executed in Berlin-Plötzensee on 4 March 1943.
Helmut Neumann, executed in Berlin-Plötzensee on 4 March 1943.
Charlotte Päch.
Heinz Rotholz, executed in Berlin-Plötzensee on 4 March 1943.
Lotte Rotholz, murdered in Auschwitz concentration camp.
Siegbert Rotholz, executed in Berlin-Plötzensee on 4 March 1943.
Lothar Salinger, executed in Berlin-Plötzensee on 4 March 1943.
Irena Walther.
Suzanne Wesse, executed in Berlin-Plötzensee on 18 August 1942.

Appendix 5

MEMBERS OF THE WHITE ROSE

First Trial, 22 February 1943, Munich
Judges
The President of the *Volksgerichtshof*, Dr Freisler
The Director of the District Court, Stier
SS Squad Leader Breithaupt
SA Squad Leader Bunge
State Secretary and SA Squad Leader Köglmaier

Accused

Christof Probst	23	Executed by guillotine
Hans Scholl	24	Executed by guillotine
Sophie Scholl	21	Executed by guillotine

Second Trial, 19 April 1943, Munich

Helmut Bauer	23	Had knowledge of the treasonous acts of the above-named accused but failed to report them, despite the fact that they are mature adults, and in contravention of the obligation of every German to report treasonous plans of this sort. 7 years in jail and forfeit of rights as citizens during that time.
Heinrich Bollinger	26	Had knowledge of the treasonous acts of the above-named accused but failed to report them, despite the fact that they are mature adults, and in

		contravention of the obligation of every German to report treasonous plans of this sort. 7 years in jail and forfeit of rights as citizens during that time.
Willi Graf	25	Collaborated with the Scholls in calling for sabotage of our war plants and in spreading defeatist ideas. They aided the enemy of the Reich and attempted to weaken our armed security. Sentenced to death and forfeit of rights as citizens.
Eugen Grimminger	51	10 years in jail
Heinrich Guter	17	Knew of the treasonous acts but failed to report them. 18 months in jail.
Falk Harnack	19	Acquitted because of lack of evidence but transferred to the Gestapo.
Hans Hirzel	19	Aided in the distribution of treasonous leaflets. 5 years in jail.
Susanne Hirzel	22	Aided in the distribution of treasonous leaflets. 6 months in jail.
Kurt Huber	50	Collaborated with the Scholls in calling for sabotage of our war plants and in spreading defeatist ideas. They aided the enemy of the Reich and attempted to weaken our armed security. Sentenced to death and forfeit of rights as citizen.
Traute Lafrenz	24	Aided in the distribution of treasonous leaflets. 6 months in jail.
Franz Josef Müller	19	Aided in the distribution of treasonous leaflets. 5 years in jail.
Gisela Schertling		Aided in the distribution of treasonous leaflets. 6 months in jail.
Alexander Schmorell	26	Collaborated with the Scholls in calling for sabotage of our war plants and in spreading defeatist ideas. They aided the enemy of the Reich and attempted to weaken our armed security. Sentenced to death and forfeit of rights as citizens.
Katharina Schüddekopf		Aided in the distribution of treasonous leaflets. 6 months in jail.

Third Trial, 13 July 1943, Munich

Harald Dohrn		Acquitted because of lack of evidence but shot on 29 April 1945 for listening to foreign radio broadcasts.
Manfred Eickemeyer		Acquitted because of lack of evidence.
Wilhelm Geyer	42	Acquitted because of lack of evidence.
Josef Söhngen		6 months in jail.

Fourth Trial, 3 April 1944, Saarbrücken

Willi Bollinger   Failed to report an act of high treason. 3 months in jail.

Fifth Trial, 13 October 1944, Donauwörth

Lieselotte Dreyfeldt
Wolfgang Erlenbach
Valentin Freise
Marie-Luise Jahn   12 years in jail
Hans Liepelt   Executed by guillotine
Hedwig Schulz
Franz Treppesch

Sixth Trial, 17 April 1945, Hamburg

Rudolf Degkwitz   1 year in prison
Frederick Geussenhainer Died in Mauthausen concentration camp
Felix Jud   4 years in prison
Heinz Kucharski   Sentenced to death but escaped
Curt Ledien   Executed by hanging
Ilse Ledien
Greta Mrosek   Executed by hanging
Thorsten Müller
Greta Rothe   Died in Leipzig-Meusdorf prison

Other members of the Hamburg White Rose Group

Elizabeth Lange   Committed suicide 28 January 1944..
Katharina Liepelt   Committed suicide 9 January 1944.
Reinhold Meyer   Died in Fuhlsbüttel prison 12 November 1944

Appendix 6

MEMBERS OF THE KREISAU CIRCLE

Dietrich Bonhoeffer, Lutheran pastor. Executed by hanging on 9 April 1945 at Flossenbürg concentration camp.
Alfred Delp, Jesuit priest. Arrested in Munich on 28 July 1944. Sentenced to death by the *Volksgerichtshof* on 11 January 1945, and murdered on 2 February 1945, in Plötzensee.
Horst Karl von Einsiedel, arrested by the Soviet secret police in October 1945. He died on 25 February 1947 under inexplicable circumstances in the Soviet internment camp in Sachsenhausen.
Otto Heinrich von der Gablentz, survived the war and became a professor of political science at the Free University of Berlin.
Eugen Gerstenmaier, theologian. Sentenced by the *Volksgerichtshof* on 11 January to seven years in a penitentiary. He later became president of the German Parliament from 1954 to 1969.
Hans Bernd von Haeften, lawyer. Sentenced to death by the *Volksgerichtshof* on 15 August 1944 and murdered only hours later in Plötzensee.
Theodor Haubach, Social Democrat Party representative in the Reichstag until 1933 and then spent a long time in concentration camps. Arrested by the Gestapo on 9 August 1944. Sentenced to death by the *Volksgerichtshof* on 15 January 1945 and murdered on 23 January 1945 in Plötzensee.
Albrecht Haushofer, educator. Murdered by SS guards on 22 April 1945.
Paulus von Husen. Arrested by the Gestapo in August 1944 and on 19 April 1945, at the last session of the *Volksgerichtshof*, he was sentenced to 3 years in prison.
Jakob Kaiser, labour union leader and member of the Reichstag. Survived the war and was later elected president of the Berlin CDU.

Albrecht von Kessel, diplomat. Survived the war.
Lothar König, Priest and professor of cosmology at the Berchmannskolleg. Survived the war.
Julius Leber, murdered on 5 January 1945 in Plötzensee.
Wilhelm Leuschner, labour union leader. Arrested on 16 August 1944, and was brought before the *Volksgerichtshof*, where he was sentenced to death on 8 September 1944. The sentence was carried out on 29 September 1944 at Plötzensee.
Hans Lukaschek, lawyer, Survived the war.
Carlo Mierendorff, Social Democrat Party representative in the Reichstag until 1933 and then spent a long time in concentration camps. Killed in an Allied bombing raid on Leipzig on 4 December 1943.
Freya Gräfin von Moltke, Survived the war.
Helmuth James Graf von Moltke. entenced to death by the *Volksgerichtshof* and murdered on 23 January 1945 in Plötzensee.
Hans Peters, professor of public law. Survived the war.
Harald Poelchau, chaplain in Tegel prison. Survived the war.
Adolf Reichwein, Educator. Arrested in July 1944, tried before the *Volksgerichtshof* and murdered on 20 October 1944 in Plötzensee.
Augustin Rösch, Jesuit priest. Arrested but survived internment.
Fritz-Dietlof von der Schulenburg, government official and army officer. Arrested on 20 July 1944 and tried on 10 August. He was executed in Plötzensee on the same day.
Ulrich-Wilhelm Graf von Schwerin, Llanded gentry and member of the *Abwehr*. Arrested and tortured, he was tried at the *Volksgerichtshof* on 21 August and executed by hanging on 8 September 1944 in Plötzensee.
Theodor Steltzer, Lieutenant colonel on the General Staff of the Commander in Chief of the Wehrmacht in Norway in Oslo. Arrested by the Gestapo. On 15 January 1945. The *Volksgerichtshof* sentenced him to death but the sentence was never carried out. Became one of the co-founders of the Christian Democratic Party (CDU).
Carl Dietrich von Trotha, economist. Survived the war.
Margarete von Trotha. Survived the war
Adam von Trott zu Solz, diplomat. Arrested on 25 July 1944. Sentenced to death by the *Volksgerichtshof* on 15 August and murdered in Plötzensee on 26 August 1944.
Marion Gräfin Yorck von Wartenburg, lawyer. Survived the war.
Peter Graf Yorck von Wartenburg, lawyer. Sentenced to death by the *Volksgerichtshof* on 8 August 1944 and murdered in Plötzensee on the same day.

Appendix 7

WHITE ROSE COURT PROCEEDINGS OF HANS AND SOPHIA SCHOLL, AND CHRISTOPH PROBST

President of the People's Court Dr. Freisler, presiding,
Director of the Regional (Bavarian) Judiciary Stier,
SS Group Leader Breithaupt,
SA Group Leader Bunge,
State Secretary and SA Group Leader Köglmaier,
and, representing the Attorney General to the Supreme Court of the Reich, Reich Attorney Weyersberg,
The Indictment of Hans and Sophia Scholl, and Christoph Probst February 21, 1943, Berlin Reich Attorney General to the People's Court Indictment
Hans Fritz Scholl of Munich, born September 22, 1918, in Ingersheim, single, no previous convictions, taken into investigative custody on February 18, 1943;
Sophia Magdalena Scholl of Munich, born May 9, 1921, in Forchtenberg, single, no previous convictions, taken into investigative custody on February 18, 1943;
Christoph Hermann Probst of Aldrans bei Innsbruck, born on November 6, 1919, in Murnau, married, no previous convictions, taken into investigative custody on February 20, 1943; all at present in the jail of the headquarters, State Police (Gestapo), Munich;
All at present not represented by counsel;
are accused:

in 1942 and 1943 in Munich, Augsburg, Salzburg, Vienna, Stuttgart, and Linz, of committing the same acts together:

I of attempted high treason, namely
1. to change the constitution of the Reich by force, and acting with intent:
2. to organise a conspiracy for the preparation of high treason,
3. to render the armed forces unfit for the performance of their duty of protecting the German Reich against internal and external attack,

II of having attempted, in the internal area of the Reich, during a time of war, to give aid to the enemy against the Reich, injuring the war potential of the Reich; and

III of having attempted to cripple and weaken the will of the German people to take measures toward their defence and self-determination.

In the summer of 1942 and in January and February of 1943 the accused Hans Scholl prepared and distributed leaflets demanding a settlement of accounts with National Socialism, disaffection from the National Socialist "gangsterism", and passive resistance and sabotage. In addition, in Munich he adorned walls with the defamatory slogan "Down With Hitler" and with cancelled swastikas. The accused Sophia Scholl participated in the preparation and distribution of the seditious materials. The accused Probst composed the first draft of a leaflet.

The transcript of the Sentence of Hans and Sophia Scholl and Christoph Probst February 22, 1943 Transcript I H 47/43 In the Name of the German People In the action against Hans Fritz Scholl, Munich, born at Ingersheim, September 22, 1918,

> The People's Court, first Senate, find that the accused have by means of leaflets in a time of war called for the sabotage of the war effort and armaments and for the overthrow of the National Socialist way of life of our people, have propagated defeatist ideas, and have most vulgarly defamed the *Führer*, thereby giving aid to the enemy of the Reich and weakening the armed security of the nation. On this account they are to be punished by Death Their honour and rights as citizens are forfeited for all time.[1]

Appendix 8

PLÖTZENSEE PRISON

> Normally the executioner came twice a week. His name was Röttger. He didn't so much walk as creep. He always wore a three-quarter length jacket. His helpers were big strong men. They had to bring the hog-tied victims to the gallows. Two wardens led the condemned from the cell to the execution shed. Each of them got eight cigarettes for doing this. A man named Appelt acted as overseer in the death building. The prisoners called him 'the fox.' He loved to pop up suddenly and check the bonds. He was always lurking around.
> Plötzensee Memorial Centre[1]

The Berlin prison on Plötzensee Lake, built between 1869 and 1879, was part of a complex covering over sixty acres that was surrounded by a twenty-foot wall. Inside was a windowless brick building with a cement floor, eight by ten metres with one door leading inside and another leading out to the morgue. Only a handful of people on the outside were aware of what went on behind the high walls at Plötzensee. The five three-storey cell block buildings could accommodate a total of approximately 1,400 prisoners.

Under the Nazis, draconian sentences and a deliberate policy of placing criminal and political offenses on equal footing became common practice with close cooperation of the military justice system with the SS-integrated security authorities, Gestapo and the Security Service of SS. Death sentences became increasingly common, and a total of some 3,000 executions took place at Plötzensee.

Wilhelm Friedrich Röttger had replaced Gottlob Bordt as first assistant to Friedrich Hehr but when Hehrs became ill in 1941, Röttger had already conducted his first twenty-six executions from 2 November 1941 until 5 December 1942. In the First World War, he had been a stoker in the boiler room of a battleship and afterwards worked as a car mechanic and assistant to an undertaker. He applied for and got the post of executioner of *Vollstreckungsbezirkes IV*, which consisted of the prisons in Berlin-Plötzensee and Brandenburg-Görden on 23 September 1942. Röttger had a reputation as a well presented and charming individual but others saw him as crude and fond of making jokes about his work. Execution might be either by hanging or beheading by guillotine. His basic remuneration was 3,000 Reichsmark a year plus a 30-Reichsmark bonus for every execution. On 7 September 1943 in a single day he carried out 186 executions, four of which, due to the chaotic proceedings, were carried out in error on prisoners who had not even been condemned to death by the courts.

Appendix 9

DRAFT OF GOVERNMENTAL DECLARATION BY BECK AND GOERDELER SUMMER 1944

Extracts

Now that the affairs of the Reich government have been assigned to us, it is our duty to announce the principles on which we will run the government and the objectives we want to achieve.

1. The first task is to restore the complete majesty of law.
2. We want to restore morality and intend to do this in all areas of private and public life.
3. We will fight against the lie; the sun of truth shall dispel its dense fog. Our people has been deceived in the most shameless way about economic, financial and political as well as military events. The true facts will be established and made public, so that every individual can check them.
4. The shattered freedom of spirit, of conscience, of religious belief and of opinion will be restored.
5. Education must once again be consciously based on the religious Christian principle, but should not violate the Christian laws of utmost tolerance towards people with other beliefs.
6. The public servant must once again become an example in his whole way of working and living.
7. During the war we owe all our work, sacrifice, and love to the men who are defending the fatherland.
8. We warned against this war that has brought so much suffering to the whole of humanity, and we can therefore speak out frankly.

May God give us insight and strength so that the meaning of these terrible sacrifices may benefit future generations!

NOTES

Prologue

1. Adam-Tkalec, Maritta, *Used in the East, hated in the West: The true story of the Red Orchestra* (berliner-zeitung.de, 2022).
2. Ohler, Norman, *The Infiltrators: The Lovers Who Led Germany's Resistance Against the Nazis* (Atlantic Books Kindle Edition, 2020), p. 235.
3. Tuchel, Johannes, *Resistance: You have to celebrate Christmas properly*, in: zeit.de. Zeit Online, November 24, 2009, accessed on 13 July 2024

Chapter 1: Internal Opposition Before 1938

1. Klemperer, Klemens von, *Reflections and Reconsiderations on the German Resistance* (Kirchliche Zeitgeschichte, Vol. 1, No. 1, Der Widerstand von Kirchen und Christen gegen den Nationalsozialismus, 1988), p. 23.
2. Klemperer, Klemens von, *German Resistance against Hitler: The Search for Allies Abroad 1938-1945* (Clarendon Press, 1992), p. 63.
3. Eltscher, Louis R., *Traitors or Patriots?: A Story of the German Anti-Nazi Resistance* (McNidder and Grace Kindle Edition, 2020), p. 7.
4. Klemperer, *Reflections and Reconsiderations*, p. 28.
5. Klemperer, *German Resistance against Hitler: The Search for Allies Abroad*, p. 2.
6. Large, David Clay, *Contending with Hitler; Varieties of German Resistance in the Third Reich, The German Resistance Movement 1933-1945* (Cambridge University Press, 1994), p. 9.
7. Zeller, Eberhard, *The Flame of Freedom; The German Struggle against Hitler* (Oswald Wolff Limited, 1967), p. 179.
8. Wistrich, Robert S., *Who's Who in Nazi Germany* (Routledge, 2013).
9. Klemperer, *Reflections and Reconsiderations*, p. 14.
10. Reynolds, Nicholas, *Treason was no Crime. Ludwig Beck, Chief of the German General Staff* (Kimber, 1976), p. 44.

11 Rothfels, Hans, *The German Opposition to Hitler*, translated by Lawrence Wilson (Oswald Wolff Limited, 1961), p. 23.
12 nationalchurchillmuseum.org/winston-churchill-and-the-gathering-storm.html
13 Leber, Annelore (ed.), *The Conscience in Revolt; Portraits of the German Resistance 1933 – 1945* (v. Hase & Koehler), 1994, p. 86
14 Schoenbaum, David, *Hitler's Social Revolution: Class and Status in Nazi Germany, 1933-1939* (Doubleday, 1966).
15 Merson, Allan, *Communist Resistance in Nazi Germany* (Lawrence and Wishart, 1986), p. 212.
16 Hill, Leonidas E., 'Towards a New History of German Resistance to Hitler', *Central European History*, Vol. 14, No. 4 (1981), p. 377.
17 Rothfels, p. 53.
18 Deutsch, Harold C. (ed.), 'The German Resistance: Answered and Unanswered Questions', *Central European History*, Vol. 14, No. 4 (1981), p. 324.
19 Ridley, Norman, *The Venlo Sting* (Pen & Sword, 2022), p. 36
20 Rothfels, p. 70
21 Stargardt, A.W., Allies Inside Germany: The German Resistance Movement against Nazi-Fascism, *The Australian Quarterly*, Vol. 16, No. 3 (1944), p. 27.

Chapter 2: Defending Traditional Values

1 Leber, Annelore (ed), *The Conscience in Revolt*, p. 133.
2 Rothfels, p. 16.
3 Eltscher, p. 101.
4 Klemperer, *German Resistance against Hitler: The Search for Allies Abroad*, p. 4.
5 Jones, Larry Eugene, 'Nationalists, Nazis, and the Assault against Weimar: Revisiting the Harzburg Rally of October 1931', *German Studies Review*, Vol. 29, No. 3, 2006, p. 484
6 Dumbach, Annette & Newborn, Jud, *Sophie Scholl and the White Rose* (One World Publications. Kindle Edition, 2023, p. 225
7 Brabner-Smith, John W., '"Hitler hated Lawyers". A Story of Resistance to Tyranny', American Bar Association Journal, Vol. 43, No. 12 (1957), p. 1105.
8 Leber, Annelore (ed.), *The Conscience in Revolt*, p. 118.
9 Ibid., p. 126.
10 Klemperer, *German Resistance against Hitler: The Search for Allies Abroad*, p. 194.

11 Ibid., p. 197.
12 Leber, Annelore (ed.), *The Conscience in Revolt; Portraits of the German Resistance*, p. 133.

Chapter 3: Left-Wing Resistance

1 Klemperer, *German Resistance against Hitler: The Search for Allies Abroad*, p. 191.
2 David, Claude, *L'Allemagne de Hitler* (Presses Universitaires de France, collection Que sais-je ?, Paris, 1954), p. 103.
3 Desroches, Alain, *La Gestapo* (Éditions De Vecchi, Paris, 1977), pp. 680, 683.
4 Shirer, William L, *Le troisième Reich des origines à la chute* (Éditions Stock, Paris, 1960), tome 2, p. 416.
5 Derbent, T., *The German Communist Resistance 1933-1945* (Foreign Language Press, 2021), p. 59.
6 Ibid., p. 49.
7 Zeller, p. 266.
8 Ibid., p. 67.
9 Rothfels, p. 64.
10 Zeller, p. 69.
11 Ibid., p. 75.
12 Ibid.
13 Zeller, p. 77.
14 Henk, E., *Die Tragödie des 20 Juli 1944* (Heidelberg, 1946), p. 46.
15 Derbent, p. 59.
16 Ibid., p. 60.
17 Henderson, J.L., *Adolf Reichwein. Eine politisch-pädagogische Biographie* (H. Lindemann, 1958), p. 64.
18 Leber, J., *Ein Mann geht seinen Weg* (Schriften, Reden und Briefe, 1952), p. 120.
19 Zeller, p. 88.
20 Ibid., p. 94.

Chapter 4: Youth Resistance

1 Leber, Annelore (ed), *The Conscience in Revolt*, p. 7.
2 Ibid., p. 5.
3 Geerling, Wayne, Magee, Gary B. & Brooks Robert, 'Faces of Opposition: Juvenile Resistance, High Treason, and the People's Court in Nazi

Germany', *The Journal of Interdisciplinary History*, Vol. 44, No. 2 (2013), p. 228.

4   Ibid., p. 230.

5   Leber, Annelore (ed), *The Conscience in Revolt; Portraits of the German Resistance 1933 – 1945*, p. 224

6   Holmes, Blair R. & Keele, Alan F., *When Truth Was Treason: German Youth against Hitler* (University of Illinois Press, 2003)

7   *Facing History & Ourselves, "Rejecting Nazism"*, facinghistory.org last updated 2 August 2016.

Chapter 5: Intellectuals against the Nazis

1   Extract from: *"Kola-Fu" – Concentration camp and Gestapo prison Hamburg – Fuhlsbüttel 1933-1945-* Hamburg Portrait Issue 18/83 of the Museum for Hamburg History, p. 6

2   Leber, Annelore (ed), *The Conscience in Revolt*, p. 29.

3   Ibid., p. 38.

4   Ibid., p. 40.

5   Ibid., p. 48.

Chapter 6: The Churches

1   Matheson, Peter, Adolf Hitler, "Policy Statement by Hitler, 23 March 1933"', in *The Third Reich and the Christian Churches* (William B. Eerdman's Publishing Company, 1981), p. 9

2   Matheson, Peter, The Catholic Church and The German Reich, "Concordant Between the Papacy and the Third Reich, 20 July 1933," in *The Third Reich and the Christian Churches* (William B. Eerdman's Publishing Company, 1981)

3   Koonz, Claudia, *Choice and Courage,* in *Contending with Hitler; Varieties of German resistance in the Third Reich*, editor David Clay. (Cambridge University Press), 1994, p. 52

4   Remak, Joachim (ed), 'Directives of the Church Movement German Christians (Movement for a National Church) in Thuringia, 1933', in *The Nazi Years: A Documentary History* (Waveland Press, 1990), p. 95.

5   Riebling, Mark, *Church of Spies: The Pope's Secret War Against Hitler* (Basic Books Kindle Editi.on), p. 11

6   Leber, Annelore (ed), *The Conscience in Revolt; Portraits of the German Resistance,* p. 144

7   Ibid., p. 150.

8   DBWE 1:34, The Dietrich Bonhoeffer Works in English, Fortress Press various editors and translators (1996–2014).

Chapter 7: The Oster Conspiracy

1. Hoffmann, Peter, 'Ludwig Beck: Loyalty and Resistance', *Central European History*, Vol. 14, No. 4 (1981), p. 345.
2. Assmann, Kurt, *Hitler and the German Officer Corps, Translated by Captain Roland E. Krause* (US Naval Institute), 1956.
3. Bullock, Alan, *Hitler, A Study in Tyranny* (Odham Press, 1952), p. 611.
4. Ridley, Norman, *Reading Hitler's Mind* (Pen & Sword, 2022), p. 78.
5. Ibid., p. 71.
6. Zeller, p. 3.
7. Ibid., p. 4.
8. Ibid., p. 56.
9. Ridley, *Reading Hitler's Mind*, p. 62.
10. Ritter, Nikolaus, *Cover Name: Dr.Rantzau* (University Press of Kentucky, 2019), p. xv.
11. Klemperer, *German Resistance against Hitler: The Search for Allies Abroad*, p. 20.
12. Nylander, Gert, *German Resistance Movement and England, Carl Goerdeler and the Wallenberg Brothers* (The Foundation for Economic History Research within Banking and Enterprise), 1999, p. 16
13. Letter from Frank Ashton-Gwatkin (Foreign Office) to S. D. Waley (Treasury), 25 June 1937, FO 371/20733/C 4714/165/18.
14. Klemperer, *German Resistance against Hitler: The Search for Allies Abroad*, p. 94
15. Steinbach, Peter, *The Conservative Resistance* in *Contending with Hitler; Varieties of German resistance in the Third Reich*, editor David Clay Large, (Cambridge University Press), 1994, p. 9.
16. Krüger-Charlé, Michael, *From Reform to Resistance: Carl Goerdeler's 1938 Memorandum* in *Contending with Hitler; Varieties of German resistance in the Third Reich*, editor David Clay Large, (Cambridge University Press), 1994, p. 76
17. Mommsen, Hans, 'The German Resistance against Hitler and the Restoration of Politics', The Journal of Modern History, Vol. 64 (1992), p. S115.
18. Rothfels, p. 59.
19. Ridley, *Reading Hitler's Mind*, p. 77

Chapter 8: The War in the West

1. Klemperer, *German Resistance against Hitler: The Search for Allies Abroad*, p. 219.

Chapter 9: Harro and Libertas Schulze-Boysen

1. Coppi, Hans, *Harro Schulze-Boysen – Wege in den Widerstand* (Verlag Dietmar Fölbach, 1993), p. 102.
2. Ibid., p. 22.
3. Ibid., p. 25.
4. Ibid., p. 29.
5. Quoted in *The Steinbart-Gymnasium* newspaper December 1927.
6. Harro Schulze-Boysen; Letter to parents from the summer of 1928 IfZ Munich ED 335/1.
7. Harro Schulze-Boysen; Letter to parents dated 31 March 1930 IfZ Munich ED 335/1.
8. Coppi, p. 41.
9. Harro Schulze-Boysen; Letter to parents 25 October 1930 335/1.
10. Ibid.
11. Coppi, p. 52.
12. Ibid., p. 57.
13. Harro Schulze-Boysen; Letter to parents dated August 1931 IfZ Munich ED 335/1.
14. *Der Gegner* magazine special edition May 1932.
15. Coppi, p. 107.
16. Berlin State Police Office's bulletin, 1 April 1933, reference 2e 7045/X.
17. Coppi, p. 127.
18. 'Harro Schulze-Boysen Letter to parents 15 Sept 1933 IfZ Munich ED 335/2.
19. Harro Schulze-Boysen; Letter dated 24 March 1934 IfZ Munich ED 335/2.
20. Letter from Elsa Nuss to Ricarda Huch 24 June 1934 IfZ Munich ED 335/2.
21. Perrault, Gilles, *The Red Orchestra* (Simon and Schuster, 1969), p. 202.
22. Coppi, p. 152.
23. Harro Schulze-Boysen; Letter to parents 12 Jan 1936 IfZ Munich ED 335/2.
24. Coppi, p. 155.
25. Hellmann, John, *Communitarian Third Way: Alexandre Marc and Ordre Nouveau, 1930-2000* (McGill-Queen's Press, 2002), p. 229.
26. Brysac, Shareen Blair, *Resisting Hitler: Mildred Harnack and the Red Orchestra* (Oxford University Press, 2020), p. 232.
27. Coppi, p. 152.

28 Ibid., p. 158.
29 Perrault, p. 113.
30 Harro Schulze-Boysen; Letter to parents 6 Sep 1936 IfZ Munich ED 335/2.
31 Kuckhoff, Greta, *Vom Rosenkranz zur Roten Kapelle, Im Schatten der Roten Kapelle* (Verlag Neues Lebel, 1972), p. 157
32 Ohler, Norman, *The Infiltrators: The Lovers Who Led Germany's Resistance Against the Nazis* (Atlantic Books Kindle Edition, 2020), p. 166.
33 Coppi, p. 180.

Chapter 10: Mildred Fish and Arvid Harnack

1 Brysac, p. 20.
2 Ibid., p. 17.
3 *Nazi Resister or Soviet Spy? The Case of Mildred Fish-Harnack, Her Husband, and the OSS* Document Number (FOIA) /ESDN (CREST): 06660827, cia.gov.
4 Knutson, Käri, 'Mildred Fish-Harnack honored as hero of resistance to Nazi regime', *University of Winconsin News*, 2019.
5 Brysac, p. 53.
6 Ohler, o.167.
7 Brysac, p. 37.
8 Knutson.
9 Brysac, p. 57.
10 Ibid., p. 65
11 Smith, Gene, 'Martha Dodd's Shining Season', American Heritage, Vol. 48, Issue 4 (1997).
12 Weinstein, Allen & Vassiliev, Alexander, *The Haunted Wood* (New York: Modern Library, 1999), p. 62.
13 Smith.
14 Brysac, p. 13
15 Scheel, Heinrich, 'Die Rote Kapelle – Widerstand, Verfolgung, Haft', in Coppi, Hans Jr, Danyel, Jürgen & Tuchel, Johannes (ed.), *Die Rote Kapelle im Widerstand gegen Hitler* (Rütten & Loenig, 1994), p. 185.
16 Brysac, p. 205
17 Ohler, p. 169
18 Andrew, Christopher & Gordievsky, Oleg, *KGB: The Inside Story: Of Its Foreign Operations from Lenin to Gorbachev* (Harper Collins, 199), p. 274.

19 Tuchel, Johannes, 'Weltanschauliche Motivationen in der Harnack/ Schulze-Boysen-Organisation', *Kirchliche Zeitgeschichte*, Vol. 1, No. 2, Theologie und Politik (1988), p. 273.
20 Brysac, p. 261.

Chapter 11: *Die Rote Kapelle*
1   Perrault, p. 15.
2   West, Nigel, *Encyclopaedia of Political Assassinations* (Rowman & Littlefield, 2017), p. 132.
3   Brysac, p. 264.
4   Ibid., p. 267.
5   Ibid., p. 273.
6   Ohler, p. 175.
7   Ibid., p. 178.
8   Brysac, p. 277.
9   Ohler, p. 182.
10 Brysac, p. 294.
11 Flicke, W.F., *Rote Kapelle; les espions de Stalin* (Verlag Welsermühl, 1957), p. 46.
12 Brysac, p. 297.
13 Ohler, p. 226.
14 Holzer, Charlotte, *Years of Defiance: The Herbert Baum Group and Jewish Resistance in Berlin* (Yad Vashem Publications, 2003), p. 149.
15 Ohler, p. 235.
16 Tyas, Stephen, *SS-Major Horst Kopkow: From the Gestapo to British Intelligence* (Fonthill Media, 2017), p. 91
17 Perrault, p. 118.
18 Ohler, p. 260.
19 Richelson, Jeffrey, *A Century of Spies: Intelligence in the Twentieth Century* (Oxford University Press, 1995), p. 126.
20 Ohler, p. 308.
21 Schad, Martha, *Mothers in the Resistance Movement* (Verlag, Opladen/ Farmington Hills, 2010).
22 Ohler, p. 344.
23 Tuchel, Johannes, 'Weltanschauliche Motivationen in der Harnack/ Schulze-Boysen-Organisation', p. 273

Chapter 12: The von Scheliha Group

1. Fikus, Sebastian, *Rudolf Scheliha. Zapomniany bohater polsko-niemieckiej przyjaźni* (W: Zeszyty Edukacji Kulturalnej. Nr 81, 2018), p. 27.
2. Wiaderny, B., *Der polnische Untergrundstaat und der deutsche Widerstand 1939–1944* (Berlin, 2002), p. 119.
3. Sahm, U., *Rudolf von Scheliha 1897–1942. Ein deutscher Diplomat gegen Hitler* (München, 1990), p. 119.
4. Pismo Elisabeth Oppersdorf z 23.05.1986 roku do Ulricha Sahma, cyt za: U. Sahm, Rudolf von Scheliha 1897–1942, p. 118.
5. Fikus, p. 27.

Chapter 13: Herbert Baum and the Jewish Resistance

1. Cox, John, *The Herbert Baum Groups:* in *Networks of Jewish, Leftist, and Youth Resistance in the Third Reich. The Human Tradition in Modern Europe, 1750 to the Present* editors, Cora Granata and Cheryl Koos, (Rowman and Littlefield), 2007), p. 143
2. Kweit, Konrad, *The Jewish Resistance* in *Contending with Hitler; Varieties of German resistance in the Third Reich,* editor David Clay Large, (Cambridge University Press), 1994, p. 68
3. Cox, p. 141.
4. Kweit, p. 70.
5. McDonaugh, Frank, *Opposition and Resistance in Nazi Germany* (Cambridge University Press, 2001), p. 9.
6. Cox, p. 146.
7. Ibid., p. 148.

Chapter 14: The White Rose

1. Scholl, Inge, *The White Rose: Munich 1942-1943* (Wesleyan University Press Kindle Edition,), p. 160.
2. Ramet, Sabrina P. & Hassenstab, Christine M., *Anti-fascism in European History: From the 1920s to Today,* Chapter 6, 'The Anti-Fascism of Hans & Sophie Scholl: Intellectual Sources of the White Rose' (Central European University Press, 2023), p. 104
3. Dumbach, Annette & Newborn, Jud, *Sophie Scholl and the White Rose* (One World Publications Kindle Edition), p. 21
4. Scholl, p. 26.
5. The White Rose; Faces of a Friendship, Katholische Universität Eichstätt Ingolstadt.
6. Dumbach, p. 301.
7. Ibid., p. 303.

8   Ibid., p. 307.
9   Ibid., p. 22.
10 The White Rose; Faces of a Friendship, Katholische Universität Eichstätt Ingolstadt.
11 Scholl, p. 22.
12 Dumbach, p. 311.
13 Ibid.
14 Ibid., p. 223.
15 Ibid., p. 228.
16 Ibid., p. 337.
17 Ibid., p. 344.

Chapter 15: The Kreisau Circle

1   Moltke, Helmuth James von, *Letters to Freya – 1939–1945*. Translated by von Oppen, Beata Ruhm (Alfred A. Knopf, 1990).
2   Moltke, Freya von, *Memories of Kreisau and the German Resistance* (University of Nebraska Press Kindle edition, 2003), location 179.
3   Mommsen, p. S116.
4   Childers, Thomas, *The Kreisau Circle and the Twentieth of July* in, *Contending with Hitler; Varieties of German Resistance in the Third Reich*, editor. David Clay large. (Cambridge University Press, 1994), p. 100
5   Mommsen p. S124
6   1934 memorandum 'Reichsreform' in the Schulenburg estate, BA Koblenz. See Heinemann, A conservative rebel, p. 264
7   Moltke, Freya von, *Memories of Kreisau and the German Resistance*, location 378.
8   Zeller, p. 114.
9   Rothfels, p. 115.
10 Ibid, p. 116.
11 Ibid., p. 119.
12 Childers, p. 111.

Chapter 16: Hitler and his Generals

1   Zeller, p. 286
2   Leber, p. 383.
3   Ibid., p. 384.
4   Hoffmann, Peter, 'Ludwig Beck: Loyalty and Resistance', p. 337.

5   Zeller, p. 16.
6   Campbell, Kenneth J., 'Colonel General Ludwig Beck: Conspirator', *American Intelligence Journal*, Vol. 31, No. 1 (2013), p. 124.
7   Hoffmann, Peter, 'Ludwig Beck: Loyalty and Resistance', p. 337
8   Ibid., p. 338.
9   Cooper, Matthew, *The German Army: 1933-1945* (Scarborough House, 1978), p. 15
10 Zeller, p. 43.
11 Hossbach, Friedrich, *Zwischen Wehrmacht und Hitler 1934-1938* (Gottingen), 1965, p. 193
12 Hoffmann, Peter, 'Ludwig Beck: Loyalty and Resistance', p. 347.
13 Ibid., p. 346.
14 Ibid., p. 385.
15 Zeller, p. 38.
16 Ibid, p. 147.
17 Zwygart, Ulrich, 'Integrity and Moral Courage: Beck, Tresckow and Stauffenberg', Military Review 74, no. 5 (1994).
18 Zeller, p. 148.
19 Ibid., p. 151.
20 Duffy, James P. & Ricci, Vincent L., *Target Hitler: The Plots to Kill Adolf Hitler*, Enigma Books, 2011, p. 122.
21 Zeller, p. 260.
22 Ibid., p. 145
23 Schrader, Helena, *Codename Valkyrie: General Friedrich Olbricht and the Plot Against Hitler* (Haynes Publishing, 2009), p. 81.
24 Zeller, p. 244.
25 MacIndoe, Kathleen Michelle, *The Forgotten Faces of Operation Valkyrie: Major-General Henning von Tresckow and General Friedrich Olbricht in the July 20 Plot to Assassinate Hitler* (University of Mary Washington, 2016)., p. 9
26 Duffy & Ricci, p. 129.
27 Hoffmann, Peter, *German Resistance to Hitler* (Harvard University Press, 1988), p. 110.
28 Zeller, p. 170.
29 Ibid., p. 178.
30 Ibid., p. 190.
31 Ibid., p. 189.
32 Fest, Joachim, *Hitler – Eine Biographie* (Auflage, 2004), p. 961.

33 Hoffmann, Peter, 'Colonel Claus von Stauffenberg in the German Resistance to Hitler: Between East and West', *The Historical Journal*, Vol. 31, No. 3 (1988), p. 633.

34 Ibid., p. 634.

35 Ibid., p. 636.

36 Ibid, p. 639.

37 Zeller, p. 211.

38 Hoffmann, Peter, 'Colonel Claus von Stauffenberg in the German Resistance to Hitler', p. 643.

39 Dulles, Allen Welsh, *Germany's Underground* (Da Capo Press, 2000), p. 172.

40 Schlabrendorff, Fabian von, *Revolt Against Hitler* (Eyre and Spottiswoode, 1948), p. 131.

41 Zeller, p. 271.

42 Ibid., p. 273.

43 Ibid., p. 286.

44 Hoffmann, Peter, *Contending with Hitler; Varieties of German resistance in the Third Reich*, editor David Clay Large, *Internal Resistance in Germany* (Cambridge University Press, 1994), p. 127.

45 Zeller, p. 299.

Chapter 17: 20 July 1944

1 Zeller, p. 101.

2 Ibid., p. 317.

3 Ibid., p. 318.

4 Hoffmann, Peter, 'Opposition Annihilated: Punishing the 1944 Plot against Hitler', *The North American Review*, Vol. 255, No. 3 (1970), p. 26.

5 Zeller, p. 364.

6 Hoffmann, Peter, 'Opposition Annihilated', p. 28.

7 Ibid., p. 32.

Postscript

1 Klemperer, Klemens von, *The Solitary Witness: No Mere Footnote to History Studies*, in, *Contending with Hitler; Varieties of German Resistance in the Third Reich*, editor. David Clay large. (Cambridge University Press, 1994), p. 134 Klemperer, Klemens von, *The Solitary Witness: No Mere Footnote to History Studies*, in, *Contending with Hitler; Varieties of German Resistance in the Third Reich*, editor. David Clay large. (Cambridge University Press, 1994), p. 134 Klemperer, Klemens von, *The Solitary Witness: No Mere*

Footnote to History Studies, in, *Contending with Hitler; Varieties of German Resistance in the Third Reich,* editor. David Clay large. (Cambridge University Press, 1994), p. 134 Klemperer, Klemens von, *The Solitary Witness: No Mere Footnote to History Studies,* in, *Contending with Hitler; Varieties of German Resistance in the Third Reich,* editor. David Clay large. (Cambridge University Press, 1994), p. 134

2   Ibid., p. 136.

3   Rothfels, p. 192.

Appendix 7: White Rose Court Proceedings of Hans and Sophia Scholl, and Christoph Probst

1   Dumbach, p. 332.

Appendix 8: Plötzensee Prison

1   Plötzensee Memorial Center www.gwd.berlin.de.

SOURCES

Adam-Tkalec, Maritta, *Used in the East, hated in the West: The true story of the Red Orchestra* (berliner-zeitung.de, 2022).

Andrew, Christopher & Gordievsky, Oleg, *KGB: The Inside Story: Of Its Foreign Operations from Lenin to Gorbachev* (Harper Collins, 1990).

Assmann, Kurt, *Hitler and the German Officer Corps, Translated by Captain Roland E. Krause* (US Naval Institute, 1956).

Brabner-Smith, John W., 'Hitler hated Lawyers'. A Story of Resistance to Tyranny', American Bar Association Journal, Vol. 43, No. 12, 1957.

Brysac, Shareen Blair, *Resisting Hitler: Mildred Harnack and the Red Orchestra* (Oxford University Press, 2020).

Bullock, Alan, *Hitler, A Study in Tyranny* (Odham Press, 1952).

Campbell, Kenneth J., 'Colonel General Ludwig Beck: Conspirator', *American Intelligence Journal*, Vol. 31, No. 1, 2013.

Childers, Thomas, *Contending with Hitler; Varieties of German Resistance in the Third Reich*, ed. David Clay large. *The Kreisau Circle and the Twentieth of July* (Cambridge University Press, 1994

Cooper, Matthew, *The German Army: 1933-1945* (Scarborough House, 1978).

Coppi, Hans, *Harro Schulze-Boysen – Wege in den Widerstand* (Verlag Dietmar Fölbach, 1993).

Cox, John, *The Herbert Baum Groups: Networks of Jewish, Leftist, and Youth Resistance in the Third Reich. The Human Tradition in Modern Europe, 1750 to the Present*, Cora Granata and Cheryl Koos, eds., (Rowman and Littlefield, 2007).

Cox, John M., *Circles of Resistance: Jewish, Leftist, and Youth Dissidence in Nazi Germany* (Peter Lang Publishing Inc, 2009).

David, Claude, *L'Allemagne de Hitler* (Presses Universitaires de France, collection Que sais-je?, Paris, 1954).

DBWE 1:34, The Dietrich Bonhoeffer Works in English (Fortress Press various editors and translators, 1996–2014).

Derbent, T., *The German Communist Resistance 1933-1945* (Foreign Language Press, 2021).

Desroches, Alain, *La Gestapo* (Éditions De Vecchi, Paris, 1977).

Deutsch, Harold C. (ed.), 'The German Resistance: Answered and Unanswered Questions', *Central European History*, Vol. 14, No. 4, 1981.

Duffy, James P. & Ricci, Vincent L., *Target Hitler: The Plots to Kill Adolf Hitler* (Enigma Books, 2011).

Dulles, Allen Welsh, *Germany's Underground* (Da Capo Press, 2000).

Dumbach, Annette & Newborn, Jud, *Sophie Scholl and the White Rose* (One World Publications. Kindle Edition).

Eltscher, Louis R., *Traitors or Patriots?: A Story of the German Anti-Nazi Resistance* (McNidder and Grace. Kindle Edition).

Extract from: "Kola-Fu" – *Concentration camp and Gestapo prison Hamburg – Fuhlsbüttel 1933-1945*. – Hamburg Portrait Issue 18/83 (Museum for Hamburg History).

Facing History & Ourselves, Rejecting Nazism (facinghistory.org, 2016)

Fest, Joachim, *Hitler – Eine Biographie* (Auflage, 2004

Fikus, Sebastian, 'Rudolf Scheliha. Zapomniany bohater polsko-niemieckiej przyjaźni', W: *Zeszyty Edukacji Kulturalnej* Nr 81, 2018.

Flicke, W.F., *Rote Kapelle; les espions de Stalin* (Verlag Welsermühl, 1957).

Geerling, Wayne, Magee, Gary B. & Brooks, Robert, 'Faces of Opposition: Juvenile Resistance, High Treason, and the People's Court in Nazi Germany', The Journal of Interdisciplinary History, Vol. 44, No. 2, 2013/

Haeften, Barbara von, *"Write Nothing about Politics": A Portrait of Hans Bernd von Haeften, translated by Julie M. Winter* (Michigan State University Press, 2018).

Hellmann, John, *Communitarian Third Way: Alexandre Marc and Ordre Nouveau, 1930-2000* (McGill-Queen's Press, 2002).

Henderson, J.L., *Adolf Reichwein. Eine politisch-pädagogische Biographie* (H. Lindemann, 1958).

Henk, E., *Die Tragödie des 20 Juli 1944* (Heidelberg, 1946).

Hill, Leonidas E., 'Towards a New History of German Resistance to Hitler', *Central European History*, Vol. 14, No. 4, 1981

Hoffmann, Peter, *German Society and Internal Resistance to Hitler* in *Contending with Hitler; Varieties of German resistance in the Third Reich*, editor David Clay Large, (Cambridge University Press, 1994).Hoffmann, Peter, 'Colonel Claus von Stauffenberg in the German Resistance to Hitler: Between East and West', *The Historical Journal*, Vol. 31, No. 3, 1988.

Hoffmann, Peter, *German Resistance to Hitler* (Harvard University Press, 1988).

Hoffmann, Peter, 'Ludwig Beck: Loyalty and Resistance', *Central European History*, Vol. 14, No. 4, 1981.

Hoffmann, Peter, 'Opposition Annihilated: Punishing the 1944 Plot against Hitler', *The North American Review*, Vol. 255, No. 3, 1970.

Holmes, Blair R., & Keele, Alan F., *When Truth Was Treason: German Youth against Hitler* (University of Illinois Press, 2003).

Holzer, Charlotte, *Years of Defiance: The Herbert Baum Group and Jewish Resistance in Berlin* (Yad Vashem Publications, 2003.

Hossbach, Friedrich, *Zwischen Wehrmacht und Hitler 1934-1938* (Gottingen, 1965).

Jones, Larry Eugene, 'Nationalists, Nazis, and the Assault against Weimar: Revisiting the Harzburg Rally of October 1931', German Studies Review, Vol. 29, No. 3, 2006.

Klemperer, Klemens von, *Reflections and Reconsiderations on the German Resistance* (Kirchliche Zeitgeschichte, Vol. 1, No. 1, Der Widerstand von Kirchen und Christen gegen den Nationalsozialismus, 1988).

Klemperer, Klemens von, *German Resistance against Hitler: The Search for Allies Abroad 1938-1945* (Clarendon Press, 1992).

Klemperer, Klemens von, *Contending with Hitler; Varieties of German resistance in the Third Reich, editor David Clay Large, The Solitary Witness: No Mere Footnote to History Studies,* (Cambridge University Press, 1994).

Knutson, Käri, 'Mildred Fish-Harnack honored as hero of resistance to Nazi regime', *University of Winconsin News*, 2019

Koonz, Claudia, *Contending with Hitler; Varieties of German resistance in the Third Reich, editor David Clay Large, Choise and Courage,* (Cambridge University Press, 1994).

Krüger-Charlé, Michael, *Contending with Hitler; Varieties of German resistance in the Third Reich, editor David Clay Large, From Reform to Resistance: Carl Goerdeler's 1938 Memorandum* (Cambridge University Press, 1994)).

Kuckhoff, Greta, *Vom Rosenkranz zur Roten Kapelle, Im Schatten der Roten Kapelle* (Verlag Neues Lebel, 1972).

Kweit, Konrad, *Contending with Hitler; Varieties of German resistance in the Third Reich, editor David Clay Large, The Jewish Resistance* (Cambridge University Press, 1994).

Leber, Annelore (ed.), *The Conscience in Revolt; Portraits of the German Resistance 1933 – 1945* (v. Hase & Koehler, 1994).

Leber, J., *Ein Mann geht seinen Weg* (Schriften, Reden und Briefe, 1952).

Lockenour, Jay, '"The Rift in Our Ranks": The German Officer Corps, the Twentieth of July, and the Path to Democracy', *German Studies Review*, Vol. 21, No. 3, 1998.

MacIndoe, Kathleen Michelle, *The Forgotten Faces of Operation Valkyrie: Major-General Henning von Tresckow and General Friedrich Olbricht in the July 20 Plot to Assassinate Hitler* (University of Mary Washington, 2016).

Matheson, Peter, 'Adolf Hitler, "Policy Statement by Hitler, 23 March 1933,"' in *The Third Reich and the Christian Churches* (William B. Eerdman's Publishing Company, 1981).

Matheson, Peter, 'The Catholic Church and The German Reich, "Concordant Between the Papacy and the Third Reich, 20 July 1933', in *The Third Reich and the Christian Churches* (William B. Eerdman's Publishing Company, 1981).

McDonaugh, Frank, *Opposition and Resistance in Nazi Germany* (Cambridge University Press, 2001).

Merson, Allan, *Communist Resistance in Nazi Germany* (Lawrence and Wishart, 1986

Moltke, Helmuth James von, *Letters to Freya – 1939–1945*, translated by Beata Ruhm von Oppen (Alfred A. Knopf, 1990).

Moltke, Freya von, *Memories of Kreisau and the German Resistance* (University of Nebraska Press, 2003)

Mommsen, Hans, 'The German Resistance against Hitler and the Restoration of Politics', The Journal of Modern History, Vol. 64, 1992

Müller, Rolf-Dieter, *Reinhard Gehlen Die Biografie* (Links Verlag, 2018).

Müller, Rolf-Dieter & Ancker, Janice W., *Hitler's Wehrmacht 1935-1945*, translated by Janice W. Ancker (The University Press of Kentucky, 2016).

Nelson, Anne, *Red Orchestra* (Bloomsbury Academic, 2023).

Nylander, Gert, *German Resistance Movement and England, Carl Goerdeler and the Wallenberg Brothers* (The Foundation for Economic History Research within Banking and Enterprise, 1999).

Ohler, Norman, *The Infiltrators: The Lovers Who Led Germany's Resistance Against the Nazis* (Atlantic Books Kindle Edition, 2020).

Perrault, Gilles, *The Red Orchestra* (Simon and Schuster, 1969).

Ramet, Sabrina P., & Hassenstab, Christine M., *Anti-fascism in European History: From the 1920s to Today*, Chapter 6, 'The Anti-Fascism of Hans & Sophie Scholl: Intellectual Sources of the White Rose' (Central European University Press, 2023).

Remak, Joachim (ed.), 'Directives of the Church Movement German Christians (Movement for a National Church) in Thuringia, 1933', in *The Nazi Years: A Documentary History* (Waveland Press, 1990

Reynolds, Nicholas, *Treason was no Crime. Ludwig Beck, Chief of the German General Staff* (Kimber, 1976).

Richelson, Jeffrey, *A Century of Spies: Intelligence in the Twentieth Century* (Oxford University Press, 1995).

Ridley, Norman, *The Venlo Sting* (Pen & Sword, 2023).

Ridley, Norman, *Reading Hitler's Mind* (Pen & Sword, 2023).

Riebling, Mark, *Church of Spies: The Pope's Secret War Against Hitler* (Basic Books. Kindle Edition)

Ritter, Nikolaus, *Cover Name: Dr.Rantzau* (University Press of Kentucky, 2019).

Romoser, George K., 'The Politics of Uncertainty: The German Resistance Movement', Social Research Vol. 31 No. 1, 1964.

Rothfels, Hans, *The German Opposition to Hitler*, translated by Lawrence Wilson (Oswald Wolff Limited, 1961).

Sahm, U., *Rudolf von Scheliha 1897–1942. Ein deutscher Diplomat gegen Hitler* (München, 1990).

Schad, Martha, *Mothers in the Resistance Movement* (Verlag, Opladen/Farmington Hills, 2010).

Scheel, Heinrich, 'Die Rote Kapelle – Widerstand, Verfolgung, Haft', in Coppi, Hans J., Danyel, Jürgen Tuchel, Johannes (eds.), *Die Rote Kapelle im Widerstand gegen Hitler* (Rütten & Loenig, 1994).

Schlabrendorff, Fabian von, *Revolt Against Hitler* (Eyre and Spottiswoode, 1948).

Schoenbaum, David, *Hitler's Social Revolution: Class and Status in Nazi Germany, 1933-1939* (Doubleday, 1966).

Scholl, Inge, *The White Rose: Munich 1942-1943* (Wesleyan University Press. Kindle Edition)

Schrader, Helena, *Codename Valkyrie: General Friedrich Olbricht and the Plot Against Hitler* (Haynes Publishing, 2009

Shirer, William L., *Le troisième Reich des origines à la chute* (Éditions Stock, Paris, 1960), tome 2.

Smith, Gene, 'Martha Dodd's Shining Season', *American Heritage*, Vol. 48, issue 4, 1997.

Stargardt, A.W., 'Allies Inside Germany: The German Resistance Movement against Nazi-Fascism', *The Australian Quarterly*, Vol. 16, No. 3, 1944.

Steinbach, Peter, *Contending with Hitler; Varieties of German resistance in the Third Reich, editor David Clay Large, The Conservative Resistance* (Cambridge University Press, 1994).

Tarrant, V.E., *The Red Orchestra* (John Wily and Sons, 1995).

Tatara, Christopher, 'Hitler, Himmler, and Christianity in the Early Third Reich', *Constructing the Past* Vol. 14 : Issue 1, 2013

The CIA's History of Soviet Intelligence and Espionage Networks in Western Europe, 1936-1945, Editor: Paul L. Kesaris (University Publications of America, 1979). nationalchurchillmuseum.org/winston-churchill-and-the-gathering-storm.html

Tuchel, Johannes, *Resistance: You have to celebrate Christmas properly* (zeit.de. Zeit Online, 40141).

Tuchel, Johannes, 'Weltanschauliche Motivationen in der Harnack/Schulze-Boysen-Organisation', *Kirchliche Zeitgeschichte*, Vol. 1, No. 2, Theologie und Politik, 1988.

Tyas, Stephen, *SS-Major Horst Kopkow: From the Gestapo to British Intelligence* (Fonthill Media, 2017).

Weinstein, Allen & Vassiliev, Alexander, *The Haunted Wood* (New York: Modern Library, 1999).

West, Nigel, *Encyclopaedia of Political Assassinations* (Rowman & Littlefield, 2017).

Wiaderny, B., *Der polnische Untergrundstaat und der deutsche Widerstand 1939–1944* (Berlin, 2002).

Wistrich, Rpbert S., *Who's Who in Nazi Germany* (Routledge, 2013

Wright, Jonathan R.C., *The German Protestant Church and the Nazi Party In The Period Of The Seizure Of Power 1932–3* (Cambridge University Press, 2016).

Zeller, Eberhard, *The Flame of Freedom; The German Struggle against Hitler* (Oswald Wolff, 1967).

Zwygart, Ulrich, 'Integrity and Moral Courage: Beck, Tresckow and Stauffenberg', *Military Review* 74, no. 5, 1994

INDEX

Abshagen, Robert 98
Adam, Karl 45
Aicher, Otto (Otl) 113
Arndt, Rudi 111

Baeck, Leo 109
Bargatzky, Emil 8
Bästlein, Bernhard 30, 98, 168
Baum, Herbert (Hebbi) 110–112, 172, 190–191, 196–197
Baum, Marianne 110, 112, 172
Beck, Ludwig August Theodor 12, 25, 30, 48, 53, 55, 58–62, 64, 134–139, 141–144, 147–149, 153–156, 159–161, 182–183, 187, 192–193, 196–197, 199–200
Becker, Hermann 79
Beek, Cato Bontjes van 101, 165, 171
Behrens, Karl 89, 168
Behse, Rudolf 82
Bell, George 127–128
Berg, Willy 100
Bergengruen, Werner 114
Birnbaum, Immanuel 106
Bismarck, Herbert von 13
Blomberg, Werner von 51, 53–54, 134, 136
Bock, Fedor von 135, 139, 142
Boese, Gero von 18
Boeselager, Georg von 145, 155
Bonhoeffer, Dietrich 46–47, 127, 147, 164, 176, 186, 196
Bosch, Robert 59
Boysen (Schulze), Marie Luise 68–69, 75
Brandt, Willy 4, 40
Brandt, Walter 24
Brandt, Heinz 145
Brauchitsch, Walter von 55, 62, 65–66, 135, 137–138, 140–141

Brecht, Bertolt 75
Bredow, Ferdinand von 51, 57, 134, 141
Brenner, Heinz 114
Brockdorff, Erika von 101–102
Brockdorff-Ahlefeldt, Walter 60
Bronin, Yakov 104
Broszat, Martin 3
Brüning, Heinrich 16, 58
Bussche-Streithorst, Axel von dem 151

Canaris, Wilhelm 12, 47, 57–58, 61, 145, 151, 154
Chamberlain, Neville 61–62
Churchill, Winston 6, 61, 67, 152,
Claussenberg, Berthold von 156
Cobb, Richard 16
Colvin, Ian 61
Cook, William 86
Cook Fish, Georgina 86
Coppi, Hans 85, 96–97, 101–102, 169, 188–189, 196, 199
Coppi, Hilde 102, 168

d'Arcy Osborne, Francis 66
Daladier, Édouard 62
David, Claude 22, 185, 196
Davilov, Anton 99
Deichmann, Freya 125
Delp, Alfred 129–130, 176
Desroches, Alain 22, 185, 196
Dimitrov, Georges 22
Dodd, William 89–90
Dodd, Martha 168, 189, 200
Dohnanny, Hans von 20
Dohrn, Herta 118
Donovan, William J. 152

Eickenmeyer, Manfred 114
Eifler, Erna 108
Einsiedel, Horst von 125, 129, 176

Eisenhower, Dwight D, 152
Elser, Johann Georg 63, 139–140
Engelsings, Herbert 85
Engelsings, Ingeborg 85
Erdberg, Alexander (see Alexandr Korotkov) 91–92
Erlanger, Henry 78,

Falkenhausen, Alexander von 5, 141, 143
Faulhaber, Michael von 45
Fish, Mildred 'Mili' Elizabeth (see Mildred Harnack) 86–87, 168, 189, 198
Fitin, Pavel 96
Franke, Joachim 112
Freisler, Roland 17, 19–20, 30–31, 122, 162–163
Freytag-Loringhoven, Wessel Freiherr von 156
Frick, Wilhelm 77
Fritsch, Werner Freiherr von 50, 53–55, 60, 134, 135
Fromm, Friedrich 'Fritz' 150, 154, 156, 159–162
Fruck, Hans 112
Fulenberg, Countess Viktoria Ada Astrid Agnes zu 80, 106
Funger, Hans 25

Galen, Clemens August Graf von 42, 46
Gall, Willi 23
Gębarowicz, Mieczysław 107
Gehre, Ludwig 154,
Gehrts, Erwin von 95, 166
Gempp, Walter 8
Germain, André 75
Gersdorff, Rudolf-Christoph Freiherr von 142, 144, 146
Gerstenmaier, Eugen 129, 131, 144, 161, 176
Giering, Karl 100
Gildisch, Kurt 46
Gisevius, Hans-Bernd 56, 62, 153, 160
Goerdeler, Carl Friedrich 12,13, 25, 27, 30, 55–56, 58–63, 109, 125–127, 129–131, 139, 143–144, 152, 156, 162, 182, 187, 198–199
Göring, Hermann 53, 57,77, 82, 93, 95, 101–102, 134, 156, 158
Graf, Willi 20, 118–121, 123, 174

Graudenz, John 98–99, 101–102, 166
Grimme, Adolf 90, 168
Grimminger, Eugen 114, 174
Groener, Wilhelm 135
Groer, Franciszek 107
Gross, Nikolaus 40
Gruhn, Erna 54
Guderian, Heinz 140, 154
Günther, Hanno 33
Gurevich, Anatoly Markovich (codename Kent) 96–97
Guter, Heinrich 114, 174

Haas-Heye, Libertas Viktoria 'Libs' (see Libertas Schulze-Boysen) 80
Haas-Heye, Otto Ludwig 80
Haecker, Theodor 114
Haeften, Hans Bernd von 128, 131–132, 152, 157–163, 176, 197
Halder, Franz 55, 62, 65–66, 138–139, 141
Halifax, Lord 61
Hallemeyer, Rudolf 23
Hammerstein-Equord, Kurt Freiherr von 27, 50, 135
Hanfstaengl, Ernst 89
Harnack, Ernst von 30
Harnack, Arvid 30, 83, 85, 87, 89, 92–97, 100–103, 168
Harnack, Mildred (see Mildred Fish) 86–87, 90–91, 101, 168, 188, 189, 196, 198
Harnack, Falk 119, 174
Hartnagel, Fritz 115
Hassel, Ulrich von 60, 139, 144, 153,
Hasselrot, Berndt 69
Haubach, Theodor 28–30, 129, 131, 155, 176
Heath, Donald 90–91
Heberie, Rudolf 74
Heilmann, Horst 94, 100–102, 166
Helfrich, Carl 106–108
Helldorf, Graf Wolf Heinrich von 60
Herrnstadt, Rudolf 104–105, 107
Heydrich, Reinhard 46, 54, 56, 60, 97, 100, 107, 162
Himmler, Heinrich 13, 24, 36, 51, 53–54, 56, 60, 62, 65, 122, 130, 137–138, 154, 156, 158, 160–161, 200
Himpel, Helmut 85, 101, 166
Hirsch, Otto 109
Hirschfeld, Alexander 92

Hirzel, Susanne 114, 174
Hitler, Adolf 2, 5–7, 9–21, 23, 26–28, 30–37, 40, 42–67, 73, 77, 82–83, 85, 89, 93–94, 98, 100–104, 107, 110, 118–121, 125, 128–151, 153–156, 158–163, 179, 183–189, 191–200
Hoepner, Erich 61, 160–162
Hossbach, Friedrich 48, 53–54, 137, 193, 197
Hübener, Helmuth 33, 35
Huber, Kurt 119–120, 123, 174
Hugenberg, Alfred 17
Husemann, Friedrich 24
Husemann, Walter 83, 166
Husen, Paulus van 130, 132, 176
Huyn, Hans Graf 105

Jacob, Franz 29, 98, 153
Jakob, Berthold 39
James, Evan 84
Jaspers, Karl 6
Jessen, Jens 144
Joachim, Heinz 111–112
John, Otto 152, 161–162
Jung, Edgar 18
Jünger, Ernst 5

Kaltenbrunner, Ernst 159
Kamy, David (see Anton Kavilov) 99
Keitel, Wilhelm 54, 157–160
Kiep, Otto 19, 40, 154
Klausener, Erich 45 46
Kleist, Berndt von 142
Kleist Schmenzin, Ewald von 19–20, 61
Kluge, Günther von 62, 141, 145, 155–156
Kochmann, Martin 110, 172
Kochmann, Sala 110, 172
Kopkow, Horst 100–102, 190, 200
Kopp, Hans 97
Kordt, Theo 61
Kordt, Erich 139
Körner, Heinrich 25
Korotkov, Alexandr 91–96
Kortzfleish, Joachim von 158–159
Kraell, Alexander 102, 108
Kuchenmeister, Walter 83, 85, 101, 166
Kuckhoff, Adam 74, 85, 87, 90, 95, 97–98, 100–101, 169
Kuckhoff, Greta 85, 90, 101, 168, 189, 198
Kuckhoff, Ule 101

Kurowsky, Fanny von 40

Lachnit, Friedrich 34
Lafrenz, Traute 114, 118, 174
Lange, Hermann 46
Leber, Annedore 4, 184–186, 198
Leber, Julius 30–31, 40, 131–132, 155, 177, 185, 198
Leeb, Wilhelm Ritter von 139
Lerch, Anni 149
Leuninger, Franz 25
Leuschner, Wilhelm 25, 27–28, 31, 129, 177
Lewinski, Karl von 125
Ley, Robert 23, 27
List, Wilhelm 62
Lorke, Greta (see Greta Kuckhoff) 87
Lortz, Joseph 45
Lukaschek, Hans 128, 177

Maas, Hermann 28, 129–130
MacEwan, David 152
Mahler, Anton 121
Meyer, Gerhard 112
Mierendorff, Carlo 28–29, 31, 128, 131, 177
Mohn, Heinrich 35
Mohr, Robert 121
Moltke, Hans-Adolf von 104–105
Moltke, Helmuth James Graf von 16, 67, 124–131, 144, 151–154, 177, 192, 199
Moltke, Asta von 128
Montgomery, Bernard 152
Mueller, Eduard 46
Müller, Hermann 16
Müller, Ludwig 43
Müller, Josef 66, 147
Müller, Heinrich 102
Müller, Franz Josef 114, 174
Müller-Otfried, Paula 43
Mussolini, Benito 62
Muth, Carl 113–114

Nebe, Arthur 5
Neurath, Konstantin von 53–54, 134
Niemöller, Martin 44–47
Nuss, Elsa 80, 188

Olbricht, Friedrich 135, 141, 143–144, 146–150, 154, 156, 158–161, 193, 198, 200

Ossietzky, Carl von 39
Oster, Hans 2, 12, 20, 30, 47, 57–58, 62–63, 65–67, 135, 138–140, 142, 147, 154

Panzinger, Friedrich 100
Papen, Franz von 16, 58, 77, 108
Paul, Elfriede 83, 101, 169
Perels, Friedrich Justus 46
Peters, Hans 128–129, 177
Pfuhlstein, Alexander von 62
Piepe, Harry 97, 99–100
Poelchau, Harald 91, 128, 177
Pöllnitz, Georgine Gisela von 84, 166
Popitz, Johannes 60, 144
Probst, Christoph (Christl) 113, 118, 121–122, 173, 178–179, 195

Quirnheim, Albrecht Ritter Werz von 154, 160

Raffray, Richard von 80
Ramdohr, Lilo 121
Reckzeh, Paul 40
Regendorf, Adolf von Harnier Freiherr von 18
Reichwein, Adolf 28–29, 128, 131–132, 177, 185, 197
Ribbentrop, Joachim von 12, 26, 54
Rittmeister, John 98, 167
Roeder, Manfred 102, 108
Röhm, Ernst 11–12, 46, 134, 136–137
Roloff, Helmut 85, 101, 167
Rommel, Erwin 155–156
Rösch, Augustin 128, 177
Rosenberg, Alfred 42, 45–46
Rotholz, Heinz 112, 172

Sacco, Nicola 88
Saefkow, Anton Emil Hermann 29–30, 168
Saefkow, Thea 29
Saefkow, Änne 30
Salomon, Ernst von 83
Sas, Gijsbertus Jacobus 66–67
Schacht, Hjalmar 13, 55–56, 58
Schäfer, Oswald 121
Scheel, Heinrich 85, 101, 167, 189, 199
Scheliha, Rudolf von 104–108, 171, 191, 197, 199
Scheliha, Renata Johanna von 105
Scherpenberg, Hilger van 40

Schlabrendorff, Fabian von 142, 146, 155, 163–164, 194, 200
Schlageter, Leo 70
Schleicher, Kurt von 16, 51
Schleicher, Rudiger 47
Schmeink, Richard 24
Schmid, Jakob 121, 123
Schmorell, Alexander 113–114, 116, 119, 121, 123, 174
Schoenbaum, David 9, 22, 184, 200
Scholl, Werner 113
Scholl, Elizabeth 113
Scholl, Sophie 113–114, 118, 121, 173, 178–179, 184, 191, 195, 197, 199
Scholl, Inge 191, 200
Scholl, Robert 122
Schomaus, Michael 45
Schönfeld, Hans 127
Schottmüller, Oda 83, 101, 167
Schulenburg, Fritz-Dietlof von der 127, 144, 160–161, 177, 192
Schulze, Heinz Harro Max Wilhelm Georg (see Schulze-Boysen) 2, 68
Schulze, Erich Edgar 68–69
Schulze, Helga Mulachiè 69
Schulze-Boysen, Heinz Harro Max Wilhelm Georg 71–79, 81–85, 93–102, 107, 151, 165, 188–190, 196, 200
Schulze-Boysen, Libertas (see Libertas Haas-Heye) 102, 165
Schulze-Buettger, Georg 142
Schumacher, Kurt 83, 96, 101–102, 167
Schumacher, Elizabeth 83, 94–95, 100–102, 167
Schwamb, Ludwig 28
Schwanenfeld, Ulrich-Wilhelm von Schwerin von 14, 20, 157
Schwarzenstein, Herbert Mumm von 40
Seeckt, Hans von 50
Shirer, William 22, 185, 200
Sieg, John 98, 102, 169
Sierra, Vincente (see Anatoly Gurevich) 96
Skorzeny, Otto 161
Skrzypczynski, Leo 90, 169
Söhngen, Josef 114, 175
Solf, Johanna Susanne Elisabeth 19
Solf, Hanna 19, 40
Solmitz, Fritz 38, 40
Speer, Albert 5
Stalin, Josef 10, 91, 95, 190, 197

Stark, Jonathan 35
Stauffenberg, Claus, Count Schenk von 5, 20, 127, 131–133, 143, 147–161, 193–194, 197, 200
Stauffenberg, Berthold 150, 152, 156, 161
Steinbrinck, Werner 112
Stellbrink, Karl Friedrich 46
Stelling, Johannes 30
Stennes, Walther 89
Stieff, Helmuth 145–146, 162
Stöbe, Ilse Friede Gertrud 104–108, 171
Strelow, Heinz 101
Strübing, Johannes 100
Stülpnagel, Karl-Heinrich von 5, 139, 142–143
Szeptycki, Andrjez 106

Tau, Max 90
Terweil, Mimi 94, 167
Terweil, Maria 85, 101, 167
Thadden, Elizabeth von 40
Thiel, Fritz 99, 101, 167
Thiel, Hannelore 101, 167
Tresckow, Henning von 64, 126, 141–147, 149–150, 154–156, 193, 198, 200
Trotha, Carl Dietrich von 125, 177
Trott zu Solz, Adam von 20, 126, 177
Tschäpe, Herbert 24

Udet, Ernst 89
Uhrig, Robert 110–111, 170

Ulex, Alexander 62
Unger-Winkelreid, Emil 73

Vansittart, Robert 59–61
Vanzetti, Bartolomeo 88
Vinogradov, Boris 90
Vishinsky, Andrei 17
Voss, Alexander von 142

Waetjens, Eduard 153
Wagner, Eduard 5
Wallenberg, Marcus 58, 152, 187, 199
Wartenburg, Peter Graf Yorck von 20, 125, 128–129, 162, 177
Wartenburg, Marion Yorck von 128–129, 177
Wartenburg, Irene Yorck von 128
Weisenborn, Margrit 82
Weisenborn, Günther 83, 168
Weissler, Friedrich 46
Weizsäcker, Ernst Heinrich Freiherr von 139
Wenzel, Johannes 100
Wiersich, Oswald 25
Wilson, Horace 61,
Witzleben, Erwin von 20, 56, 60, 135, 141, 160, 162
Wolff, Theodor 104
Wolter, Marta 83
Wunderlich, Rudi 24

Zarden, Irmgard 40